D0153123

This book was purchased with
U.S. Department of Education
Title III grant funds.

OIL IN THE GULF

Oil in the Gulf

Obstacles to Democracy and Development

Edited by
DANIEL HERADSTVEIT
Norwegian Institute of International Affairs, Norway
HELGE HVEEM
University of Oslo, Norway

Library
Southern Maine Community College
2 Fort Road
South Portland, Maine 04106

ASHGATE

DS
236
.O35
2004

© Daniel Heradstveit and Helge Hveem 2004

All rights reserved. No part of this publication may be reproduced, stored in a retrieval system or transmitted in any form or by any means, electronic, mechanical, photocopying, recording or otherwise without the prior permission of the publisher.

Daniel Heradstveit and Helge Hveem have asserted their right under the Copyright, Designs and Patents Act, 1988, to be identified as the editors of this work.

Published by
Ashgate Publishing Limited
Gower House
Croft Road
Aldershot
Hants GU11 3HR
England

Ashgate Publishing Company
Suite 420
101 Cherry Street
Burlington, VT 05401-4405
USA

Ashgate website: http://www.ashgate.com

British Library Cataloguing in Publication Data
Oil in the Gulf : obstacles to democracy and development
    1. Petroleum industry and trade - Persian Gulf Region
    2. Democratization - Persian Gulf Region 3. Persian Gulf
    Region - Politics and government 4. Persian Gulf Region -
    Economic conditions
    I. Heradstveit, Daniel, 1940- II. Hveem, Helge
    320.9'53

Library of Congress Cataloging-in-Publication Data
Oil in the Gulf : obstacles to democracy and development / edited by Daniel Heradstveit
    and Helge Hveem.
      p. cm.
    Includes bibliographical references and index.
    ISBN 0-7546-3968-1
     1. Persian Gulf Region--Politics and government--20th century. 2. Persian Gulf
    Region--Economic policy. 3. Democracy--Persian Gulf Region. I. Heradstveit, Daniel,
    1940- II. Hveem, Helge.

    DS236.O35 2003
    320.953--dc22

                                    2003058289

ISBN 0 7546 3968 1

Reprinted 2004

Printed and bound in Great Britain by Antony Rowe Ltd, Chippenham, Wiltshire

9/05 BT
89.95
Title III

Contents

List of Figures and Tables

Figures

Tables

List of Contributors

Dr. G. Matthew Bonham is Professor of Political Science and Chair of the International Relations Program in the Maxwell School of Syracuse University. He has held academic positions at the University of California, Berkeley, and the School of International Service of the American University. He has published three monographs, 14 referred journal articles and 10 chapters in anthologies, including "Attribution Theory and Arab Images of the Gulf War" (with Daniel Heradstveit), *Political Psychology*, 17 (1996) and "The Limited Test-Ban Agreement: Emergence of New Knowledge Structures in International Negotiation" (with Victor Sergeev and Pavel Parshin), *International Studies Quarterly*, 41 (1997).

Mehrzad Boroujerdi is Associate Professor and Director of Graduate Studies in the Department of Political Science at Syracuse University's Maxwell School of Citizenship and Public Affairs. Most recently, he has been a scholar-in-residence at the Middle East Institute in Washington, DC. Boroujerdi is the author of *Iranian Intellectuals and the West: The Tormented Triumph of Nativism* (Syracuse University Press, 1996), general editor of the series *Modern Intellectual and Political History of the Middle East* at Syracuse University Press and the book review editor of the *International Journal of Middle East Studies*.

Ådne Cappelen is Head of the Research Department at Statistics Norway. An economist by profession, he has researched and published extensively on macroeconomic issues. In his research for Petropol, he has applied his expertise to the case of Saudi Arabia, using data not usually accessed by researchers. Among his recent publications are several chapters in books on economic and social issues: *The Economic Challenge for Europe* (Elgar, 1999) and *Evolutionary Economics and Income Inequality* (Elgar, 2001).

Robin Choudhury is an adviser at the Research Department of Statistics Norway, where he has been working on the development of macroeconometric models. Since 2001 he has held a 20 per cent position, spending the rest of his working hours at EDB Fellesdata developing software for the banking sector. He is an economist from the University of Oslo, Norway. More recently he has also done work for the Ministry of Planning in Riyadh, Saudi Arabia.

Daniel Heradstveit is Professor and Senior Research Associate at the Norwegian Institute of International Affairs. He has been Ford Foundation Fellow at Stanford and Harvard Universities and held positions as Professor of International Relations at Johns Hopkins University, Bologna, and Professor of Comparative Politics at the

University of Bergen. Heradstveit has also served as a consultant and political analyst for the Norwegian oil company Statoil. He is the author or co-author of 11 books on the Middle East, semiotics and political psychology. His most recent book is *Democracy and Oil: The Case of Azerbaijan* (Reichert Verlag, 2001).

Helge Hveem is Professor of Political Science at the University of Oslo. He served as Chairman of the Board of the Petropol program at the Norwegian Research Council from 1996 to 2001. Hveem has published extensively on the geopolitics of natural resources, including *The Political Economy of Third World Producer Associations* (1978), and on the political economy of globalization and regionalization processes. He is represented in a wide range of anthologies during the last few years. He has been Visiting Professor at the European University Institute in Florence and the University of Bordeaux.

Åshild Kjøk is a Researcher at the Norwegian Defence Research Establishment, where she works for the Terrorism and Asymmetric Warfare Project. She has an M.I.A. in Middle Eastern and Security Studies from Columbia University. Kjøk is the editor of *Terrorism & Human Rights After September 11 – Towards a Universal Approach for Combating Terrorism and Protecting Human Rights* (Cairo Institute for Human Rights Studies, 2002).

Brynjar Lia is a Research Fellow at the Norwegian Defence Research Establishment, where he heads the Terrorism and Asymmetric Warfare Project. He was a Visiting Fulbright Scholar at the Center for Middle Eastern Studies at Harvard University 2001–02. Lia has published works on political Islamic movements as well as contemporary terrorism. He is the author of *The Society of the Muslim Brothers in Egypt 1928–42: The Rise of an Islamic Mass Movement* (Ithaca Press, 1998) and co-author of the forthcoming book *Globalisation and the Future of Terrorism: Patterns and Predictions* (Frank Cass, 2003).

Øystein Noreng is TotalFinaElf Professor of petroleum economics and management at the Norwegian School of Management. He is also a consultant to the IMF, the World Bank and numerous governments and oil companies. Noreng has researched and published extensively on petroleum markets and resource policies, national oil companies and other aspects of industry organization. His book *Oil and Islam* (Wiley, 1997) is today an authoritative book on the subject. Noreng has just completed a new book, *Crude Power*, published by I.B.Tauris & Co. (2002).

Reidar Visser is a Research Fellow at the Norwegian Institute of International Affairs. He recently completed his doctorate at the Faculty of Oriental Studies, University of Oxford.

Introduction

Daniel Heradstveit and Helge Hveem

Why this Book?

The world has grown accustomed to hearing politicians talk about promoting democratic values outside their own territory. Today we are witness to radical
changes in the United States, where even neo-conservatives have enthusiastically
adopted what used to be the terminology of the Left – civil society, rule of law and
democracy – and now propose to apply this discourse to Iraq.

Some argue that the real reasons for the war in Iraq are to be found elsewhere,
primarily in the establishment of a new regional power-base for the United States.
They contend that Washington's new desire to introduce democracy in Iraq is
merely a rhetorical device to maintain and strengthen the legitimacy of US policy in
the Gulf – a kind of psychological warfare ultimately as transparent as the code-
name for the war, "Operation Liberate Iraq".

Unlike those critics, we are willing to take US decision-makers at their word
and give them the benefit of the doubt. The task of nation-building and promoting
stability in the region will not be easy, however, and the United States has an obli-
gation to make a sincere effort. Will this create a "window of opportunity" for democratic forces in the Gulf? It seems too early to say. This is a region where the
rule of law and democratic norms are particularly weak. The building of civil societies in the Gulf is a daring venture, and many people are justifiably skeptical.

We hope that this book can inject into the debate new knowledge about political
and economic forces, including the complex relations between oil, politics and
economic development, the role of religion, cultural factors, and, above all, the
mentality of the people themselves. The oil-producing countries of the Gulf need
modernity and its values, to help them deal with the problems their oil economies
are creating. And yet, any political system that can manage its oil wealth for the
common good – as opposed to enriching a small elite – is likely to find itself on a
collision course with local traditions. The result may well be frustration, alien-
ation... and a backlash that benefits anti-democratic forces.

The main purpose of this volume, which consists of seven chapters written by
contributors from a range of disciplines, is to offer an original analysis, based on
new research, of the relationship between domestic political forces, religion, culture
and identity, the role of the petroleum industry, economic development, and geopolitics in the core region of the global oil industry. In today's world, many of the
old rules no longer apply. Once, the great powers might have fancied that they
could contain and control domestic politics in the Gulf, as elsewhere – but this is no

longer the case, unless they also change their views of the region. The mentalities that are shaping international affairs today, especially in the West, project a world view that has failed to take adequate account of the Iranian revolution of 1979, the Palestinian *intifadahs,* and recent revelations that the al-Qaida network has been largely recruited from a growing opposition in Saudi Arabia.

Prospects for Democracy

What are the main obstacles to democratic development? Where do we find the best prospects? These issues can be observed in the cases of Iran and Iraq.

Generational conflicts characterize the region, not least in these two countries. There are the uneducated but rich old people, the frustrated middle-aged people, and the educated but impoverished and largely disenfranchised young people. The three groups have been molded by very different formative political experiences: for the first group, it was independence from the colonial powers, for the second the 1967 Arab defeat in the Six-day war with Israel, and for the third, the Gulf War. In particular the last is taken by the younger generation as proof that the West is bent on keeping them down.

In contrast to Iran, the question is whether post-war Iraq can move from dictatorial secularism to a renewal of Islamist rule. A key determinant for the future of Iraqi politics will be developments within the country's majority Shi'i community. This is also the field of Iraqi politics where the gap between US policies and the wishes of the population seems greatest, thus adding to the potential for instability in the future.

Writing on the Shi'i Islamist parties and their attitudes to the territorial integrity of the modern state of Iraq, *Reidar Visser* points out that historically separatist options or schemes for a merger with Iran have been of only marginal importance for the Shi'is. In fact, their reluctance to challenge the territorial integrity of the country has been such that many Shi'i Islamist parties have been unenthusiastic even about the various schemes for a future Iraqi federation which materialized during the 1990s. However, a new and more radical current within Shi'i politics emerged in Iraq during the final years of the former regime, and this political movement was considerably strengthened by the security vacuum that followed in the months after the fall of Saddam Hussein. Largely based in the urban areas where it enjoys substantial support among the urban poor, and with close links to hardliners in Iranian and Lebanese politics, this new tendency in Iraqi politics looks set to become one of the less predictable forces in the years to come, with a potential for challenging traditional Shi'i approaches even to the Iraqi state as such.

In his chapter on Iran, *Mehrzad Boroujerdi* notes that, although the outcome of the series of Iranian elections since 1997 has given the world hope that a modified democracy was right around the corner, the continued factional deadlock has forced us to think again. Boroujerdi's depressing conclusion is that the battle is still undecided. Both Khatami's power and the popular mandate are being marginalized by a clergy that claims a monopoly on knowing the will of God. And what are the people and their elected president compared with Him? Boroujerdi brings to the surface the eclectic qualities of Iranian politics that are often lost on Western analysts unfamiliar with its nuances and complexities, and explains why Iranian politics should not be reduced to a case of a power struggle between two men, President Khatami and Supreme Leader Khamenei. He maintains that the revolutionary slogan, "Islam is the solution", has now been emptied of meaning and lacks the power to mobilize the younger generation. Nevertheless, Boroujerdi offers us a glimpse of hope by pointing out that Iranian society is undergoing a rapid and fundamental transformation, from a traditional-authoritarian to a modern-democratic society. If neighboring Iraq goes democratic, this will probably strengthen democratic forces in Iran – and this could be the straw that breaks the back of the "theocratic camel".

Daniel Heradstveit and Matt Bonham focus on the new strategy pursued by foreign oil companies in the field of human rights and corporate social responsibility. Western companies have come under pressure from activists at home to become forces for good in the corrupt and autocratic states where they pump oil. However, an oil company is not a political reform association – it is a corporation formed for the purpose of finding, extracting and distributing petroleum; it is staffed by engineers and financial officers, who do not necessarily understand the local culture and the policy instruments necessary to promote the political and moral values of Western countries.

Western oil companies can become a positive influence, but they must first make up their minds to do so. Up to now their motto seems to be, "We take care never to be mixed up in corruption, we can do no more than that". Or: "*We* are not corrupt, corruption is part of the local culture, we're against it but we're not responsible". Measured against the ethical codes now being formulated by the most progressive multinationals, such thinking is obsolete. Heradstveit and Bonham point out that Western oil companies have moral responsibility to become more transparent if, as respondents in Azerbaijan and Iran assert, their activities have led to increased corruption. There is much to suggest that the Western oil industry is – perhaps unknowingly and inadvertently – indirectly helping to maintain this culture of corruption, and as a consequence, supporting forces that work against secularization and democratization in both Azerbaijan and Iran.

The oil companies, however, should not have to take all of the blame for the culture of corruption found in most oil-producing companies. The political leadership is directly responsible for the pervasive corruption that enslaves its inhabitants, impedes economic growth, erodes respect for law, destroys social cohesion and prevents the development of democratic institutions. The political leadership of Azerbaijan and Iran should look to other countries that can serve as models, such as Slovakia and Latvia, where the top leadership has displayed the willingness to eliminate corruption. They have appointed anti-corruption committees and commissioners to enhance the effectiveness of investigation procedures and to amend the tax, labor and penal laws. Honest officials are rewarded. In Azerbaijan and Iran, such a step would represent a radical break with tradition. As long as the top political leadership remains hopelessly corrupt, honesty may seem a lost cause, but it is worthwhile to take the offensive.

The research of Heradstveit and Bonham also suggests that the local mentality needs to be changed, especially in Azerbaijan. Here, Iran can serve as a model. Instead of blaming corruption on "the system" – an attribution that makes any effort to change seem impossible – people in Azerbaijan should shift the focus of their understanding to dispositional factors, which are easier to control and manipulate. In Iran, for example, elites tend to see corruption as being caused by individuals, rather than by the culture or the system. Armed with this dispositional perspective, they feel more empowered to make changes, by simply exposing and removing the corrupt individuals. Such an attributional pattern is exactly the type of understanding that is associated with modern secular democracies.

The Prospects of Economic Development

Paradoxically, one major obstacle to economic development and to establishing some degree of a true market economy in the Gulf could be the predominance of oil. As gold may have been destructive to Spain some centuries earlier, and diamonds still plague parts of Africa, so may oil be a curse and not a blessing to the people of the Gulf region. In general, a monocultural export economy is not the best basis on which to base long-term economic development or a functioning market economy. According to *Øystein Noreng,* the economies of the oil-producing states are a "predicament", because oil first brought prosperity and then unmade it. The combination of an economic monoculture, a rising population and political rigidity is presenting the countries of the Gulf with the difficult choice between painful reform and ultimate collapse.

A Gulf country is typically a *rentier* state – a protected concessionary and distributive economy directed by the elite or the clan through control of the state apparatus. In such an economy, citizens expect to receive gifts rather than earn their income through exchange in the market. Although these countries differ greatly, the course of the "*rentier* cycle" is similar: first the *rentier* state is established, creating a new class, then the technocracy is consolidated, third the ruling class hangs on in the teeth of mounting opposition, and finally (seen so far only in Iran) the new class is overthrown. In the 1970s, the oil states appeared to outsiders well managed and economically promising. But then two big price hikes brought revenues that led to conspicuous consumption but bypassed the groups that were already underprivileged, while rapid population growth meant that per capita oil revenues actually fell sharply.

The paradox is perhaps most visible in the case of Saudi Arabia. *Ådne Cappelen and Robin Choudhury* present three alternative economic and political scenarios for that country. The first scenario is one of no change at all: this is unsustainable and therefore unlikely. The second is a measure of reform, not least in connection with entry into the World Trade Organization (WTO), including privatization or at least deregulation of, for example, transport and telecommunications, measures to diversify the economy and the introduction of tax. However, there will be no solution to the problem of falling per capita GDP without female emancipation, which still seems unlikely.

The third scenario they identify is an "oil market grab" following a failure of liberal reform. Such an outcome has been considered for OPEC as a whole, meaning a huge production increase. However Cappelen and Choudhury find that a market grab on the part of Saudi Arabia alone would be more feasible, as the kingdom has a capacity for a huge increase at little cost – but such a strategy would mean the end of OPEC and Arab unity. After the war in Iraq, some representatives of the occupation power have indicated that Iraq could be taken out of OPEC in order to finance a speed-up of reconstruction. Such a move would probably be even more politically controversial in the Gulf and could cause devastating harm to OPEC.

The Economy-Democracy Linkage

All Gulf states would experience an easing of their economic problems if oil prices were to remain high. Prospects for that to happen remain, however, quite uncertain. And if either Saudi Arabia or Iraq were to choose the "oil market grab" option, the price of oil would drop. Herein lies an apparent contradiction: If Saudi Arabia organizes the grab in order to save the political system from collapse, Iraq and Iran will be in a squeeze that may reduce their prospects for democracy. If Iraq, under US control, organizes it, and even if this is motivated by the need to stabilize the country and not by geopolitical considerations, the regime in Saudi Arabia could collapse, and the country might become very unstable.

It therefore appears more likely that the Gulf countries will have to consider domestic reforms rather than any attempt to grab the oil market. One obvious obstacle is that there is little or no taxation. Back in the late 1770s, the American revolutionary slogan read "no taxation without representation". In the Gulf it has been reversed to read "no representation without taxation". Lack of such a linkage makes processes of change very difficult to handle, as is obvious in the case of Saudi Arabia, where the state lives on its centralized petroleum revenues and uses them to purchase loyalty and legitimacy. But even in Iran the state buys popular support by keeping petrol prices extremely low.

The military, once a radical and reformist social force, has become a conservative one, writes Noreng. Oil revenues, arms salesmen and external and internal threats have led to a high degree of militarization. While the military appears to have secured for itself a position of relative economic wealth and political power, a varied range of other groups has remained on the outside.

It is in Saudi Arabia that the linkage between the economy and the political system is at its most intimate. The country has three main interest groups: the huge royal family, with its burden of luxury and danger of faction; the religious community; and the emergent business community. There is no clear line between the royal family and business, as contracts are considered part of a "gift" system. The drying-up of oil revenues, maldistribution and hidden unemployment are turning the business community "liberal".

The early 1980s saw production cuts that resulted in plummeting revenues and fiscal deficits, while the 1991 Gulf War led to an increased military burden. Recent years have seen some improvement in the oil price and public finances, as well as in domestic borrowing as a strategy. Short of a high long-term oil price, however, Saudi Arabia has no real options for increasing its revenues other than taxation, with the concomitant pressure for democracy. The problems of stagnation in the non-oil economy and the low economic participation of native Saudis have not yet been addressed adequately.

The Role of Geopolitics: Terrorist Threats and Superpower Responses

In none of these cases are economic development and democratization solely dependent on domestic or regional factors. Geopolitics and the policy of the great powers, in particular the US superpower, are still central elements. Throughout history they have played a dominant role, although they were reduced or became more contingent with the emergence of Arab oil power. With terrorism and the present tough and assertive policy pursued by the United States in what it calls a response to terrorism, might we discern the beginnings of a new period of imperial policy?

The strategy pursued by the current Bush administration has such profound effects and implications for the region and its position in the global political economy that it is beyond the scope of the present book to discuss the matter in depth. Will the US administration use its policy of pre-emptive strike to attack more countries? Will it pressure Israel to make a fair deal with the Palestinians? How will it pursue its recent policy of engaging itself politically and militarily in Central Asia – a matter of serious concern not only to Iran, but also to other countries in Asia? And, perhaps most importantly in the short run: how will it deal with the post-war challenges in Iraq?

With respect to terrorism, *Brynjar Lia and Åshild Kjøk* analyze patterns of contemporary terrorism against petroleum infrastructure targets. Studies of terrorist strategies, as opposed to target vulnerabilities, have hitherto been neglected. The research of Lia and Kjøk is based on a comprehensive database in which "terrorism" is defined as "acts of political violence committed by non-state groups with some degree of transnational ramifications". However, threats of attacks are under-reported in the database and have been excluded from this study. Their database also covers only transnational terrorism – but, given the international nature of the petroleum industry, this is not a serious problem.

Attacks on petroleum targets have been relatively rare over the past three decades. Nor have such strikes been particularly damaging. About half of the world's producer countries have been spared from serious terrorist strikes against their installations. The most common types of attack have involved blasting of pipelines (these have been the most lethal and destructive incidents); kidnapping of personnel and bombings of offices. Pipelines are unguarded; they are easy to attack and escape from afterwards. Kidnappings have not been particularly lethal, being more oriented to ransom or other demands and confined to a few countries. Armed attacks on personnel have been carried out mostly in a civil war context, especially in Algeria. Office bombings have taken place mostly at night, thus serving a symbolic function, by domestic terrorists outside a situation of armed conflict. Strikes against terminals, depots and petrol stations have been quite rare. The good news for some countries is that there have been very few recorded attacks against oil platforms and offshore installations, and virtually all of these occurred in Nigeria, the only country to have suffered the armed seizure of a platform.

Their data suggests that "petroleum terrorism" is a strategy pursued more often by insurgents or rebel groups than by political terrorists and extremists. The former aim to weaken the government physically, by striking at targets vital to the national economy, and by controlling sources of revenue, whereas the latter's use of violence is often characterized by strikes against highly symbolic but militarily irrelevant targets. Not surprisingly, "petroleum terrorism" is especially widespread in countries involved in armed conflict. An increase in the number of incidents can be attributed to the petroleum industry's own expansion into areas that were in any case suffering from insurgency and civil war. The most frequent motives are opposition to the political regime in the country and to the presence and activities of foreign petroleum companies, followed by economic motives – which includes fundraising for the insurgency.

Domestic groups, in particular leftist and ethno-separatist groups, are responsible for most attacks on petroleum production infrastructure; only rarely are foreign groups involved. There are no known cases of transnational petroleum terrorism by right-wing or environmental groups. Separatist and leftist groups seem to attempt to avoid casualties, while Islamists have been more ruthless.

Concluding Remarks

As can be seen from the above summary, this book goes far beyond a narrow political-economy perspective. The contributors represent a range of different disciplines, and they illuminate the issues from different perspectives: economics, political science, history, political psychology, and international relations. They also consider the prospects for economic development, which will be shaped by domestic social, political and cultural factors, as well as by geopolitics and the strategies pursued by global business actors – all in some kind of interaction with oil.

All of the contributors to this book describe the obstacles to democracy that are rooted in the mentality of the people who live in the Gulf. In Iraq, for example, the outcome of the struggle to maintain the viability of the country is related to attitudes about the territorial integrity of the state. Democracy in Iran is blocked by a conflict between very different conceptions of legitimate authority, theocratic and secular. Many of the Gulf states are paralyzed by the mentality of the *rentier* state, and find it difficult to break out of the *rentier* cycle. In Saudi Arabia, beliefs about the role of women in society limit the prospects for democratic reform, and the leadership is divided about the future role of the country in the region and OPEC. Elites in Azerbaijan attribute corruption to "the system" and consequently feel helpless to initiate any reforms. The oil companies could help to reduce corruption, but they believe that corruption is simply part of the culture and is something they cannot do anything about. Finally, the United States still has a relatively unsophisticated view of the region. Its perspective lacks an understanding of the complexity of introducing democratic reforms, but at the same time attempts to maximize its narrowly defined interests. There is still hope for the future, however, because these obstacles to democracy are largely rooted in beliefs and values – and these are mental images that are open to change.

Chapter 1

The Predicament of the Gulf Rentier State

Øystein Noreng

The Salience of the Middle East

The world remains vitally dependent on Middle Eastern oil. Almost three decades after the first oil price shock of 1973–74, oil remains of critical importance to consumers and producers alike. OPEC, the Organization of Petroleum Exporting Countries, is still alive and doing well in spite of repeated announcements of its demise and the sometimes alleged irrelevance of oil. Despite concerns about greenhouse gas emissions from burning fossil fuels, the world economy remains highly dependent on oil, which provides 40 per cent of the world's primary energy. Despite the extensive search for oil elsewhere over the past 30 years, more than half of the world's oil reserves are located in Middle Eastern OPEC member countries.

Middle Eastern politics directly affects the United States and the rest of the world, at times in most unexpected ways. The study of potential links between oil exports and the rise of Islam is empirically difficult. Oil exports and their revenues are easy to define and figures are publicly available, but Islamism is hard to define. Many diverse groups are difficult to compare. They range in quality from gradualist and pragmatic through revolutionary to Messianic. Most are non-violent, but some are extremely violent, as demonstrated by the terrorist attacks on New York and Washington, DC, on September 11, 2001. Groups also differ in size. Most are small, but some are part of wide networks. Most Islamist groups operate clandestinely because they are illegal or subject to police surveillance. Their life-spans vary because of repression, in-fighting and competition, as well as mergers and takeover cases.

One view is that the attacks on New York and Washington, DC, were carried out by fanatics motivated by violent religious sensibilities, unrelated to the economic, social and political problems of the Middle East, such as poverty or Israel's occupation of Palestine (Simon and Benjamin, 2001). In this perspective, fighting terrorism means eliminating individuals and small groups. Oil is not an issue, neither as a cause of terrorism nor as a potential target. Another view holds that a terrorist network has thrived on the political and economic bitterness felt in much of the Arab world and the Middle East (Khalaf, 2001). In this perspective, terrorists are motivated by oppression and by their opposition to corrupt, authoritarian Arab governments that are supported by the United States and other Western powers. In this case, fighting terrorism means not only eliminating individuals and small groups, but also undertaking comprehensive economic, social and political reforms.

In this perspective, oil is a key factor: it has provided huge revenues for the rulers, but neither political reform nor sufficient prosperity for the people. Since 1970, oil revenues have profoundly changed the societies of the Middle East, but there has been little political change that can cope with the ambitions of more numerous, younger and better educated generations. The outcome has been a society with rising social and economic inequalities and generational conflicts. The bitterness has also been caused by Arab defeats against Israel, by the plight of Palestinians and by the enduring sanctions against Iraq.

It is hard to assess the extent and the intensity of the resentment against the rulers in place and their Western allies and protectors because of the lack of freedom of assembly and expression in most, if not all, Arab countries. The West has become a victim of its own trap in the Middle East. By supporting corrupt and dictatorial regimes for immediate economic and strategic advantages, the West has prevented the kind of change necessary to stabilize these countries through representative government (Moïsi, 2001). Western oil interests and economic stability are shaky when dependent on moribund political systems and paralyzed societies. The United States has provided military, political and at times economic support in return for access to oil. At times the United States, again often supported by allies, has actively destabilized Middle Eastern governments with a popular mandate, as happened in Iran in 1953.

Rising Western dependence on Middle Eastern oil since the 1960s has not been matched by efforts to stabilize the region politically. Although the United States is increasingly dependent on oil imports and on the Middle East supplying the world market with volumes sufficient to stabilize prices, there has, so far, been little interest or insight into Middle Eastern affairs. The wisdom of giving unquestioning support to corrupt and authoritarian regimes because they export oil is not evident. The error has been to equate secure oil supplies with regimes more dependent on Western backing than on a popular mandate. Such a policy can backfire – as it did for the United States in Iran. In this perspective, the September 2001 terrorist attacks may appear as the forerunner of more trouble insofar as they express a widespread but so far hidden discontent. In that case, oil supplies and prices could be at stake.

The Middle Eastern Rentier State

This chapter discusses the internal pressures that have been building up in the oil-exporting countries of the Middle East due to rising population pressures, an economic monoculture and political rigidity. In the 1970s and early 1980s, huge oil revenues distorted economic development and caused political centralization within the state. Regardless of oil prices, the economic basis for this mode of development is no longer present. Economic restructuring away from oil is urgent, but success will depend on political power shifting from the state to the private sector, and from the rulers to the ruled.

Historically, in the key Middle Eastern oil-exporting countries there has been at least some connection between rising oil revenues and lagging political reforms. Today's regimes depend on oil revenues to prevent or delay reforms in the short run, and to survive in the long run. Rentier states need access to economic rent to survive. The politically conditioned need for revenues, to buy support and legitimacy, reduces oil policy discretion. The alternative is economic reform, with a more independent private sector and direct taxation, followed up by political reforms aiming at a more representative form of government.

Rising prosperity based solely on oil is a phenomenon of the past in the Middle East. With few exceptions, today's Gulf oil exporters face a race against time, as they have to develop away from oil dependence and their populations are rising quickly. Political implications are important, as rulers financed by erstwhile plentiful oil revenues are coming under increasing pressure to share power with representatives of the private sector – not only its bosses, but also its workers.

In the Middle East, oil has caused a special, capital-intensive mode of development. With high oil revenues, capital accumulation could take place at a much higher rate in the public sector than in private business. Control of the accumulation process moved from private capitalists to public sector bureaucrats and autocratic rulers. Oil money strengthened the state and the bureaucracy in relation to private business, creating a distinctive political system based on the centralization of petroleum revenues within the state (Cause III, 1994, p. 42 f).

Briefly put, the political process is that the rulers do not tax citizens or businesses, but hand out selective privileges, financed by oil revenues, against loyalty and support from a largely parasitic private sector (ibid., p. 43). Access to large oil revenues channelled through the treasuries is a distinctive feature of the state in the oil-exporting countries of the Middle East. These oil revenues make the state a distributor of economic rent from oil and therefore of privileges and transfers, instead of being a tax collector and redistributor (Pawelka, 1991). Most economic activities outside the petroleum sector depend on government permits, contracts, support and protection. This is usually coupled with an absence of taxes on property and income, except for the religious tax, *zakat*. Consequently, the Middle Eastern oil exporters have had no market economy, but rather a protected concessionary and distributive economy that is directed by the government. Private production, exports and investment have received reduced importance in the context of the state-run oil economy. The private sector has lost political weight.

The contrast with the independent capitalist development of the Western world is striking. In the developed capitalist economies, organized economic interests use the state for their political purposes. In the Middle Eastern oil-exporting countries, the state uses private business for its political purposes. This is a basic feature of the *rentier state*.

The result is the two-tiered economy. The public sector represents the developed part. It consists of the state apparatus, the national oil company, other key state enterprises and the leading financial institutions, all owned or controlled by the state. It accounts for most of the value added. The private sector, however, is less developed. It is dependent upon selective favors and transfers. Private businesses usually operate in imports, trade or services, but seldom in large-scale manufacturing. Agriculture is generally marked by low productivity and is dependent upon public support. The merchant class, the traders and craftsmen in the bazaar, needs differentiation. Some merchants have succeeded, through public favors and concessions, in gaining considerable wealth. Others have been marginalized by imports and large-scale trading.

The absence of direct taxation has reduced the need for the state to prove its legitimacy to the population through democratic institutions. Instead, the state buys legitimacy by spending oil revenues. When the state does not impose taxes on wealth and income, the need for liberal and democratic reforms diminishes. Instead, the state can buy legitimacy and support by granting selective economic privileges (Bierschenk, 1991). These selective favors have their counterpart in equally selective measures of discrimination. Those groups that do not benefit from the selective favors find themselves as second-class citizens. In the Gulf states,[1] unlike the situation in Iran and Iraq, there are a large number of foreign workers with inferior economic, political and social status. As an instrument of power, oil money is supplemented by the military.

The Military Pillar of Power

The growth and power of the military are salient features common to most countries of the Middle East, whether oil-exporting or not (Humphreys, 2001, p. 113). Military officers have repeatedly intervened to keep countries and political systems together, so that military government has often been the rule rather than the exception (Richards and Waterbury, 1990, p. 353 f). Iraq is a good case in point. The social origins of the military, especially the junior officers, are largely in the urban middle and lower middle classes. This is the case not only in Iraq. Historically, the military has been an exponent of social and political change, but over time, the military establishment has become a conservative force in the Middle East, defending its own privileges and its budgetary priorities. At the outset, military rule was socially radical, motivated by the aim of redistributing wealth and income, of carrying out profound reforms and asserting national interests against the colonial legacy. It has over decades acquired its own vested interests – meaning budgetary appropriations, training and the most modern equipment, apart from personal fringe benefits and political influence. In the oil-exporting countries the sudden influx of

---

1   The Gulf states – understood as Saudi Arabia, Kuwait, Oman, Qatar, Bahrain and the United Arab Emirates.

large oil revenues proved an irresistible temptation for the military establishment to demand more money. The military establishment represents a salient part of the new class of technocrats – wielding power, but not the ability to earn revenues. Like the technocrats of the public sector, the military establishment is largely professional, recruited by merit.

Indeed, the rise in military expenditure seems easier to explain by the level of oil revenues than by any sudden internal or external threats. Middle Eastern oil exporters have a preference for military spending not shared by oil exporters elsewhere. In 1998, Mexico spent less than one per cent of its gross domestic product, GDP, on the military, Indonesia about one per cent, Malaysia, Norway and Venezuela about two per cent and, Iran about three per cent. By contrast, in Oman and in Saudi Arabia some 13 per cent of GDP went to the military (SIPRI Military Expenditure Database). In Islamic Iran the military evidently enjoys far less influence, privileges and money than was the case under the Shah.

External threats, internal enemies, the pressure from foreign arms manufacturers as well as the military complex can explain the military priority. The political instability of the Middle East means that practically all countries of the region face actual or potential threats from neighbors. Political instability also means that almost all Middle Eastern governments face internal threats as well. Foreign arms dealers, assisted by their governments, do their best to convince oil-exporting Middle Eastern rulers that they need to buy the most sophisticated and expensive military hardware. Finally, local officers, friends and family members of the rulers also promote arms purchases, for a commission. High military expenditure helps the armed services compete for personnel, drawing competence away from more productive civilian tasks. In theory, the military burden means that the oil-exporting countries have some flexibility in budgetary policies, provided that it is politically possible to cut expenditures on the armed forces and that no serious threats appear on the horizon.

The Rentier Cycle

The lack of representative political institutions exacerbates the problem of accommodating social and generational change and of redistributing income. Autocratic governments, exercising varying degrees of repression, have traditionally gained legitimacy by offering public services financed by oil revenues, without imposing taxes on the population (Ismael, 1993, p. 81 ff Rising oil revenues at first financed rising public expenditure, but the recent decline in oil revenues has led to cuts in public services. The political effect has been a gradual weakening of political legitimacy. The lesson is that only the distribution of oil revenues can buy legitimacy. Algeria and the Shah's Iran are telling examples of how oil revenues can serve to undermine legitimacy if distribution is insufficient. The rapid population growth since the mid-1970s has exacerbated the problem of declining oil revenues. The sudden rise in oil revenues first led to rising investments in health, which in turn meant falling mortality rates, but without a parallel decline in birth rates. Subsequently, investment in education benefited large youth cohorts, but they could not always find suitable jobs in a labor market that was depressed due to falling oil revenues. Throughout its war with Iraq, Iran promoted population growth. Only in the 1990s did the country embark on a policy to limit population growth.

In countries as culturally and historically different as Iraq, Iran and Saudi Arabia, the economic monoculture has caused remarkably parallel economic, social and political problems. However, they are at different stages of maturity within a cycle of stages and events which in substance, if not in form, has strikingly similar features. The basic common problem is the rentier economy, its exposure to oil market risk and the consequent income discontinuities (Luciani, 1994). Because of differences in oil resources in relation to population, Iran was the worst hit by low oil prices in 1997–99, but Saudi Arabia was also badly affected. The 1986 oil price decline had had less dramatic effects because Iran and Iraq were at war and their civilian economy was already damaged. Seen in historical perspective, Iran is the most advanced case, Iraq the least, among the Middle Eastern oil exporters in a cycle of oil dependence where oil first brings prosperity, then unmakes it. The following is a brief exposition of a theory of the rentier cycle.

The first stage is the establishment of the rentier state and the rise of the new class. The high oil revenues in the 1970s and early 1980s caused profound social change, uprooting traditional society in the Middle East. In Iran this process started as early as in the 1960s. During this initial period, the distributive rentier state was established, with an increasingly parasitic private sector. At this time, the merchant class became largely marginalized by the rising technocratic and military classes. The rentier state made substantial efforts in infrastructure, housing, health and education. Distribution of wealth and income was not yet an important political issue, except in Iran, where the rentier state was more established and inflationary pressures exacerbated the distribution issue. Here, it culminated in the 1979 revolution. By contrast, in Iraq and in Saudi Arabia, the consensus in the 1970s was that the entire nation benefited from the oil boom.

The second stage comes with the consolidation of technocratic power at the expense of the merchant class and poorer parts of the population. In Iran this happened back in the 1960s and the early 1970s; in Kuwait, Iraq and Saudi Arabia, ten years later. With stagnant or declining oil and gas revenues, the distribution of wealth and income suddenly became an important political issue.

In the third stage, the new class refuses to give up privileges and power, in the face of rising opposition. In Iraq the new class has an important military component, in Saudi Arabia a royal part that cherishes privileges. In Iran confrontation took place in the late 1970s, whereas in the other countries it has been less acute. The problem of accommodating social and generational change and of redistributing income becomes exacerbated by the absence of representative political institutions.

In the fourth stage, the new class loses power. So far, this has happened only in Iran, where most of the technocratic groups at the core of the Shah's regime have fled the country. Others have reached compromises with the Islamic regime. In Iran, power has been taken over by a heterogeneous coalition of interests, including the clergy of varying opinions and vested interests, Islamic foundations, merchants and technocrats. Elsewhere in the Middle East, the position of the new class, civilian and military, seems precarious unless compromises can be made with the various forces of opposition.

Within this general cycle there are deep-seated differences between countries. The outcome is not determined, but conditioned by oil prices and political skills. Low oil prices put the rentier regimes under severe pressure, but they also represent a challenge for reformers. This has been evident in Iran, Kuwait and Saudi Arabia since 1998. High oil prices dampen political pressure to change and can strengthen conservative forces that resist economic and political reform.

When put under severe pressure – that is when resources are insufficient to satisfy the client groups and support is withering – rentier states may collapse or turn to internal repression combined with external aggression. Iraq is an evident case. Insufficient oil revenues paved the way for the collapse of the Shah's regime in Iran through social unrest. The fiscal crisis of the rentier state, due to insufficient oil revenues, easily becomes a survival crisis for the regime (Aziz-Chaudhry, 1997). A salient example is Iran in the late 1970s; another is Iraq in the late 1980s. The high petroleum revenues of the 1970s and early 1980s acted to stabilize the rentier states, whereas subsequent low oil prices have contributed to political destabilization. The Iranian regime collapsed under stress in 1978–79, because of falling oil revenues, the high priority given to the military and heavy industry, and a particularly unequal income distribution. The Iraqi regime in 1989–90 suffered from falling real oil revenues. With a commitment to high military expenditure, it found itself unable to import food and service the foreign debt as well. Even if the Iraqi debt to other Arab countries was unenforceable, the Iraqi government was in a precarious financial situation. This was one of the motives for choosing external aggression – attacking Kuwait – so as to avoid a social and political upheaval, with the prospects of a bloody end to the regime. A third way out, economic and political reform, seemed out of the question at the time.

The highly centralized political leadership of the Middle Eastern oil-exporting countries is vulnerable to low oil prices and insufficient oil revenues. Rising population means an increasing pressure to change. The lack of consensus about the rules of the game in politics and the absence of democratic institutions build up pressures for political change, which potentially could be of a revolutionary character insofar as there are no institutions to handle them, nor able to suppress them. The power structures put in place by high oil revenues cannot survive long with low oil revenues, unless it adapts to the new situation. Unless its base is enlarged, the coalition of the military and the technocrats risks losing power. Iran is but one historical example of an apparently strong regime suddenly crumbling. The fates of the Soviet Union and the East European Communist regimes have also shown that political monopolies carry high risk.

The Apparent Economic Miracle of the Middle East

From the early 1970s to the mid-1980s, the Middle East was considered the economically most promising part of the world in spite of its numerous political tensions and open conflicts. Thanks to the revenues from oil, the oil-exporting countries of the region had made an economic quantum leap, sometimes going from dire poverty to extreme wealth within a decade. Their economic growth rates were exceptional, and their relative position in the world had improved tremendously.

Around 1980, Kuwait's per capita GDP was higher than that of most European countries, while, by the same measure, Iraq and Saudi Arabia were at the level of Central Europe. The Middle East had become an important market for goods and services. The region also had the economic resources to make it a politically significant part of the world community. The general impression was that the oil wealth was reasonably well managed and that the oil-exporting countries of the region were making the transition to modern economies. The wise use of an important natural resource, it was thought, could apparently propel a group of countries into the modern world. These countries also gave the impression of having sophisticated and visionary leaderships that combined wisdom and power (Roberts, 1995, p. 23 ff).

The oil price rises of the 1970s made everyone in the oil-exporting countries of the Middle East much richer, but some citizens became much richer than others. The mechanisms of particular enrichment were many. In some countries, there was little or no distinction between the coffers of the state and those of the royal family, so the rulers, their families and favorites were the first to benefit. Leading officials in government and the national oil company could amass vast fortunes through a mixture of private and official interests. Businesses dealing with the government and the oil industry could also profit disproportionately, as could some lucky landowners. In the aftermath of the first oil price rise came the beginning of ostentatious wealth and conspicuous consumption. This inspired grandiose and megalomaniacal development plans, as for example in Iran. By the 1970s it was becoming evident that the distribution of wealth and income was growing less and less equal. However, this was relatively easy to bear, because even the poorest parts of the population also enjoyed rapidly improving living conditions. The exception was Iran, where the rapidly rising income inequality in the late 1970s proved to be an important factor behind the revolution.

The immediate effect of the second oil price rise of 1979–80 was to flood the Arab oil exporters of the Middle East with easy money. This money was even less equally distributed – but that did not matter much politically. Everyone experienced rising prosperity. For a few years, these countries experienced an acute embarrassment of riches. This came to an end when they had to cut oil export volumes to defend the price of oil before it fell, and export volumes were still fairly low. The contraction that began at various points in the early 1980s, depending upon how much money had been saved during the boom years, was not equally distributed. Budget cuts hit the poor much more than the rich. By around 1980 the distribution of wealth and income had become extremely unequal in most Arab oil-exporting countries, and during the late 1980s and early 1990s income distribution became even more skewed. The poor were getting both more numerous, and more impoverished. The rich refused to relinquish their money and privileges – and they had the means to defend their interests.

In oil-exporting Middle Eastern countries, social services for the bulk of the population have improved since the early 1970s, but they have mostly benefited the already privileged parts of the population, the people from whom the rulers wanted political support. Declining oil revenues since the 1980s should have caused a reduction in these transfers and special services, but most governments have not dared to do so, fearing opposition from resourceful groups. Instead, the budget cuts have hit hardest those groups that were already the most underprivileged. This has been accompanied by a vast array of subsidies and transfers to the private sector. Recent attempts at reintroducing taxes and withdrawing subsidies and transfers to the privileged have caused effective protests from the groups concerned. In Saudi Arabia, it has been politically difficult to cut the military budget, although the country evidently possesses more military hardware than it can use. Some key people get commissions from arms purchases. Because of the political dependence of the regime on these groups, the proposed measures have been withdrawn. Persistent quarrels over the budget in the Kuwaiti parliament are but one example. Consequently, the new austerity has hit hardest those groups that have been the least privileged, as they are considered less dangerous by the regime. An example is the decline of health service and education quality in Saudi Arabia.

The vision of the Middle East progressing has faded, gradually emerging as a mirage. Part of the reason can be found in the international conflicts plaguing the region, for example over Palestine, Lebanon, Iraq, Iran, Yemen and Kuwait. The reason is also that autocratic leaders use conflicts with neighbors to entrench their power and to refuse or delay reforms.

The Unmaking of the Miracle

By the late 1990s it was evident that the Middle East had fallen behind economically. It is continuing to do so, although high oil prices around 2000 have provided some relief, which may be temporary. Average income is high by Western standards only in Kuwait, Qatar and the United Arab Emirates. Countries such as Oman and Saudi Arabia have an average income level about that of poorer European countries, such as Greece or Portugal. Income distribution is less unequal among citizens than among the working population, which includes a large number of foreign workers. In Iran and Iraq, average income levels are much lower. Living conditions for the majority of the population are difficult by European or North American standards.

The oil price decline of 1986 led to a serious drop in oil revenues for most oil-exporting countries and a subsequent deterioration in social conditions. The oil-exporting countries, as a rule, are poor and getting both relatively and absolutely poorer as their population grows. Indeed, it is difficult to overemphasize the threat of the population time bomb ticking away, which has meant a rush against time in the effort to develop the Middle Eastern oil-exporting economies (Fargues, 1994). Algeria finds itself in the same predicament.

All Middle Eastern oil exporters are now facing basic economic problems and difficult decisions in their oil policies, conditioned both by their own needs and interests and by relations to their neighbors. All these countries need high oil revenues, but they also need to reduce their dependence on oil revenues. Low oil prices in 1998 revealed their economic vulnerability and political problems. Iran and Saudi Arabia experienced a dramatic deterioration of the balance of payments, making clear that the alternative to drastic budget cuts and deep-going economic and political reform was to stabilize oil prices at a significantly higher level. On the other hand, in both countries, low oil revenues triggered a process of economic reform, which does not seem to have been halted by the subsequently high oil prices during 1999 and 2000. The combination of lower imports and higher oil export revenues has improved the economic situation. In 1999, Iran had a balance-of-payments surplus, Saudi Arabia a much-reduced deficit that turned into a surplus in 2000.

The leaps in oil revenues in the 1970s and early 1980s enabled the rulers of most Middle Eastern countries to disengage their domestic economies from the world economy. Although this was especially the case with the oil exporters, similar tendencies were also present in the other countries. For the oil exporters, oil revenues were evidently seen as the ultimate solution to any budgetary or balance-of-payments problem.

Huge rentier revenues from the windfall profits from oil enabled the rulers to square the circles of economic policy. Oil revenues permitted investment and consumption to increase simultaneously at high rates. Public expenditure could be raised as taxes were reduced. Oil revenues permitted selective and generous subsidies to consumers and producers alike. Domestic prices were to a large extent decoupled from those of the world market. Heavy investment was made in both human and real capital, especially in ambitious infrastructure projects, but structural rigidities and market distortions were maintained.

The return on this investment has been generally poor (Pakravan, 1997). Since the early 1980s the countries of the Middle East have had low economic growth rates, except for the late 1990s, when oil revenues rose suddenly. The reasons for these low economic growth rates are stagnant or declining productivity and the absence of structural reforms. The outcome is declining average living standards and increasing social inequalities. Poverty is advancing quickly, and unemployment rates are among the world's highest. Equally seriously, the Middle East oil exporters do not seem to manage any substantial diversification of their income base. With a few honorable exceptions, the region sells almost only crude oil, oil products and natural gas to the outside world. For this reason, the Middle East is missing out on commercial and industrial opportunities in a more open and economically interdependent world.

In the Middle East the illusion of unlimited access to capital made the rulers overlook other problems on the road to economic development (Penrose and Penrose, 1978, p. 166). The high oil revenues in the 1970s and early 1980s prevented measures and reforms that could have prepared the development of a more diversified economy. Consequently, oil also prevented a more stable economic growth in the longer run.

The first cardinal error was the neglect of agriculture and domestic food supply. This was based on the illusion that oil-financed food imports were the long-term solution. Today, food imports weigh heavily in the trade balance of all Middle Eastern oil exporters – also in Iran and Iraq, which have a potential for higher self-sufficiency in food.

The second major error was the neglect of mass education in many countries of the region. This was the case in Iran under the Shah, but not under the Islamic republic, nor in Algeria, Iraq, Kuwait or Saudi Arabia. It was based on the illusion that the oil economy needed only a small number of experts, not mass literacy. Imperial Iran provided higher education to a small elite, neglecting mass literacy, but the Islamic republic has emphasized education of the people. In other countries, such as Saudi Arabia, education is universal, but there are important quality differences.

The third error was to give priority to capital-intensive heavy industry instead of labor-intensive manufacturing. This choice was based on the illusion that the state should and could provide employment.

The fourth error was an overvalued exchange rate that stimulated imports at the expense of local businesses. Also this choice was based on an illusion – that the oil economy did not need a productive and prosperous local merchant class. The illusion proved fatal to the Shah's regime in Iran, providing grounds for the alliance of clergy and merchants that overthrew the regime.

Today, the results of mistaken economic policies are rising import dependence, rising unemployment and an economic monoculture with a critical exposure to the risks of the oil market. The deteriorating distribution of income has impaired political stability and the access to capital. The oil exporters of the Middle East made a great leap forward in the 1970s and early 1980s. Since then, what they risk is a leap backward.

The key economic problems of the Middle East relate to population growth, inequity and economic stagnation. The unequal distribution of wealth means that the fruits of progress are unequally shared. Over time, this impedes the creation of a home market for industrial products and industrialization itself. The increasing concentration of wealth and income in a small number of people is unproductive. The very rich tend to expatriate part of their wealth, and concentrate demand on imported luxury items, impeding the growth of a wider home market for less sophisticated products. The very rich tend to keep part of their wealth idle, as in numerous luxury dwellings and cars, thereby diverting capital from more productive uses.

The unequal distribution of wealth means that the fruits of progress are unequally shared. Although statistics are not readily available, income distribution seems to have been particularly unequal in imperial Iran, where the merchants were marginalized by the free-spending state. In Islamist Iran, income distribution appears less unequal, although good data is not available. In Iraq, income distribution seems to have become more equal after the 1958 revolution and until the Gulf War in 1990, but has since become much more unequal under the impact of sanctions. The ruling families of the Gulf states (see footnote 1), including Saudi Arabia, had the resources both to enrich themselves and to let the oil wealth benefit their populations (Owen and Pamuk, 1999, p. 207). Here, the problem has become how to give priority to income distribution as oil revenues fall.

The impact of declining oil revenues to the Middle East has been exacerbated by the rising need to import food, due to insufficient output and productivity growth in agriculture. This problem is critical because most countries of the region have hardly any manufactured exports. Persistent high fertility rates, together with declining investment in physical capital and low domestic savings and insufficient investment in human capital, are paving the way for a further decline in productivity growth.

Since the first oil price rise in the early 1970s, the oil exporters of the Middle East have achieved an unusual inequality of wealth and income. Before the first oil price rise, most Middle Easterners were poor by European or North American standards. Some were less poor than the rest, but there were fairly few cases of extreme wealth. There was little ostentatious wealth or conspicuous consumption, even in Kuwait and the Emirates that were to become the UAE in 1971. Even in Iran, with the most stratified society at the time, personal wealth was comparatively modest. Hence there was some equity in the poverty. The poverty was easier to bear because it apparently afflicted all. Even Saudi princes were not rich by European or North American standards before 1973. At the time, there was much more ostentatious wealth and conspicuous consumption in Latin America and even parts of sub-Saharan Africa.

The experience of low oil prices in 1998 and early 1999 revealed the vulnerability of the Middle Eastern rentier states and provided strong incentives to reach agreement to raise oil prices substantially. Saudi Arabia was a case in point. The lesson is simply that high oil prices stabilize the regimes and that low oil prices undermine them. Insofar as high oil prices – above $25 per barrel – are not sustainable, the regimes concerned are facing a countdown to a crunch where there seems to be only two options: deep-going reforms, or collapse.

The need to create jobs is urgent. Youth unemployment is in many cases running at between 30 and 50 per cent. The need to replace foreign workers with locals, as in Saudi Arabia, raises difficult issues of labor productivity and income distribution. Iraq has traditionally been the exception, as a welfare state with relatively good social conditions. This no longer holds true, due to the Saddam Hussein regime, the war against Iran, the Gulf conflict and the subsequent embargo.

Population Growth and Economic Stagnation

In 1970, the six leading oil exporters on the Gulf – Iran, Iraq, Kuwait, Qatar, Saudi Arabia and the Emirates – had a total population of about 45 million. By 2000, this figure had more than doubled to about 117 million. Over the same period, their total oil output rose by about one half, from about 13 million barrels a day in 1970 to about 20 million barrels a day in 2000. This means that average per capita oil output has been almost halved, from 0.30 barrels a day per person in 1970 to 0.18 barrels a day per person by 2000. Measured in constant 2001 prices, by the price of Saudi Light crude, average per capita oil output value in these six countries was $1.84 in 1970. By 1985 it had more than tripled to $5.87, but by 2000 it had declined again to $4.58. This latter figure is misleading as a rising proportion of the oil is consumed locally at low prices, especially in Iran. Population growth and uncertain oil prices mean that per capita oil revenues in the Middle East are far more likely to fall than to rise. The revenue squeeze limits choice in oil policy, as a larger population requires more money. This also means a risk of social distress and political instability, with potential repercussions for the oil market.

Table 1.1 Population and oil output 1970, 1985 and 2000

	Population		
	1970	*1985*	*2000*
Iran	28 429 000	47 100 000	66 129 000
Iraq	9 356 000	15 317 000	23 332 000
Kuwait	744 000	1 712 000	2 042 000
Qatar	111 000	358 000	769 000
Saudi Arabia	5 745 000	12 379 000	22 757 000
UAE*	220 000	1 379 000	2 408 000
Total	44 605 000	78 245 000	117 437 000

	Oil output (thousand bbl/day)			*Oil output per capita* (bbl/day)		
	1970	*1985*	*2000*	*1970*	*1985*	*2000*
Iran	3 829	2 250	3 770	0.13	0.05	0.06
Iraq	1 549	1 433	2 625	0.17	0.09	0.11
Kuwait	2 990	1 023	2 150	4.02	0.60	1.05
Qatar	362	301	795	3.26	0.84	1.03

Saudi Arabia	3 799	3 388	9 145	0.66	0.27	0.40
UAE*	780	1 193	2 515	3.55	0.87	1.04
Total	13 309	9 588	21 000	0.30	0.12	0.18

	Oil output value per day (thousand US$ 2001)			*Oil output value per capita per day (US$ 2001)*		
	1970	*1985*	*2000*	*1970*	*1985*	*2000*
Iran	23 674	107 760	96 517	0.83	2.29	1.46
Iraq	9 577	68 631	67 203	1.02	4.48	2.88
Kuwait	18 487	48 995	55 043	24.85	28.62	26.96
Qatar	2 238	14 416	20 353	20.16	40.27	26.47
Saudi Arabia	23 489	162 262	234 123	4.09	13.11	10.29
UAE*	4 823	57 136	64 387	21.92	41.43	26.74
Total	82 288	459 199	537 625	1.84	5.87	4.58

* UAE: United Arab Emirates

Figures are calculated on the basis of oil output figures given above and the assumption of a single oil price, that of Saudi Light, in 1970 $1.35/bl., in 1985 $29.00/bl. and in 2000 $24.78/bl.

Economic monoculture has made the Middle Eastern oil exporters highly vulnerable to the cycles of a single commodity market. Periodically high revenues have not led to any diversification of the economic basis, except in small rentier economies such as Kuwait and the United Arab Emirates, where a substantial part of the economic surplus has financed foreign investment. For this reason, discontinuities are the trademark of the economic development of the Middle Eastern oil exporters. Breaking out of this pattern is a political rather than an economic problem. It will require changes in power structures rather than incremental resources.

In recent years, the economic and political system has been under stress in practically all oil-exporting countries of the Middle East. Since the mid-1980s, low oil prices have forced severe cuts in public budgets. One example is Saudi Arabia in 1994 and 1995 and again in 1998. Budget constraints have led to transfer cuts and declining living standards for large parts of the population. They have also diminished the bargaining power of the established rulers. In many cases economic growth rates have been lower than population growth rates, so that average incomes have fallen. Unemployment has risen, especially among young people, as governments no longer have resources both to educate and to employ them. During the 1970s and 1980s expenditure on education had increased drastically in all oil-exporting countries. Today, the result is a large number of young people who often cannot find work commensurate with their qualifications (Ende, 1991). This has become an increasingly acute problem in Saudi Arabia, whose young people often have high expectations, as well as in Iran.

In practically all oil-exporting countries, budget cuts are painful, but have not been sufficient to reduce deficits, especially since the governments have not dared tax income and property. Hence the economic leverage of governments declines sharply in times of social and political unrest.

All Middle Eastern oil-exporting countries have become increasingly dependent on oil revenues as populations grow and the development of other sources of income is lagging. The low oil prices of 1998 revealed economic and political vulnerabilities that could be potentially fatal to the regimes in place, unless they could manage political change. Budget and trade deficits suddenly reached unsustainable levels. The high oil prices in 1999–2000 have markedly improved budget and trade balances, but these mask structural problems due to economic monoculture, high risk exposure to oil prices, together with population growth. Against this backdrop, the current organization of economic life does not appear sustainable, except perhaps in Kuwait, Qatar and some of the United Arab Emirates, which can supplement oil revenues with investment income. These countries have small indigenous populations, large oil revenues and huge financial resources.

After 20 years of war economy, Iraq has an urgent need for civilian investment, but the country also has a considerable potential for developing a more diversified economy. Iran already has a more diversified economy, but also has a large population and low self-sufficiency in food supplies and a need to create employment outside oil. Saudi Arabia's economy is not much diversified, and the country remains dependent on oil revenues. High population growth, rising unemployment and stagnant or declining living standards make an ever more urgent need for economic reforms.

For these reasons, low oil prices in 1998 gave rise not only to a critical economic situation for Iran and Saudi Arabia, but also to some political change. In Iran, the outcome was further liberalization and a weakening of the conservative forces within the clergy. In Saudi Arabia, low oil prices strengthened reformist forces inside and outside the royal family. In Iraq, by contrast, rising oil revenues following the agreement with the United Nations apparently strengthened the regime, dampening the immediate need for economic and political reforms, and therefore also the basis for opposition against the regime.

In the Middle Eastern oil-exporting countries, political stability requires high oil revenues and a gradual development of representative institutions. On this latter point, Iran is the most advanced, Iraq the least. The risk of instability is embedded in a sudden decline in oil revenues before representative institutions are more developed, or in an external political event. Recent experience indicates that for Iran, a possible decline in oil revenues would help provoke a more liberal and democratic trend in politics and strengthen the private sector over the rentier state. This process has already been put in motion by generation change and globalization. The risk is, however, that internal strife could strengthen the conservative forces within the Iranian clergy, who, in order to survive politically, would take an ideologically more aggressive stance against neighboring oil exporters.

For Iraq, lower oil revenues could strengthen opposition to the regime, but also make it more aggressive. A destitute Iraq can be a more serious menace than a prosperous one, as was made evident in 1990 by the attack on Kuwait.

Also for Saudi Arabia, lower oil revenues would probably accelerate economic and political reforms and eventually open up for more foreign investment to create employment and income, but there are alternative outcomes (Cappelen and Choudhury, 2000, p. 17). This would require, however, consensus within the royal family on the need for change and its direction, and that the elite surrounding the royals voluntarily relinquish important privileges. Another way out could be to boost oil output, regardless of the consequences for oil prices and relations with Iran and Iraq. There is also a possibility of a more Islamist political development.

The 1997–98 oil price decline caused a severe economic predicament among the world's oil exporters, not least in the Middle East. The 1999–2000 oil price rebound has again improved the situation, but serious basic problems remain.

In its 1999 budget, Saudi Arabia, the world's largest oil exporter, cut spending by 12 per cent. Oil revenues were estimated to be the lowest since 1990. The 1998 actual fiscal deficit soared to SR 46 billion, nine per cent of gross domestic product. The 1999 fiscal deficit caused domestic borrowing by the government. Nominal Saudi GDP declined by nearly 13 per cent in 1998, leading to lower public spending, lower subsidies and reduced living standards.

Continued domestic borrowing lessens the resources available to the private sector. Only a serious effort to restructure loss-making state enterprises, as well as to cut state subsidies further, enabled the Saudi government to keep within its projected deficit for 1999. The stated goal of a balanced budget by 2000 seemed unattainable, unless oil prices should unexpectedly shoot up – as they in fact did.

Iran's predicament is worse, as the country does not have a prosperous private sector with resources to lend to the state. The government in 1998 again resorted to a budget funded by printing money. Despite owning nearly ten per cent of proven global oil reserves and nearly one-fifth of the world's gas reserves, Iran in 1998 defaulted on repayment of interest and principal on its short-term debt to Italy, Germany and Japan. Successive governments have covered the deficit in the state industries budget, which comprises 60 per cent of the total, by the simple expedient of printing money.

Only a few non-oil manufacturing companies and private or family-owned trading and agricultural companies in Iran are free from state control. Most nationalized companies lose money; but they are financed by the central bank. Because of the money printed to finance state industries, inflation reached 40 per cent in 1999. The only certain sources of revenue to cover annual budget expenditure are export sales of oil, gas and petrochemicals, which historically comprise 75 per cent of state earnings.

The low oil prices enhanced underlying demographic and economic pressures and the consequent political risk in the Middle East. There is no more money to distribute, unless wealth is taxed. There is an urgent need to cut expenditure and imports, but the governments hardly seem able to choose cuts in a way that can protect the basic standard of living. The cuts made are often too timid to reduce the trade balance substantially, but they do contribute to social deterioration.

The common feature in all these states is an economic crisis building up without the governments being able to act. The Saudi financial improvement of 1995 was but the first part of a long process which again was compromised in 1998. Population growth puts the system under persistent pressure to cut unnecessary expenses. Therefore, military requirements will increasingly conflict with civilian needs. Kuwait is the only country of the region where internal demographic and economic pressures do not seem to be building up to a critical level. This is little consolation, however, for a tiny city-state squeezed between potentially unstable or hostile neighbors. The pressures building up in Iran are such that oil certainly is no option, unless real oil prices move substantially above present levels and stay there. Otherwise, Iran seems to have no choice but to industrialize – with important political implications, including opening up to the world. Any delay or failure in the process of simultaneously redistributing wealth and opening up to the world would represent a risk to the oil market.

Postponing reforms through high oil revenues is hardly a durable solution. Maintaining high oil prices will require a persistently robust demand or agreement between the major oil exporters, preferably both, but neither is assured. Insofar as oil demand stays high and no significant investment is made in capacity expansion outside OPEC, and the leading Middle Eastern oil exporters agree on price levels and market shares, conditions could be favorable for oil prices to stay higher than during most of the 1990s (Morse, 2000). If oil demand falls, significant investment is made in capacity expansion outside OPEC, and the leading Middle Eastern oil exporters disagree on price levels and market shares, then the conditions could be ripe for another oil price decline.

The bad omen for Middle East politics is that high oil revenues in 1999 and 2000 have caused military spending to increase again. Indeed, after the end of the Cold War, the Middle East has become the world's leading market for arms, and is now its most militarized region. For internal politics, high military expenditure means a lasting conflict between civilian and military priorities, resulting from a persistently powerful political position of the armed forces and a consequent unproductive use of scarce resources. Iran is currently an exception. For external politics, the rearmament indicates the persistence of regional threats, tensions and conflict potential.

Economic Stagnation, Political Opposition and Islamism

The Islamist movements in the Muslim countries would appear to represent a social revolt as well as an assertion of cultural and national identity in the wake of an unsuccessful or incomplete modernization based on oil. The background is dynamic demographics in a strained economic situation within a rigid political context. These three aspects are closely linked. Rapid population growth creates conflicts of distribution, positions, priorities and values. The immature and unstructured political systems keep ageing leaders in power without accountability to the public. Autocratic political systems do not facilitate dialogue and compromise, but provoke conflict instead.

The outcome is intense social and generational tensions. They arise partly out of a conflict over distribution and economic positions, especially jobs, partly out of a conflict of views on how to organize society, and partly out of conflicts of power. Put simply, the older generation got little education, but jobs, wealth and power when the new Muslim states arose after independence. It benefited greatly from the influx of large oil revenues in the 1970s and early 1980s. Members of this generation were at least 30 years old at the time of the first oil price rise in 1973. The next generation is more numerous. It has got more education and many jobs, but less wealth and little power. It benefited more moderately from the oil wealth. Its members were at most 30 years old in 1973. The youngest generation makes up the majority of the population. Its members have got education, but few jobs, no wealth and no power. They were born too late to benefit from the high oil revenues. Indeed, employment is the test failed for the Muslim states a generation or two after independence and with declining oil revenues (Kepel, 1994, p. 26). This is a recipe for intergenerational conflict with a social and cultural accent (Fargues, 1994). The social crisis leads to a cultural crisis with religious references and political significance. It prepares the ground for Islamist movements.

The older generation, those over 60, are usually the ones who took power at independence and used it for their own economic benefit. The middle generation, those below 60 and above 30, has been barred from power by their elders and have received fewer economic benefits. The exceptions are Iran, Iraq and Libya, whose rulers are younger than in most of the rest of the Middle East and North Africa. The youngest generation, those under 30, has arrived too late for power, economic benefits or adequate social services in a stagnant economy.

A generational perspective on politics should take into account important historical events. Middle Eastern or North African Arab citizens born in the 1920s would have experienced independence as fairly young people after the Second World War. This was their major formative political experience. The military nationalist regimes that took power in the 1950s consolidated their positions and influence. In their forties, they experienced the emerging prosperity of the 1960s as well as the shock of the Arab defeat by Israel in 1967. In their fifties, they benefited from the oil boom of the 1970s and early 1980s. For them, the Iranian revolution represented a threat. In their sixties and seventies they now refuse to give up power or privileges.

For the next generation, born between the 1940s and the 1960s, the major formative political experience was military defeat by Israel in 1967. They saw it as an Arab defeat at the hands of the West. The 1973 war and the subsequent oil price rise represented a settling of scores and new opportunities. The Iranian revolution was another major formative event for young adults. In their late thirties or early forties, since the mid-1980s they have suffered from low oil prices, dwindling resources and blocked opportunities. This stimulates frustrations. Only in Iraq and Libya does this generation have substantial political power.

For the youngest generation, born since the 1970s, the major formative political event was the Gulf War. They easily associate the subsequent low oil prices with Iraq's defeat by the West. Even more than for the preceding generation, dwindling resources block opportunities and stimulate frustrations. That the West went to war for oil, was victorious and has hence benefited from low oil prices – this invites a confrontational outlook.

Against this backdrop, political leaders have in their youth experienced different historical events as critical in their formation. In the Arab world, critical events were the Suez invasion in 1956, the Arab defeat by Israel in 1967, the 1973 war and the subsequent oil price rise. They also include the Iranian revolution and the second oil price rise of 1979–80. By a simplistic division, members of the older generation of leaders were above 20 in 1956 and the middle generation were above 20 in 1980. For the present young Arab generation, the 2003 Iraq war is likely to be a major critical event in the formation of political thinking.

In the Arab world, radical Islamism took off as local movements in the mid-1980s. This coincided with the fall in oil revenues. The movements largely had the form of social welfare organizations, which supplemented the deficient and often corrupt public services. These organizations enjoyed the active support of young intellectuals. The governments found these organizations more difficult to prosecute than the preceding Islamist armed guerrilla movements, as their welfare work was making them popular. The next step was for the multiple Islamist organizations to present political grievances. The ideological references often go back to the Middle Ages, when the leading learned would at times question the rulers' legitimacy when their rule was unjust.

The Arab countries are experiencing an increasing political polarization, because the cleavages of class, age and culture tend to coincide. Simply put, many Muslim countries have old rulers who control the government and the economic surplus. They also to a considerable extent represent Western ideas and lifestyles. In opposition to them are a frustrated middle generation and an impoverished youth. In social terms, their origins are usually in an urban lower middle class with recent rural roots but with education (Toscane, 1995, p. 33). They want influence and prosperity and are keen to assert national cultural traditions against Western influence on attitudes and lifestyles. This may be particularly relevant to the oil-exporting Arab countries. In the aftermath of the 2003 Iraq war, the key question is to what extent the educated urban lower middle class will aspire to Western-style consumer prosperity and Western inspired democracy, or will reject Western economic and political models. The outcome in Iraq is likely to have a wider influence in the Arab Middle East.

In most Arab countries the established political leadership is not accountable to the population through democratic processes. In many cases it appears to the younger generation and the poorer parts of society to be excessively favorable to the West or even corrupted by the West. The absence of democratic institutions means that a peaceful transition of power appears blocked to the opposition. With rising economic problems, the opposition is no longer only the cause of the younger generations, but becomes an alliance of diverse groups.

The alleged original social project of Islam readily emerges as an ideal in a strained economic situation. In brief, Islam promises equality and social welfare, but respects private property. In a society with rising social tensions but without democratic institutions, its message falls on fertile ground. Indeed, traditional Muslim society apparently enjoyed some degree of egalitarianism and social welfare. Then, with European colonization and domination, came economic inequality and marked social differentiation, especially in the rural areas. As a result, the pursuit of social justice naturally gets an anti-Western accent.

The reference to the past concerns the centuries after the Prophet Mohammed, when the Muslim world enjoyed a remarkable and original development of religion and government, science and civilization (Mantran, 1989, p. 58). Therefore the issue is social, concerning the distribution of income, wealth and power. It is also cultural and national, concerning political identity within fairly recent borders. Finally, it is generational, affecting conflicts of power and outlook between age groups with different experiences and expectations, and national, affecting the search for a cultural and political identity.

In this connection, the issue is not what Islam says on economic, social and political issues, but how it is being referred to and used politically. This is of particular relevance in the present economic and social turmoil in the Middle East and North Africa. Potentially, this could become the case in Central Asia as well. If Islamism has its causes in mounting conflicts of income distribution, exacerbated by rising social and generational tensions, then oil is clearly neither a necessary nor a sufficient condition. Conflicts of income distribution as well as social and generational tensions may arise in any society, independently of oil. However, oil may reduce the conflict potential when revenues rise, and subsequently enhance it when revenues fall. Insofar as rising oil revenues have postponed structural economic and political reforms, the reckoning tends to be crude. Most important, the oil industry and its revenues have strengthened the public sector at the expense of the private sector. When oil revenues decline, the public sector suffers from diminishing resources and a frustrated private sector. This is perhaps the major reason why there could be a link between oil and Islamism. Finally, declining oil revenues in an undiversified economy leave young people with reduced chances and with greater disappointment. This is particularly important when oil revenues decline and the population continues to grow at a rapid pace.

No Representation without Taxation

In hindsight, high oil revenues have provided a substitute for democracy in the Middle East oil-exporting countries. Because the rulers did not have to tax their subjects, they did not need representative governments either (Crystal, 1990, p. 6 ff). Indeed, the rulers implicitly countered demands for democracy by turning around the rallying slogan from the American war of independence, by replying: "No representation without taxation." That the rulers have not needed to tax their subjects has, it can now been seen, proved a curse for the development of political institutions. Oil revenues are an important reason why the wave of democracy that swept over much of the world in the 1980s and 1990s has not yet reached the Middle East and North Africa. Oil is partly responsible for the retarded political and institutional development of the Middle East and North Africa. With declining per capita oil revenues the Gulf oil exporters not only face the challenge of economic restructuring, but also that of political reform. Less oil money simply means that governments will have to tax wealth and income, and that raises the issue of representative government. This is both a domestic issue in the various countries, and a regional one.

The absence of strong regional co-operation, democratic governments and a regional hegemonic power impedes political stability in the Middle East. The various states and regimes have competing and conflicting interests that complicate mutually responsive regional co-operation. In part, this is linked to the positions of individuals and ruling groups that have resulted from the absence of stable democratic institutions. Since the collapse of the Ottoman Empire, no single state has been able to dominate the Middle East, to exercise hegemony through a combination of geography, population, economy and organization. This absence of hegemony or close political co-operation aiming at regional economic integration necessarily means instability and temptations to establish dominance. Any attempt at establishing hegemony has an impact on oil supplies and oil prices, as was demonstrated by the 1990–91 Gulf crisis. It has also provoked foreign intervention.

The Middle East is split and unstable with a weak Iraq. After Iraq was defeated, Iran is no candidate for hegemony, even with its large population and lack of foreign debt. Language and religion set Iran apart from the Arab mainstream. Liabilities are political instability and rising income requirements. Pressing financial constraints could make Iran a potential source of instability in the Middle East, or could lead it to attempt to play a dominant role in the region. Nevertheless, through religion Iran has important cultural features in common with the majority of the population of neighboring Iraq. These cultural links have a political significance (Kubba, 2001, p. 80).

Iraq is geographically, economically and culturally, by the level of education, the heartland of the Arab Middle East. The potential Arab leadership may make Iraq the key to control the Middle East. The United States evidently realized this when deciding to occupy the country. Iraq has the world's second largest oil reserves. Water provides agricultural potential. Traditionally, Iraq is the major

Middle Eastern country with the most secular tradition, where religion has had the least influence in public life as in politics. Iraq has been the closest candidate for regional hegemony, through its combination of a central geographical position, a sizeable population, the potential for a diversified economy, a high level of education and a comparatively efficient administration, at least until the 2003 war. France and the Soviet Union must have realized this, since they chose Iraq as their essential partner in the Middle East. In hindsight, they bet on the right horse, but with the wrong rider, Saddam. Since the country's creation in 1920, internal tensions have led to authoritarian government. Open questions are how to keep Iraq together and who shall control Iraq.

Iraq has a particularly violent history, with political change generally involving bloodshed. The present regime has built its power on crude force, but in doing so it embodies a national tradition. The reason may be the ethnic and religious cleavages of the country, which make violence and repression appear as the most effective means of defending the state. Here, oil revenues seem to accrue directly to the military. It would appear that the country could have resources to opt for a different path of development, but this would require rulers willing to share power and privileges.

Iraq had strong economic motives for invading and subsequently annexing Kuwait in 1990. Even if Iraq is a rich country, notwithstanding the foreign debt and the massive military build-up, the country found itself in a desperate economic situation. Before the August invasion, the immediate economic outlook for Iraq was dismal, with a huge foreign debt and high expense for the import of food and investment goods (Amuzegar, 1999, p. 135). Iraq did not have the means to service the foreign debt and feed its population, let alone make new investments or maintain the military hardware. During 1989–90, Iraq had attempted to renegotiate its foreign debt and to defer interest payments. With a few minor exceptions, these attempts failed, as Iraq's creditors had little confidence in the ability of the regime to improve its financial performance; at the same time they were unhappy with the regime's continued military build-up. Military imports could have been reduced only at the risk of alienating the regime's domestic basis, the armed forces. Reducing civilian imports would have led to social unrest. In the spring and early summer of 1990, Iraq was quickly approaching bankruptcy. In this situation, the physical survival of the Iraqi leadership was at stake. In order to avoid a collapse, a leap forward was seen as necessary.

Richer neighbors had frustrated Iraq's desire for higher oil prices, and it had practically no capital to invest in additional capacity, but there seemed to be other ways out. Neighboring Kuwait had for a long time been seen as provocatively countering Iraqi oil price interests, through its policy of producing above OPEC quotas (ibid., p. 39). In addition, Kuwait was Iraq's major creditor. It had equally large oil reserves, but a tiny population. Combining the oil reserves of the two countries with Kuwait's port facilities and small number of people could not but appear as an attractive proposition to an economically beleaguered Iraqi regime. In the early summer of 1990, Iraq had explicitly threatened Kuwait unless the latter agreed to enforce higher oil prices. Iraq also wanted part of the debt to Kuwait, at least $15 billion, to be written off (Roberts, 1990).

Put together, Iraqi and Kuwaiti oil revenues should have been more than enough to provide the regime of Greater Iraq with a comfortable economic situation. Greater Iraq would have been a regional economic power, in addition to its military power, making it the indisputable leader of the Gulf area. In this perspective, Iraq would not have needed to invade more countries in order to dictate the oil policies of Saudi Arabia and the United Arab Emirates, so that oil prices could stay at a level desirable to Iraq. A plausible Iraqi motive, not only for invading Kuwait, but also for embarking upon a strategy of achieving regional hegemony in the Gulf area, was to influence the future oil supply pattern from the Middle East. The objective was evidently to acquire both a larger market share and a higher economic rent.

Iraq still has the potential for agricultural development, for feeding its own population and for exporting food, besides a potential for industrial development and large oil resources. For this reason Iraq may yet become a rich country, provided it can get its politics right. Since independence, it has developed an urban merchant class. Iraq in the 1970s also embarked on a capital-intensive economic strategy outside oil, but it neglected agriculture and food supplies less than many others did (Amuzegar, 1999, p. 133). The country raised military expenditure in 1978, after Saddam took power. The military effort increased in 1980, after Iraq attacked Iran, earning higher oil prices. During the 1980s Iraq stepped up its oil production substantially, to finance the war against Iran and to keep civilian life running as undisturbed as possible.

Since the 1990s, sanctions and isolation have made the regime liberalize the economy, selling off state industries, services and agricultural land (Aziz-Chaudhry, 1997, p. 368). Privatization has enlarged and consolidated a capitalist class. In the rural areas, privatization of state farms has reconstituted the class of large landowners originally put in place by the Turkish and the British and swept away by the 1958 revolution. The outcome is a new social structure with private capitalists in a prominent position and a stake in political stability and the survival of the regime, although with reforms when conditions permit. The viability of the new social structure will probably depend on the recruitment to and composition of the new propertied class. If constricted to the presidential entourage or the Sunni Arab military and civilian technocrats, then it may not survive the demise of the Saddam regime, but if recruited on a broader base, with Shi'i and Kurdish elements, chances for survival improve and it may strengthen Iraq's integrity.

The Saddam regime has also had its foreign allies, but since the 1958 revolution Iraq has never been dependent on a single foreign supporter. Britain was the major loser at the fall of monarchy. The new republic at first developed close links with the Soviet Union, then France became the preferred partner. Both the Soviet Union and France found large arms markets in Iraq. By contrast, relations with the United States remained at a low level throughout the 1960s and 1970s.

The Iranian revolution of 1979 and the termination of US influence in Iran suddenly increased the political value of the Iraqi regime to both the United States and the conservative Gulf states. The Iranian revolution appeared as an ideological threat to political stability throughout the Middle East, so it was in the interest of both the United States and the conservative Arab regimes to topple the new Iranian regime. It is an open question to what extent Iraq in September 1980 went to war against Iran entirely on its own initiative, or whether there had been US and possibly Arab encouragement. That war proved to be an economic catastrophe for Iraq, although there was no clear-cut military winner or loser (Amuzegar, 1999, p. 136). The subsequent attack on Kuwait was an Iraqi attempt at compensation, aiming at a military and economic victory.

Any discussion of Iraq's future must be speculative, especially after the 2003 war and the subsequent US-led occupation. The duration of the occupation is an open question, as well as the chances of success or failure in establishing a new regime acceptable to the population and able to keep the country together. The alternatives are briefly a successful US occupation creating a democratic regime that is welcomed by the population or an unsuccessful US occupation leading to a US-backed dictator and eventually a slide into strife and chaos. The outcome is pertinent to petroleum policy and to Iraqi economic development.

An occupation regime has the right to maintain and repair oil fields already producing, but not to license new development. To restore the historical capacity of 3.5 million barrels per day (mbd) would require a minimum of 18 months and $3–5 billion. This is within the legal competence of an occupation regime. The next phase, to raise the capacity to six mbd would require seven years and at least $40–50 billion in investment in equipment and infrastructure. This is outside the legal competence of an occupation. No serious oil company would invest huge amounts in oil fields without a clear legal basis. Otherwise, the political risk would be unacceptable. Less serious oil companies might take such a risk, but they would hardly have the money and they would scarcely be creditworthy to the banks.

Any stable and legitimate Iraqi regime would have a strong bargaining position with the international oil industry, due to the limited geological risk as reserves are proven and comparatively low cost. This leaves the US occupant with an uncomfortable dilemma; to ensure new oil development, the occupation regime must be replaced by a legitimate Iraqi regime, which could be a democracy, a UN-supervised regime or an Iraqi dictator, eventually backed by the United States.

The Saddam regime managed to survive until the 2003 war in spite of or because of the sanctions and isolation (Roberts, 2003, p.2). The country has immense problems of reconstruction and is burdened by a huge foreign debt and war reparations, its major creditors being Kuwait and Saudi Arabia. France and Russia also have outstanding debts. There is a potential for anti-Western sentiment caused by the isolation and ensuing hardship of the population during the 1990s, which could be exacerbated by an unsuccessful US-led regime change. The political balance between the different ethnic and religious groups in Iraq remains unsettled; ultimately Iraq's integrity could be at stake, with Kurdish secession being the major risk. The invasion of Iraq by US-led UN forces in 1990 provoked revolts by both the Shi'i and the Kurdish population. The traditionally close links between the Shi'i Iraqi clergy and the Iranian clergy represent a potential for closer political relations. The situation of the Shi'i majority will be critical to any US attempt at regime construction. Any serious attempt at democracy must accept the likelihood of Shi'i majority rule and the subsequent impact on regional politics in the Gulf region as well as on internal politics in the Gulf states (see footnote 1). In any case, due to the Shi'i majority, neighboring Iran will weigh heavily on the political reconstruction of Iraq.

Iran is in a different situation. The country's assets are a large population, considerable oil and natural gas reserves and a geographical position on the Gulf, together with limited foreign debt. Historically, Iran has played an important role in international oil politics. This is also likely to be the case in the future, even if Iranian oil exports will probably be lower than they were in the 1970s. Political moderation has led to Iran gradually renewing relations with outside powers and opening up for international trade. Iran's reintegration into the international community means that Iranian interests and problems will have a greater significance for Middle Eastern politics. Nevertheless, and despite improved relations with the rest of the world and high oil revenues during 1999–2001, Iran seems to be heading towards domestic political instability, as the forces of change clash with the guardians of the Islamic republic (Dinmore, 2000).

Iran is a contradictory case. The Islamist revolution has matured and Iranian society has changed profoundly, as a new generation is taking over. Within a narrow political framework the Iranian regime combines apparently democratic institutions with an absence of basic human rights (Naïm, 1992). Oil revenues have enhanced the ability of the theocratic rulers to trade off various interests and survive politically. The local merchant class has strengthened its position, but has become more diversified and heterogeneous. Islamic foundations retain considerable power in an alliance with the clergy. Differences in wealth and income are again rising. Social inequities may be approaching the level reached under the Shah's regime (Ehteshami, 1995, p. 119 ff). Because the theocratic rulers represent important vested interests, they are unwilling and unable to fulfil the social promise of Islam. The Iranian Shi'i clergy has interests in conflict with its ideology. The Iranian regime is under increasing pressure. Oil revenues are at a low level by historical standards, and the economic and social situation is deteriorating. The outcome seems to be political unrest with challenges from both secular, liberal forces and a more egalitarian Islamist opposition.

Iran's liabilities are considerable. From 1980 until about 1995, annual population growth was at around three per cent, outstripping economic growth, so that per capita income declined by perhaps one half. Food supplies remain precarious for the bulk of the population. Iran's economic predicament is due largely to the eight-year war against Iraq, but also to the attempt at imposing an administrative economy, which has led to distorted prices, inefficiencies, low capacity utilization and lack of investment (Amuzegar, 1999, p. 132). Since 1980, Iran's productive capital and infrastructure have seriously deteriorated. There is an urgent need for investment capital in all sectors of the economy. Foreign capital, however, is reluctant to invest in Iran on a large scale, so oil will remain the predominant source of foreign exchange and investment capital for many years. Iran has huge gas reserves, but no large-scale gas export project is likely to be realized for years.

The major problem of post-revolutionary Iran has been isolation and continued economic stagnation. Although this is no longer the case, except for economic isolation from the USA, the effects linger on. The isolation caused technical and organizational stagnation, rising costs and loss of competitiveness. The Iranian oil industry suffers from technical obsolescence due to the US embargo. The development of agriculture and manufacturing suffers from obsolescence and the isolation of the country. Overcoming the obsolescence will be necessary if employment, food and industrial products are to be provided for a rapidly increasing population. This in turn will require overcoming the isolation, implying more open contacts with the outside world, not least Europe and North America. Iran's isolation is partly a result of US pressures that often have causes in domestic US politics. In Iran, mounting social pressures in a strained financial situation could in the worst case lead to an isolated regime that would represent a rising risk for its more prosperous neighbors. The US moves to isolate and weaken the Iranian regime have backfired.

The political instability in Iran has potentially severe repercussions for the neighboring countries. Even if the present Iranian regime represents no threat to its neighbors, it may lose power. One alternative is rapid reform, more or less discarding the ideology of the past 20 years, aiming at restoring a market economy and international trade. Another alternative is a backlash to a more fundamentalist regime that could present an ideological and political threat to the neighboring countries. In the first case, Iran could contribute to stabilizing the Middle East, in the second case to unsettling the area. Political unrest in Iran, leading to a more fundamentalist government in Teheran, could inspire a similar political development in Iraq, or parts of Iraq. By contrast, a successful reformist regime in Iran, leading to a market economy and subsequently democracy, could also inspire corresponding trends in Iraq and elsewhere.

The Gulf states – Saudi Arabia, Kuwait, Oman, Qatar, Bahrain and the United Arab Emirates – possess enormous riches such as oil and gas in the ground and assets invested abroad, but they cannot defend themselves against poorer and more populous Iran and Iraq. They attract hostile attention, as was evident during the 1990–91 Gulf crisis, and they have to rely on foreign protection (Kemp and Pressman, 1997, p. 131). Interests are reciprocal, with the Gulf states needing to settle a security problem and the outside protector getting compensation through access to oil. Since the British withdrawal from the Gulf, this protector has been the United States.

The Saudi monarchy in principle enjoys religious legitimacy as the defender of the holy cities. In practice it acquires political support through elaborate alliances with various regional and merchant interests. Royal marriage policy has traditionally been a key instrument in tying the country together, as the royal family has neutralized potential regional opponents through wedlock. Large oil revenues have historically provided the rulers with ample resources to satisfy a multitude of requirements. Today, however, rapid population growth and large youth cohorts, together with an increasing urbanization, are putting the system under increasing pressure.

The Kuwaiti monarchy also has historical legitimacy as the defender of the independence of the state against the Ottomans and recently Iraq. However, it lost some of its perceived legitimacy for failing to foresee the Iraqi attack in 1990 and for fleeing the country. Huge oil revenues have made the royal family financially independent of merchant interests, while the merchant class has apparently renounced political influence for the benefit of economic privileges (Owen, 1992, pp. 237–8). Recent parliamentary elections under government control do not change this picture. The result is a three-tier society.

The first tier is the extended royal family that controls both oil revenues and political power Economically prosperous, but politically disenfranchized Kuwaiti citizens are the second tier. They essentially make up the merchant class. Foreign workers without economic privileges or political rights make up the third tier (Bierschenk, 1991, p. 102). For decades, immigrants without any political rights have carried out practically all manual work and much clerical work in Kuwait. These workers are often in a difficult social situation (Halliday, 1974, p. 431 f).

Kuwait has a fairly important technocratic class in the national oil company and the Kuwait Investment Office. As employees of the public sector, they are probably politically more loyal to the royal family than to parliament and the merchant class (Ismael, 1993, p. 100). The armed forces in Kuwait are fairly insignificant.

The situation in the United Arab Emirates is fairly similar to that in Kuwait. Also Saudi Arabia has elements of this stratification, even if the number of foreign workers is relatively less important. In theory, the Saudi government could expel foreign workers in cases of political unrest, but the damage to the economy would be substantial. This social stratification is hardly a good basis for political stability.

The International Dimension

The United States fought the Gulf War in 1990–91 essentially over oil (Sèbe and Le Bras, 1999, p. 111). The United States saw an immediate need to safeguard Saudi oil reserves and supplies, to keep them from Iraqi control, because Kuwait, then occupied by Iraq, bordered on the oil-rich eastern province of Saudi Arabia (Gillespie and Henry, 1995, p. 12). The United States also wanted to prevent a strong Iraq emerging from the fusion of Iraqi and Kuwaiti assets in the ground and in the financial markets, which would dominate the Gulf and eventually the Middle East.

Some ten years after the Gulf War, Iraq was re-emerging as a force in Middle East politics and in the oil market. Iraq had regained some political initiative, especially with the deterioration of the Israeli–Palestinian conflict since the autumn of

2000, and the United States was essentially being forced to consider reactive measures. As the United States did not manage to unseat Saddam, the choice was overthrowing the regime by force, meaning invasion and occupation – with a high political risk. The alternative would have been to tacitly accept the Saddam Iraq and see sanctions erode. For the United States, Iraq under Saddam represented an immense risk. US oil companies risked remaining outside as Asian, European and Russian oil companies moved into Iraq. French Total had signed a letter of intent for oil development with the Saddam regime. Russian Lukoil maintains it had a contract, although cancelled by Saddam. In the Middle East, the United States risked facing, on hostile terms, an economically progressing and politically more influential Iraq, which would ultimately represent an oil market risk.

The US motives for going to war against Iraq appear multiple and complex, but the desire to control the Middle East seems to have been an overriding concern. Oil, directly and indirectly, evidently has been a significant factor (Roberts, 2003, p. 19). In hindsight, the alleged weapons of mass destruction may appear as a pretext for invading Iraq. The concern about regime change will be tested by a successful transition to democracy in Iraq and the eventual willingness of the United States to accept Shi'i majority rule. A more material motive may have been to establish Iraq as an alternative and a competitor to Saudi Arabia as a large oil supplier and price maker in the oil market, and thus to diversify the oil supply and price risk. Another motive could have been to secure positions for US oil companies and to avoid Asian, European and Russian oil companies making an inroad, as happened in Iran and Libya due to the US-imposed ban on investment in those countries. Finally, the desire to secure Israel from a potentially dangerous enemy to the east and divert attention from the Palestinian crisis should not be forgotten.

During the 1990s, oil in the Caspian region and Central Asia figured prominently in US policy. More recently, high oil prices have served to renew US interest in Caspian and Central Asian oil (Kalicki, 2001). At stake for the United States is not only access to the region's oil and gas, but also trade and political positions. The campaign against Afghanistan following the September 2001 terrorist attacks has for the first time provided the United States with a military presence in Central Asia, in Uzbekistan. For the United States, fighting terrorism in this way can go together with securing oil interests. In the mid-1990s, US gas interests were actively pursuing pipeline projects to bring oil and natural gas from Central Asia, in particular Turkmenistan, through Afghanistan to Pakistan and eventually India (Rashid, 2000, p. 157 ff). At that time, US oil companies were on speaking terms with the Afghan Taliban regime. Today, Central Asian oil and natural gas provide motivations for the United States to secure a position in Afghanistan, although the outcome is uncertain and there is competition with Chinese and Russian interests.

With rising security concerns, the Gulf states (see footnote 1) became more attentive to US oil interests. These states had an interest in exchanging US protection for other favors. Insofar as Iraq or Iran or both represent a military or political threat to the Gulf states, they also provide incentives to the latter to improve their relations with the United States. Oil policy is their major instrument, other means being investment and military purchases. Against this backdrop, Saudi Arabia and Kuwait, as well as the United Arab Emirates, have a security policy interest in the United States needing their oil, whether directly for physical supplies or indirectly to stabilize the market. The external threat, perceived or real, and the subsequent need to maintain close links with the United States hamper political development in the Gulf states, because of the risk that truly representative institutions might choose differently.

For Saudi Arabia and Kuwait a major risk, in the future as in 1990, is to be caught between US and Iraqi interests, or perhaps a coalition of Iraqi and Iranian interests. Saudi Arabia, apart from being politically threatened by Iraq, is also likely to feel threatened in its long-term economic interests. Saudi Arabia has an equally strong interest in not provoking Iraq, or Iran and Iraq together. After Iraq's withdrawal from Kuwait, there has been a legacy of distrust, even though Iraq was forced to disarm. In the case of a successful US-led regime change in Iraq, the risk for the Gulf states is to be of less importance to US interests.

The persistence of real or perceived foreign threats and tensions between the major Middle Eastern oil exporters is likely to retard both economic and political development. The best way to secure a more harmonious economic and political evolution therefore is to secure regional stability and peace, preferably through comprehensive disarmament. Especially important here are Iraq and Israel, the two most heavily armed countries. This is a long haul, requiring the active participation of the various countries of the region as well as the major foreign powers (Katzman, 1998, p. 27).

Securing oil supplies demands comprehensive political reform in the Middle East, reform that can promote democracy and peace. Today, there is hardly any Arab or Middle Eastern democracy. The Middle East is the world's most militarized region, with a huge and complex conflict potential. Promoting democracy in the Middle Eastern oil-exporting countries is in the West's interest, even though it would mean discontinuing support for old friends and would involve transitory risks. Promoting democracy would also mean building institutions to secure the rule of law, with an independent judiciary, freedom of expression and assembly, including the right to organize independent labor unions, which could help in reducing the disparities of wealth and income, and promoting a private sector to provide alternative income sources and jobs. Such measures would come at the expense of the West's old friends, but could make many new, young ones. Oppressive regimes that leave no hope for peaceful change foster terrorism, and should be condemned and contested by the West (Ibrahim, 2001). The risk for the West is that oppressive governments will use terrorism as a pretext for more oppression, provoking more opposition, instability and eventually more terrorism. In this perspective, consistently promoting democracy and the rule of law is also the best strategy for the West to combat terrorism and secure oil supplies at the same time.

Likewise, promoting peace in the Middle East is in the West's interest. It can stabilize oil supplies, although it would mean taking Arab interests seriously, putting pressure on Israel to give up Palestinian land and terminating sanctions that hit Iraq's civilian population, not the rulers. Promoting peace would also mean discontinuing massive arms sales and actively engaging in a policy of regional disarmament that would include both Iraq and Israel.

Finally, promoting peace and securing oil supplies would mean including Iran and Iraq in a framework of regional co-operation, not excluding them, as has been US policy until now. To safeguard oil interests, the United States needs friends and allies, not foes. It cannot, as the only surviving superpower, defend important interests unilaterally. Russia until the 2003 war seemed to be a winner here (Peel, 2001). Iran may forego a historical opportunity to become more closely integrated economically and politically with the outside world because of the conflict between reformers and conservatives. In this perspective, the continuation of the US sanctions against Iran, embodied in the Iran–Libya Sanctions Act, ILSA, renewed in the summer of 2001, appears both thoughtless and contrary to US economic and political interests. In the redefinition of the United States' friendship needs, Israel may lose, especially as the Sharon government has managed to embarrass the United States and appear as an active force of instability in the Middle East (*Financial Times*, 2001). By changing policies in this direction, the West can hope to reduce the motivation and potential for terrorism, while enhancing the basis for economic and political co-operation and interdependence, as well as securing oil supplies. Unless a more comprehensive settlement can be reached in the Middle East, Saudi Arabia, until the 2003 war, seemed likely to be torn between fears of a stronger Iraq, motivating closer links with the United States, and the perceived need to improve relations with Iraq, motivating more political distance from Washington. After the war, Saudi Arabia's position may be more precarious, especially if the US occupation of Iraq is politically successful, making Iraq the favored partner of the United States in the region. An unsuccessful US occupation would have repercussions on Saudi internal politics as well as on foreign policy, leading to more distance from Washington. A way out of the dilemma for Saudi Arabia seems to be closer links with Iran. Against this backdrop, US–Saudi oil relations may also have to change. The need to keep some distance from the United States for the sake of domestic political balancing may induce Saudi Arabia to be a less compliant residual oil supplier, opting for a lower output and higher oil prices. That would help Iran, but not the United States. Whereas it will take a decade at least to make Iraq an oil power, Saudi Arabia is and will remain the arbitrator of the oil market and oil prices. Moreover, France and especially Russia could delay new Iraqi oil development through the international court system in case an Iraqi regime should favor US oil interests.

References

Amuzegar, Jahangir (1999), *Managing the Oil Wealth*, I.B. Tauris, London.

Aziz-Chaudhry, Kiren (1997), "Economic Liberalisation and the Lineages of the Rentier State", in Nicholas S. Hopkins and Saad Eddin Ibrahim (eds), *Arab Society*, The American University in Cairo Press, Cairo, pp. 345–58.

Bierschenk, Thomas (1991), "Die Golfstaaten: politische Stabilität trotz ökonomischem Wandel", in Pawelka, Pfaff and Wehling (eds), pp. 95–108.

Cappelen, Ådne and Choudhury, Robin (2000), *The Future of the Saudi Arabian Economy*, Statistics Norway, Oslo.

Cause III, F. Gregory (1994), *Oil Monarchies*, Council on Foreign Relations Press, New York.

Crystal, Jill (1990), *Oil and Politics in the Gulf*, Cambridge University Press, Cambridge.

Dinmore, Guy (2000), "Iran's Unsteady Ship", *Financial Times*, December 12.

Ehteshami, Anoushiravan (1995), *After Khomeini*, Routledge, London.

Ende, Werner (1991), *Auf der Suche nach der Idealen Gesellschaft*, in Pawelka, Pfaff and Wehling (eds), pp. 64–72.

Fargues, Philippe (1994), "Demographic Explosion or Social Upheaval?", in Salamé (ed.), pp. 156–79.

Financial Times (2001), "U.S. Rebukes Israeli Leader as Coalition Tensions Rise", October 6–7.

Gillespie, Kate and Henry, Clement M. (1995), *Oil in the New World Order*, University Press of Florida, Gainesville, Florida.

Halliday, Fred (1974), *Arabia Without Sultans*, Penguin Books, Harmondsworth.

Humphreys, R. Stephen (2001), *Between Memory and Desire*, University of California Press, Berkeley, California.

Ibrahim, Anwar (2001), "Growth of Democracy Is the Answer to Terrorism", *International Herald Tribune,* October 11.

Ismael, Jacqueline S. (1993), *Kuwait: Dependency and Class in a Rentier State*, University Press of Florida, Gainesville, Florida.

Kalicki, Jan H. (2001), "Caspian Energy at the Crossroads", *Foreign Affairs*, Vol. 80, No. 5, pp. 120–34.

Katzman, Kenneth (1998), *Searching for Stable Peace in the Persian Gulf*, U.S. Army War College, Carlisle, Pennsylvania.

Kemp, Geoffrey and Pressman, Jeremy (1997), *Point of No Return*, Brookings Institution Press, Washington, DC.

Kepel, Gilles (1994), "Le monde arabe après l'accord israélo-palestinien", in Gilles Kepel (ed.), *Exils et Royaumes*, Presses de la Fondation Nationale des Sciences Politiques, Paris, pp. 21–9.

Khalaf, Roula (2001), "Why They Hate Us", *Financial Times*, October 5.

Kubba, Laith (2001), "Domestic Politics in A Post-Saddam Iraq", in Joseph A. Kechichian (ed.), *Iran, Iraq and the Arab Gulf States*, Palgrave, New York, pp. 65–82.

Luciani, Giacomo (1994), "The Oil Rent, the Fiscal Crisis of the State and Democratisation", in Salamé (ed.), pp. 130–55.

Mantran, Robert (1989), *L'expansion musulman*, Presses Universitaires de France, Paris.

Moïsi, Dominique (2001), "Tragedy that Exposed a Groundswell of Hatred", *Financial Times*, September 24.

Morse, Edward L. (2000), "Oil Price: Turning Point?", *Middle East Economic Survey,* Vol. 43, No. 50, December 11.

Naïm, Mouna (1992), "Les contradictions des héritiers de Khomeiny", *Le Monde*, December 6–7, pp. 1 and 7.

Owen, Roger (1992), *State, Power and Politics in the Making of the Modern Middle East*, Routledge, London.

Owen, Roger and Pamuk, Sevket (1999), *A History of the Middle East Economies in the Twentieth Century*, Harvard University Press, Cambridge, Massachusetts.

Pakravan, Karim (1997), "The Emerging Private Sector: New Demands on an Old System", in Gary G. Sick and Lawrence G. Potter (eds), *The Persian Gulf at the Millennium*, St. Martin's Press, New York, pp. 115–26.

Pawelka, Peter (1991), "Der Irak als 'Rentierstaat'", in Pawelka, Pfaff and Wehling (eds), pp. 38–63.

Pawelka, Peter, Pfaff, Isabella and Wehling, Hans-Georg (eds) (1991), *Die Golfregion in der Weltpolitik*, Verlag W. Kohlhammer, Stuttgart.

Peel, Quentin (2001), "Washington's Balancing Act", *Financial Times*, October 1.

Penrose, Edith and Penrose, E.F. (1978), *Iraq, International Relations and National Development*, Ernest Benn, London.

Rashid, Ahmed (2000), *Taliban*, I.B. Tauris, London.

Richards, Alan and Waterbury, John (1990), *A Political Economy of the Middle East: State, Class and Economic Development*, Westview Press, Boulder, Colorado.

Roberts, John (1990), "Piecing together the Peace Jigsaw", *The Energy Compass*, December 14.

Roberts, John (1995), *Visions and Mirages*, Mainstream Publishing, Edinburgh.

Roberts, John (2003), *Oil and the Iraq War of 2003*, ICEED, Boulder, Colorado.

Salamé, Ghassan (ed.) (1994), *Democracy without Democrats?* I.B. Tauris, London.

Sèbe, Charles and Le Bras, William (1999), *Indomptable Iraq*, Le Sémaphore, Paris.

Simon, Steven and Benjamin, Daniel (2001), "Myths of American Misdeeds", *Financial Times*, October 2.

Toscane, Luiza (1995), *L'Islam, Un autre Nationalisme?* L'Harmattan, Paris.

Chapter 2

The Future of the Saudi Arabian Economy: Possible Effects on the World Oil Market

Ådne Cappelen and Robin Choudhury

Introduction

The vast oil resources of Saudi Arabia have enabled the country's population to enjoy a standard of living much higher than they otherwise would have experienced. Domestic production of other tradable goods and services is quite minimal. Domestic demand has been kept afloat by government budgets, even though the government budget and the current account have been in deficit since 1985–86. This lack of funds restricts the government's maneuverability in policy-making. There has generally been poor economic development during the 1990s. Gross domestic product (GDP) per capita has been stagnant or even declining over the past ten years and severe financial imbalances have subsequently emerged. Saudi Arabia's current political and social structure is probably not adequate to handle severe economic problems that perhaps cannot be avoided much longer. These economic problems could lead to changes in policies or in government.

This chapter focuses on alternative economic and political developments that could reshape the future of Saudi Arabia. We start with a brief summary of the historical, political and economic background followed by a description of two scenarios for the Saudi economy. First we outline a future based upon the continuance of the current policies for another decade; this is the baseline. The first alternative scenario explores possible effects from policy reforms in taxation and privatization. The second alternative scenario explores possible effects from changing oil policies. The chapter finally discusses what these domestic scenarios might imply for the relations between Saudi Arabia and the Organization of Petroleum Exporting Countries (OPEC). In our opinion it is not likely that Saudi Arabia will act on its own within OPEC and there are both economic and political arguments that lead us to conclude that Saudi Arabia is likely to maintain its support for OPEC.

Historical and Political Background

Saudi Arabia in its present form was created in 1932 as an absolute monarchy with the Al-Saud family as the ruling power. The legitimacy of this family's rule has its origin in a religious and political compromise established in 1744 when the Muslim leader Mohammed bin Abdel-Wahhab sought refuge with Mohammed bin Saud. At that time, the latter was leader of a geographically central but small portion of what today is Saudi Arabia including the area of Riyadh. Together they started a campaign across Arabia aimed at attaining wider control of Arabia for the Al-Saud family and concurrently giving supremacy to orthodox Wahhabism. By 1810 Saudi forces had gained control over much of what today is Saudi Arabia. However, in 1818, the Saudi forces had lost most of their territory to Ottoman Empire counter-attacks. During the nineteenth century Saudi forces tried once again to recapture lost territory but were thwarted by the Al-Rashid (another Arabian tribe from an area north of the Al-Sauds) who received the support of the Ottoman Empire. For a time the Al-Sauds were even forced to take residence in what today is Kuwait.

In 1902 the Al-Sauds succeeded in winning back Riyadh from the Al-Rashid and in 1932 Abdel-Aziz bin Abdel-Rahman, or Ibn-Saud, declared himself King of Saudi Arabia. When he died in 1953, his 34 surviving sons inherited the Kingdom. Ibn-Saud's successor, King Saud, established the first Council of Ministers, a collective system of government among the sons of Ibn-Saud. The Council of Ministers has both legislative and executive power although the final word is with the King. The council is generally composed of members of the Royal family, families related to it and in some cases technocrats such as Oil and Mineral Resources Minister Ali bin Ibrahim al-Nuaimi.

In 1992, following the Gulf War, political opposition and pressure from Western governments resulted in King Fahd issuing three government-related decrees. The first was the Basic Law of Government, which could be viewed as the present constitution of Saudi Arabia. In this decree, human rights are guaranteed by the state as long as they are in accordance with Islamic sharia. The second decree established the Consultative Council that now consists of 90 members appointed (not elected) by the King. The members of this council are mostly former senior government officials or highly educated individuals associated with tribal leaders, but the council also includes a few members from religious opposition groups. Its function is strictly advisory and decisions are accepted only if approved by the Council of Ministers and ultimately the King himself. The third decree instituted regional authorities in order to create a clearer hierarchy within regions and between central and local government. The members of the regional councils are also chosen by the King and are mainly tribal leaders and members of prominent merchant families.

The changes in government that took place could be seen as responses to political pressure both of domestic and foreign origin. One the other hand, they could be regarded as adaptations of the traditional system of governing by consensus. The population of Saudi Arabia was some 12 million (nationals) in 1992, twice the population from the time of the first oil price hike in 1973 ("OPEC I"). When Ibn-Saud died in 1953, the population was less than four million. This population explosion will put a government of consensus under pressure to develop new institutions for making political compromises. How should the various interest groups be allowed to and able to express their interests? The two new councils based on the 1992 decision can be seen as attempts to address this question, though the late King Faisal had already proposed these councils in 1962.

What are the main interest groups in Saudi Arabia and how might they shape future policies? We shall distinguish between three main groups: the Royal family, the religious community and the emerging business community. The main political force in Saudi Arabia is the Al-Saud family, amounting to some ten thousand depending on how far from the main line of inheritance one chooses to draw the line. Rivalry and factions within the family are likely, causing some uncertainty concerning succession. These factions could form alliances within the family or with factions of the religious or emerging business communities. The Royal family enjoys a material standard of living and privileges that are possible only for a minority in any country. As the family rapidly increases in size, the financial burden increases. This burden, combined with the Westernized and affluent lifestyles, provokes hostilities among other citizens and particularly among religious groups. Governing by consensus will be increasingly difficult if the living standard of the members of the Royal family must be financed by taxes on ordinary people. According to the Basic Law of the Kingdom, "taxes and fees are to be imposed on the basis of justice and only when the need arises". Even if not taken literally this will limit the potential increase in resources spent by the Royal family as a whole.

The present Saudi compromise builds upon the historical compromise between the Royal family and religious Wahhabism, and implies that the Saudi population in general should benefit from the oil revenues of the Kingdom through generous provision of public services and subsidies. In practice this has largely been achieved by providing well-paid jobs to Saudis in the government or in companies controlled by the government or by the Royal family.

With the present King Fahd being ill, his half brother, Crown Prince Abdullah, is regarded as being in charge of daily policies and is the most likely successor to King Fahd. Abdullah is considered to be less pro-Western than King Fahd, particularly in light of his very active and quite successful foreign policy and specifically in his pro-Arab policy. The 1997 Iranian election of Mohammed Khatami as president has helped to bring Iran closer to the Arab countries; and Saudi Arabia and Iran have signed agreements to increase both economic and cultural links. The closer contact between the two countries was probably also important in establishing cutbacks in oil production within OPEC; a step which led to more than a doubling of oil prices during 1999.

It is important to the purpose of this chapter to examine Saudi Arabia in a wider context and specifically to examine its relationship to the "Arab nation". The final collapse of the Ottoman Empire at the end of the First World War and the release of territories resulting from the 1920 peace accord in Sèvres allowed the emergence of the territorial states of the region. The new states in the region have not, however, been able to establish themselves as strong nation-states. One superficial indication of this phenomenon is that the Egyptian, Syrian and Iraqi national anthems and flags have changed four times since the Second World War. The question of a successor to the Ottoman Empire is still considered viable in some circles and, according to El-Harmassy (1987), there is more loyalty to the idea of a large Arab nation than to the present Arab states. It is in this perspective that one could understand the surprisingly large Arab popular support that Saddam Hussein received when he occupied Kuwait.

The majority of Muslims in Saudi Arabia are Sunni but there is a significant Shi'i minority in the eastern oil-rich region. The government began to suspect this minority of having links to Shi'i groups in Iran when riots in the Shi'i region coincided with the Iranian revolution in 1978–79. However, with the establishment of closer ties to Iran and political changes there, religious opposition cannot be considered a Shi'i phenomenon. Instead, during the first half of the 1990s there was a growing religious opposition within the Sunni majority and a more radical clergy emerged. One issue the religious critics often focus on is the close relationship between Saudi Arabia and the United States. In particular the government's reliance on United States troops to defend the country against Saddam Hussein was seen by many Saudis as a loss of honor in that a non-Muslim army had to defend Islam's Holy Land. Another issue is that large sums have been spent for many years to build up Saudi military capacity apparently without much success. The car bombs in 1995 and 1996 were additional indications of the anti-Western and anti-American sentiments present in Saudi Arabia. The Royal family has hoped that the religious leaders (ulema) would be able to control the critics and thereby maintain the historical compromise between Wahhabism and the Royal family. It is therefore of some interest to note that Crown Prince Abdullah's foreign policy focuses on improving relations with other countries around the Gulf, including Iran. His policy in this respect is regarded as quite successful and popular.

Economic development in Saudi Arabia since the 1970s has not only brought higher income for the country as a whole, but has also created a Saudi business class. Government policy has been to nationalize not only oil companies but also to provide beneficial conditions for national companies generally. Therefore, until recently it has been difficult for foreign companies to establish themselves without a Saudi national counterpart. However, the policy does seem to be changing as reflected in the following actions. In June 2001 three large areas of virgin desert were opened to foreign consortia, allowing them to tap and use whatever natural gas they may find. The deal also enables upstream development of hydrocarbons that earlier were the preserve of the nationalized Saudi Aramco. Oil reserves are, however, still in the control of the state, even what may be found in these new areas. International companies have also been commissioned to develop downstream uses; plans include building power, desalination and petrochemical plants. But still the government will have to open up the economy more and policies must be changed if Saudi Arabia is to become an additional Arab Gulf state accepted by the World Trade Organization (WTO).

The Royal family and other Saudi nationals are the main entrepreneurs in the economy. The links formed between the Royal family and the business class can be seen partly as an attempt to widen the political basis for the government in a country without parties or civil society in any Western sense. However, these links are put under strain as oil revenues have diminished and the government must delay payments to the private sector. Other complexities arise because there are no clear borderlines between the government and the private economy of the Royal family. Contracts are widely believed to be part of a "gift" system rather than being market based. Competition is thus limited, thereby driving up costs for the government. A last component of discontent with the government is the increasing hidden unemployment and unequal distribution of income and wealth. The business class is therefore generally in favor of liberal reform.

Economic Structure and Development 1970–1999

Not only as a major source of export revenue is oil the key to the Saudi economy; it is also the primary source of the government's revenue (see Figure 2.1). From 1990 to 1997 other sources of revenues have fluctuated between 21 and 27 per cent of total revenues. The government revenues rose from Saudi riyals (SR) 6.6 billion in 1970 to more than SR 300 billion in 1980. The reason for this strong growth in revenues was a more than threefold increase in the oil price resulting from the trade embargo following the Yom Kippur war. The Iranian revolution caused a new steep rise in prices, levelling the oil price at almost 30 United States dollars (USD) per barrel.

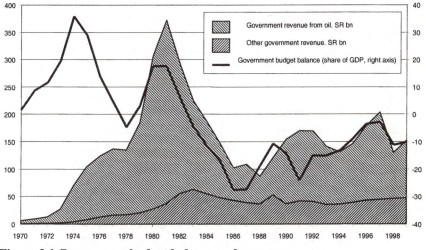

Figure 2.1 Government budget balance and revenues

This ever-increasing price trend was adversely affected during the third development plan (1980–84), as world demand for oil declined in response to the high prices. In an attempt to keep up the price level, Saudi Arabia drastically reduced its production, thereby creating a significant decline in total government revenues. From Figure 2.1 it appears that 1981 marked a turning point in the fiscal history of Saudi Arabia. The budget surplus was reduced from 17.6 per cent of GDP in 1980 to 6.1 per cent in 1981. In 1982 the government's revenue from oil exports was reduced by 29 per cent from the previous year, dropping from a peak level of SR 335 billion to 237 billion. In 1983 the budget showed a deficit of 4.1 per cent of GDP and Saudi Arabia has been running fiscal deficits ever since. The reasons for deficit are reduced income from oil exports and a continuous high level of expenditure.

During the winter 1985–86 Saudi Arabia abandoned its policy of being the ultimate swing producer in the oil market and shortly thereafter a large drop in the oil price took place. The fiscal balance continued to deteriorate in 1986, but then gradually improved during the late 1980s. However, the invasion of Kuwait and the subsequent outbreak of the Gulf War posed enormous financial challenges to the Saudi economy. The Gulf crisis led to increased expenditure on weapons and other military equipment, and both in 1990 and 1991 expenditure rose more than 30 per cent from the previous year. More than one-third of public funds were used for military activities and strengthening of Saudi Arabian defenses. To make matters worse, Saudi Arabia paid a significant share of the belligerent countries' expenses by drawing down foreign assets. Lastly, expenditure on some subsidies, introduced during the Gulf War, remained in place for domestic political reasons. In 1992 and through most of the 1990s government finances improved slowly. The UN embargo on oil imports from Iraq and occupied Kuwait enabled Saudi Arabia to increase its oil production from less than 5.5 million barrels daily (mbd.) at the beginning of 1990 to more than eight mbd. at the end of the year. This increase in production volume more than offset the effect on revenues from falling prices at the beginning of the decade.

The gradual improvement in the budget balance during most of the 1990s was partly due to higher oil prices, but additional contributions were made by the decisions to reduce government spending and to raise charges on utilities. Then in 1998, the oil price dropped more than 34 per cent and the fiscal deficit rose to more than 11 per cent of GDP. The recent high oil prices have contributed to a significant improvement in the budget balance for 2000 and 2001.

The authorities have opted to finance budget deficits through domestic borrowing. This has resulted in a rapid rise in the stock of domestic debt. According to the International Monetary Fund (IMF), total domestic debt increased from 52 per cent of GDP in 1992 to 86 per cent of GDP in 1995. The amount of domestic borrowing to finance the large fiscal shortfall in 1998 is estimated to have pushed this figure to over 100 per cent of GDP. A long period of budget deficits has eliminated much of the room for maneuverability in fiscal policies and also limits the possibility for buying off domestic political unrest by increasing expenditure.

In retrospect, the government has attempted to use its massive oil revenues to finance an ambitious development program. The aim has been to build up and develop the infrastructure, the industrial and agricultural sectors, and modernize the health and education systems. The Saudis have also allocated massive amounts of money to build up the armed forces. The achievement of these goals was possible in the aftermath of the first oil shock in 1973, but from the mid-1980s lower oil prices have squeezed government finances, and have led to rising domestic debt and delayed payment to government contractors and suppliers. Cuts in subsidies and other efforts to curb government expenditure in 1995, in combination with higher oil prices in 1996 and 1997, contributed to reduce the fiscal imbalances substantially in those years. The difficulty for the Saudi government is that, short of a buoyant oil market, there are no other immediate methods to increase revenues. To introduce a general tax system that could finance government expenditure would probably demand political reforms that so far have not really been on the domestic political agenda, in spite of the fact that other Gulf states are moving slowly towards some form of democratic rule.

While growth rates of non-oil GDP reached double digits during the 1970s, growth was minimal during the early 1980s and was even negative during some years. During the 1990s non-oil GDP growth was generally very slow and on average for the decade just above one per cent. Slow growth in investment has dominated the changes in the structure of domestic demand accompanied by more moderate growth in public spending compared to previous decades. There has also been little change in the industrial structure with growth rates for most sectors close to the average. All in all the 1990s has been a period of economic stagnation and falling per capita GDP. The latter is due to population growth close to four per cent annually, the result of which is a very young population that finds it harder and harder to get well-paid jobs.

Another factor influencing the economic environment is that the Saudi labor market is dominated by foreign employment, cf. Figure 2.2. The rapid economic growth made possible by oil income could not have been realized without a massive import of foreign labor since there has been a traditionally low participation of Saudis in the labor market. In particular Saudi women have an extremely low degree of labor market participation. Labor was imported from neighboring countries, as well as Asian countries such as the Philippines, Pakistan, India and Sri Lanka. Since 1979 employment of non-Saudis has outnumbered Saudi employment, and this development has worried the authorities. A principal and controversial element of government efforts to change this feature is the so-called "Saudization" program, the process of replacing foreigners with Saudi manpower. The Saudization program was introduced in the fourth development plan (1985–89), but as is evident from Figure 2.2, the results have been modest so far. The main reason for this is the wage differentials between Saudi and non-Saudi workers. A widening wage gap between the two groups has become a serious obstacle to the expansion of Saudi employment in the private sector, especially for Saudis with low skills.

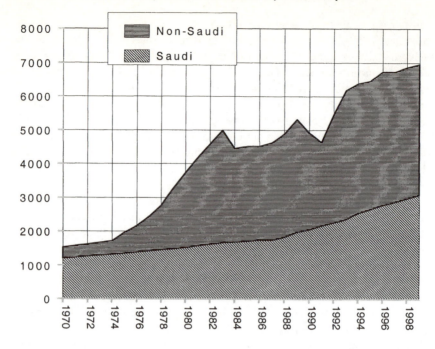

Figure 2.2 Employment of Saudis and non-Saudis. 1,000 persons

Scenarios for the Saudi Economy 2000–2010

The Saudi economy developed poorly during the 1990s. GDP per capita was stagnant or even declining and severe financial imbalances emerged. The country has a political and social structure that is probably not adequate in handling severe economic problems that cannot be avoided much longer. This may lead to substantial changes in policies but also to changes in government that are very difficult to predict. What are the economic prospects for Saudi Arabia? In order to analyze these, we study two alternative political and economic scenarios for the Kingdom. The reference case or the "baseline" assumes no major changes in government policy or oil policy. Historical trends are carried forward with no fundamental shift in policy. We do not think this is a particularly likely alternative; it rather shows that something needs to be done to improve the economic performance for the country as a whole.

The first alternative scenario, which we consider more likely than the baseline, is called "policy reform". We assume that Saudi Arabia will enter the WTO, and therefore will reduce subsidies, privatize or at least deregulate some industries/companies and introduce some measures of taxation in order to increase non-oil revenue of the budget. This alternative, which in many ways is in line with the kind of policy reforms the World Bank has been advocating for a long time, will be politically difficult to implement. It may well be only partially effectuated and not able to meet material demands of large sections of the Saudi population.

A more dramatic scenario in terms of oil policy is then presented, where lack of funds "forces" the government to take on a more aggressive oil policy in an attempt to avoid financial imbalances. This second alternative, called "oil market grab", could be combined with the previous alternatives. In terms of historical events, however, we see it as more likely following a failure of liberal reform. This oil market grab scenario is, in reality, unlikely for many reasons. First of all, its success will depend on changing the Saudi share of OPEC oil supply. Saudi Arabia is able to increase its oil production substantially within a few years and at very low costs; not many other OPEC countries are in a similar position. This scenario then would most likely lead to a complete breakdown of OPEC, having huge political effects in many countries, particularly Arab countries. Those OPEC countries that cannot strongly increase output will see their oil revenues dwindle and what Arab unity there is would most likely be ended. It is also a politically risky business for the Saudi government because it could be seen as an attempt to rescue its own economic and political position at the expense of others. In a country where many people say "First Muslim, then Arab, and finally Saudi", a nationalist Saudi policy move may not gain much support from the public in general nor from the religious opposition.

As suggested above, our baseline scenario is based on assumptions of no major changes in policies or economic trends. We also assume that the recent OPEC policy of moderate production in order to keep the crude oil price above 20 USD per barrel continues.

The Saudi riyal (SR) is pegged to the USD at a rate of 3.745 per dollar. We assume the exchange rate to be constant over the coming decade. Although some speculation against SR took place during 1998–99 when oil prices plummeted, there was no devaluation. With consumer price inflation in the OECD of around two per cent a year we assume Saudi import prices to grow by one per cent annually.

The Saudi population as of 1999 consisted of roughly 16 million Saudi nationals and some four million foreigners. Nearly all non-nationals are employed (3.95 million to be precise) while the employment of Saudis is estimated to be roughly three million. The birth rate is very high and population growth is assumed to be 3.5 per cent over the next decade, one of the highest in the world. We assume that the supply of Saudi labor will grow in line with population while the amount of foreign labor will be kept constant. The official policy has for some time been that of Saudization, meaning the absolute decline in the number of foreign workers. This has however, been difficult to achieve and in the baseline scenario we assume that only relative Saudization will take place due to population growth. Labor supply by Saudis and non-Saudis is shown in Figure 2.2. Total labor supply will on average grow by 1.7 per cent anually from 2000 to 2010 based on these assumptions.

For many years both productivity as measured by total factor productivity and the real rate of return on capital has been falling in the private non-oil economy of Saudi Arabia. This is a major reason for the drop in GDP per capita. It implies that the country is getting less and less in return for its labor and capital. In our baseline scenario we assume that this decline will end and that both factor productivity and real rate of return will be constant. For more details on the assumptions we refer to Cappelen and Choudhury (2000).

With these assumptions, non-oil GDP per capita will grow at a rate roughly half of population growth during the present decade. To be more precise non-oil GDP will grow less than two per cent annually while total GDP growth will be around two per cent. The assumption of 1.5 per cent growth in government consumption will result in a similar growth rate for government GDP while our assumptions regarding oil and gas supply will imply a somewhat higher contribution to total GDP growth from the oil sector than for the non-oil sectors. GDP per capita will fall by 1.5 per cent annually over the coming decade. This is indeed a bleak prospect for any economy and even more so for Saudi Arabia with a GDP per capita of roughly 7,000 USD (approximately 30,000 SR) in 1999. Real disposable income for the country will grow somewhat more than GDP because export prices will grow about 0.5 per cent more than import prices, but this will only moderate the fall in national real income per capita slightly.

With no growth in productivity, there is little scope for increases in real wages. Traditionally rapid wage growth in the public sector has carried over to other parts of the Saudi labor market although not for foreign workers. We assume that the government manages to keep wage growth quite low in the years ahead partly in response to the large budget deficit and partly due to the large inflow of young Saudis who traditionally have been looking for jobs in the government sector. Consumer prices are estimated to increase by 1.2 per cent annually so that real wages increase only marginally. Note that in this baseline scenario no policy reforms are carried out such as reducing government subsidies of utility prices.

We assume expenditure on social sectors to increase in line with population in real terms while expenditure on defense and administration are constant in real terms. Government consumption will thus grow by 1.5 per cent annually over the next decade. Government investment on the other hand is assumed to be constant in real terms. There is no direct taxation in the Saudi economy except for the *zakat*, which is very small. There is no indirect taxation either, but some customs duties exist that amount to less than two per cent of GDP. Duties are held constant in value terms. Taxes and subsidies on factor incomes are also small and all rates are assumed to be constant.

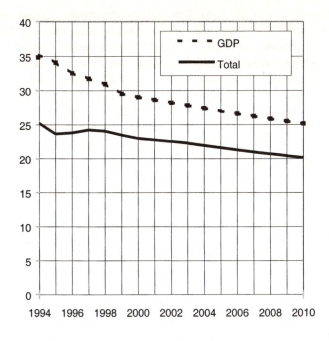

Figure 2.3 GDP and total consumption per capita. 1,000 SR. Baseline

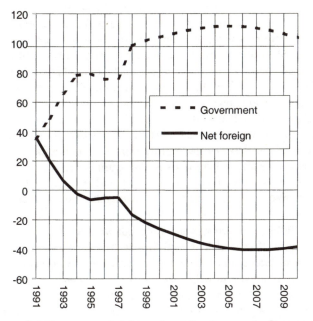

Figure 2.4 Government debt and net foreign assets. Per cent of GDP. Baseline

With oil prices above 20 USD per barrel the Saudi current account deficit could be considerably diminished over the coming years. One reason for this is a very moderate growth in imports accompanied by slow growth in domestic demand and output. However, the government budget deficit will remain in spite of very slow growth in government expenditure. This has to do with the fact that this deficit has been a much larger share of GDP during the second half of the 1990s and it increased considerably due to low oil prices in 1998 and the beginning of 1999. We assume that the interest rate on government loans will stay close to seven per cent and that government debt probably passed 100 per cent of nominal GDP during 1999. Thus the present deficits are clearly not sustainable when nominal GDP increases by roughly 3.5 per cent as in our simulations. Indeed, government debt to nominal GDP will reach 111 per cent in 2005 before slowly decreasing, though still over 100 per cent in 2010 according to our calculations, cf. Figure 2.4.

The baseline scenario tells us that present policies are probably not sustainable. The major problem with this scenario is that the Saudi economy becomes even more dependent on oil as the private non-oil sector grows very slowly. Also large budget deficits continue for many years as we have assumed constant per capita supply of government social services. This may well be considered too optimistic or perhaps careless. The deficits have so far been financed domestically by the banking sector and with loans from government-owned companies. It is a question of how much longer this can go on. Politically it may be difficult to sustain a decade of negative income growth and negative private consumption growth per capita, as the 1990s have also been a period of slow growth. There is a need for policy reforms and we now turn to an analysis of some likely proposals.

The policy reform scenario includes some policy changes that are likely to be implemented in Saudi Arabia although it is difficult to fix the exact date for these reforms. Some of these have been on the agenda for some years already and some are likely to be discussed more openly in the years to come as the necessity of reforms becomes clear. Some of the reforms will have to deal with the serious macroeconomic imbalances while others are more typical supply-side reforms that hopefully will affect growth in a positive way.

Saudi Arabia has been negotiating with the WTO on the terms that might apply if the country is to become a member of the organization. A crucial issue in these negotiations is the degree of openness that Saudi Arabia will have to accept. So far the demands from the WTO have been more comprehensive than the Kingdom has been willing to accept. We assume, however, that a membership will become effective in the near future.

From the baseline scenario it is apparent that although government debt is gradually reduced as share of GDP in the long run, the short to medium deficits are large. Possible policy measures would be either to introduce some taxation or to cut expenditure. One obvious candidate would be to cut military expenditure but that may be more wishful thinking than realistic policy in the present conditions. What we have assumed is the introduction of some excise taxes mainly on consumer goods that either have a high import content or damage health (smoking) or pollute (petrol). The goods that are mainly imported are also luxury goods. It may be argued that it is not acceptable to introduce these taxes under present political circumstances ("no taxation without representation"). However, the government could claim with some justification that social services are still relatively generous so that some taxation is justifiable. In addition the taxes introduced could be defended on other grounds than pure fiscal ones as suggested earlier.

To diversify the economy has been a slogan for some time in Saudi Arabia. The idea is to become less dependent upon oil extraction in addition to rolling back the role of government control in the economy. Some steps in this direction have recently been taken by the June 2001 decisions that are expected to result in more foreign direct investments in the economy. We have assumed that foreign investors start developing both the mining and tourist sector of the economy.

Finally, the policy reform scenario includes some privatization measures in the form of sale of government assets in telecommunications and air transportation. We assume also that the privatization scheme will improve productivity as the companies cut their labor force, leading to lower prices on services. The latter assumption is reasonable only if government-controlled sectors are not simply replaced with privately controlled sectors, dominating enough to institute monopolistic pricing.

In Table 2.1 we show the main effects from the compound shift constituting the partial analyses discussed so far. In Cappelen and Choudhury (2000), each of the policy changes is studied separately. In comparison with the baseline scenario, we see that most of the adjustment to new equilibrium levels takes place during the first half of the period, and we observe no major changes in the long-term growth rates. Figure 2.1 shows the deviation from the baseline scenario, showing GDP for the private sector 2.8 per cent higher in 2010 in the policy reform scenario than in the baseline. This increase creates room for an increase in both private consumption and private investments. Private consumption shows a bell-shaped improvement over the baseline scenario. In 2000 it is 1.3 per cent higher, the difference reaches 1.8 per cent in 2005, before it drops back to 1.1 per cent in 2010. The WTO scenario alone worsens the trade balance by SR 7.3 billion at the end of the period. The partial effects from the other scenarios improve the trade balance, resulting in a SR 3.2 billion overall improvement in the current account balance. In the policy reform scenario, the growth in the consumer price index is 1.3 percentage points higher in 2000; then, for the next four years it is 0.3–0.4 percentage points lower. For the rest of the period growth rates are the same. The effect on the consumer price is mostly due to the introduction of some taxes on consumer goods. However, WTO membership leads to lower prices and so does privatization (by assumption).

Figure 2.5 Government debt (left axis) and net foreign assets (right axis). Baseline and policy reform. Per cent of GDP

In Figure 2.5 we compare government debt and net foreign assets in the two scenarios. In the policy reform scenario, we observe a considerable reduction in the government debt, from 104 to 88 per cent of GDP in 2010. Net foreign assets turn for the worse during the first half of the simulation period, and then are just reaching the same level at the end of the period. This should not be a concern as this is due to higher investment, leading to a higher capital stock.

To conclude, it is worth noting that the policy reform scenario has not led to sustained higher growth but a higher level of GDP with improved financial balances, particularly for the public sector. The problematic feature of falling consumption per capita has not been resolved. In our view, one possibility to overcome this feature would be to increase female labor participation; that is, however, a controversial issue in Saudi Arabia.

Table 2.1 Main effects of the policy reform scenarios. Deviation from baseline scenario

	2000	2001	2002	2003	2004	2005	2006	2007	2008	2009	2010
Per cent deviation											
GDP	0.5	0.7	0.8	1.0	1.2	1.2	1.2	1.2	1.2	1.3	1.3
GDP private sector	1.3	1.6	1.9	2.3	2.7	2.7	2.8	2.8	2.8	2.8	2.8
Private consumption	1.3	1.7	1.8	1.8	1.7	1.8	1.6	1.4	1.3	1.1	1.1
Private investments	11.8	6.0	3.7	2.8	2.5	2.6	2.5	2.4	2.4	2.5	2.6
Exports	1.6	2.0	2.3	2.6	2.9	3.0	3.1	3.2	3.3	3.4	3.6
Imports	5.8	4.4	3.6	3.1	2.8	3.0	2.9	2.8	2.7	2.7	2.8
Import market share	2.7	2.0	1.6	1.2	1.0	1.0	1.0	0.9	0.8	0.8	0.8
Public debt	-2.5	-3.4	-4.3	-5.3	-6.3	-7.4	-8.5	-9.8	-11.2	-12.8	-14.6
Consumer price	1.3	0.9	0.5	0.2	-0.1	-0.1	-0.1	-0.1	-0.1	-0.1	-0.1
Absolute deviation											
Current account balance (mill. SR)	-7323	-4079	-1977	-520	776	571	1182	1894	2440	2836	3184
Government budget balance (mill. SR)	4338	6423	7092	7876	8750	9495	10477	11537	12697	13966	15347

Can Saudi Arabia Benefit Economically from a More Aggressive Oil Policy?

Saudi Arabia is a major supplier of crude oil to the world oil market with a market share of more than ten per cent. The country has on a number of occasions acted as the main swing producer within OPEC. The OPEC market share has gradually increased to around 40 per cent of world supply after having fallen to only 30 per cent in 1985. The combination of the Asian crisis and the OPEC decision of November 1997 to increase production quotas is usually thought of as the main cause for the oil price collapse during 1998. A somewhat neglected factor was the substantial increase of crude production in Iraq. From December 1997 to December 1998, Iraqi production increased by 1.7 mbd. and reached volumes not seen since the invasion of Kuwait. Several attempts by OPEC to restrict supply finally succeeded in March 1999 and the oil price increased during 1999 to a level close to the previous peak price during the winter of 1996–97. The war in Iraq has again called on OPEC and Saudi Arabia in particular to stabilize the oil market. It is probably fair to say that the recent OPEC successes in restricting oil supply have surprised most experts in the oil market.

In this section we study the potential benefits to Saudi Arabia and OPEC of a more aggressive production policy. We discuss first what we will refer to as the baseline scenario for the world oil market. Then we present an analysis of a scenario where OPEC capacity and production are increased in order to grab a larger share of the world market than in the baseline. The idea is to study if such a policy could reduce those fiscal imbalances for the Saudi economy presented above. For more details of our analysis we refer to Cappelen and Choudhury (2000).

Our simulations are based on a small model of the world oil market where world demand is disaggregated by two regions, OECD and the rest of the world except former centrally planned economies, where net crude supply to the world market is exogenous. Demand depends on real income (GDP) and the real oil price adjusted for refining costs and taxes. Supplies from OECD and other market economies depend positively on the real oil price and technological change. OPEC production balances the market. The crude price is modelled as a function of capacity and production in OPEC so that higher capacity utilization in OPEC will increase the crude price. In our alternative scenario, the OPEC countries are assumed to increase their production capacity. This drives the price down and OPEC production as well as capacity utilization increases. This will in turn lead to higher prices. We shall return to this scenario below.

GDP growth in the OECD countries is assumed to be 2.5 per cent while the growth rate for the rest of the world is assumed to be 4.5 per cent. In the baseline, production capacity in OPEC is assumed to grow by nearly two per cent annually. Net supplies from former planned economies, the most important being Russia and China, are assumed to be constant at approximately two mbd.

The average crude price per barrel in 1999 is estimated to be 18 USD and OPEC supply is 31 mbd. In 2000 and most of 2001 oil prices have been much higher than this, but during the fourth quarter of 2001 prices have come down just above 20 USD. This is at the lower end of the price bracket that OPEC has recently targeted and we use this as a level in accordance with our model simulations. Before the war started in Iraq in 2003 prices were again well over 30 USD per barrel, but declined to meet the OPEC target bracket in April 2003.

In 2010 OPEC supply is estimated to be 37 mbd. and the crude price 24 USD assuming two per cent inflation. Thus, in the baseline, the crude price in real terms is roughly constant with the actual level late in 2001. The growth rate of non-OPEC crude supply is estimated to be roughly equal to that of OPEC. The market share of OPEC, reaching 40 per cent in the late 1990s, will be fairly constant according to the baseline scenario. The main characteristics of the baseline are presented in Table 2.2.

Table 2.2 The world oil market. Baseline scenario

	1990	1995	2000	2005	2010	1990–2000	2000–2010
						Average growth rates	
World demand (mbd.)	66.4	70.1	76.0	82.5	90.0	1.4	1.7
OECD	41.6	44.9	48.0	50.7	54.0	1.4	1.2
Other market econ.	12.8	16.5	19.5	22.8	27.0	4.3	3.3
World supply (mbd.)	66.9	70.1	76.0	82.5	90.0	1.3	1.7
OPEC	25.0	27.7	30.5	33.5	37.0	2.2	1.8
Market economies	27.4	32.0	34.5	38.0	41.0	2.3	1.7
Crude oil price (USD)	22.3	17.2	26.0	22.0	24.0		

This scenario is of course subject to large uncertainties. One important uncertainty is related to the non-OPEC supply potential. Recently there has been a renewed interest in the relation between oil reserves and long-run production capabilities in the world. Contributions to this debate are Campbell and Laherrère (1998), Bakthiari (1999) and Martin (1999). The main argument in Campbell and Laherrère and earlier studies by Campbell is that the world is running out of cheap oil and that conventional oil production will peak very soon. The arguments supporting these conclusions are summarized in Bakthiari (1999) as:

- 80 per cent of total world output comes from fields discovered before 1973
- There is now a tendency to overestimate reserves rather than the opposite
- The last giant oil field was discovered in 1986
- It is unlikely that the world contains any major undiscovered oil province.

These arguments, usually made by geologists, are of course met with skepticism from economists who tend to argue that technological progress will reduce extraction costs and increase recoverable reserves. If a scarcity should appear and the oil price increases substantially, more exploration will take place and more oil will be found so that a long-term major price increase will be avoided. When the Club of Rome launched its resource scarcity view more than 30 years ago, it was met with criticism and soon sunk into oblivion. There are relatively large unexplored provinces, such as the Caspian Sea, that could prove to be major areas for new growth in production outside OPEC. Even within OPEC the return of Iraq to the scene and the possibility of a normalization in the political situation of that country could prove that low-cost reserves are as high as suggested by the non-geologists.

In our model, OPEC is not modelled as a single rational body that tries to maximize net revenues from oil. Given the behavior of OPEC during the last 30 years, this is probably not a very controversial assumption. OPEC is assumed to set prices so that a target level of capacity utilization is met. This behavioral assumption has some empirical foundation. However, the model leaves the OPEC capacity unexplained and is consequently only a partial model. In this section we analyze what happens to the world oil market and the crude oil price in particular if OPEC decides to increase its capacity substantially compared to our reference scenario. Instead of the assumed two per cent annual growth over the next decade, we now assume that OPEC increases its capacity by another five mbd., then lowers the crude price in order to increase demand for OPEC production. Over time the increase in capacity will gradually be followed by higher output so that capacity utilization is roughly constant. By comparing the two alternatives, we see if OPEC has any incentive to change its decisions compared to the baseline.

Let us start with a simple theoretical model in order to understand the main mechanisms of our simulation. OPEC production (XO) is assumed to be the difference between total demand (D) and non-OPEC supply (S). Demand depends negatively on the real consumer price (PC) while supply increases when real producer prices (PS) increase.

$$XO = D(PC) - S(PS)$$

The real consumer price of oil (PC) is given by

$$PC = (\alpha*PS + (1 - \alpha)*P)*(1 + t)$$

The consumer price of oil depends on the producer price (PS) or the crude price multiplied by a share α that captures the share of crude in total refinery costs. Other costs are simply taken to depend on the general price level (P=1) or the GDP deflator. Since oil products are heavily taxed in most countries, the indirect tax rate (t) has been incorporated into the formula.

OPEC revenue is given by

$$R = PS*XO - C*XO$$

where C is production cost per unit in OPEC. Inserting the first two equations into the revenue function and differentiating gives

$$dR = [(1 + (D - S)/(\alpha*(1+t)*\varepsilon*D - \sigma*S))*PS - C]*dXO$$

The first term inside the brackets is OPEC marginal revenue taking into account the supply response of non-OPEC producers and the last term inside the brackets is marginal costs of increasing OPEC production. This model of the oil market treats OPEC as a Stackleberg leader, and has certain shortcomings, but is simple and transparent in the short to medium run.

If we define the OPEC market share (*ms*) as

$$ms = XO/D$$

the condition that has to be fulfilled if OPEC is to benefit from higher output is

$$C/PS < 1 + ms/[(\alpha*(1+t)*\varepsilon - (1-ms)*\sigma)]$$

The denominator on the right hand side will always be negative as the price elasticity of demand (ε) is always negative and the supply elasticity (σ) is always positive. Thus the right hand side will always be less than one. The cost-price margin for OPEC on the left hand side of the inequality sign will also be less than one so it is not obvious how to conclude. We must take into account that all the parameters on the right hand side are not parameters in a strict sense because they will all depend on the crude oil price (PS). One obvious qualitative result is that if the oil price is low, the OPEC cost-price margin will be high. That in itself will make it less probable that the inequality sign is fulfilled. This is also reasonable because OPEC is more likely to decrease output when the oil price is low than when it is high. Indeed, this is also what we observe and has led many observers to state that OPEC functions better as a cartel when the oil price is low than when it is high. The other side of this argument is just as obvious. For producers within OPEC with high marginal costs, the cost-price margin will be high. Thus higher output is not seen as the best OPEC strategy for these countries. The opposite is the case for low cost producers within OPEC. They would most likely earn more if OPEC expanded output where only low-cost producers are allowed to expand production. This difference in policy within OPEC has been observed a number of times and limits the effectiveness of OPEC as a cartel particularly in times of high prices when low-cost producers would benefit the most from higher output on the margin.

It is also worth noting that the higher the tax on oil products (t) in consumer countries, the more likely it is that OPEC will gain from higher output. This is because there is less demand response due to the large gap between consumer and producer prices. Thus the tax rate acts just as a high price elasticity of demand (in absolute terms). It produces a "flat" demand curve that makes demand very responsive to higher prices. Therefore, when OPEC increases supply, prices will not have to go down much since consumers are so flexible. Also the more elastic the supply is outside OPEC the more likely OPEC is to benefit from higher output; a small reduction in price will lower non-OPEC output more than when supply responds less.

Let us now turn to the model simulations. The model we use is of course not the "truth" in any sense. However, any OPEC strategy will have to be based on a set of empirical assumptions regarding the oil market and a model is a useful tool in organizing the discussion and in performing sensitivity analyses. Ideally we should have compared the results from many different models of the oil market in order to study "optimal" OPEC behavior, as there are large uncertainties with regard to the important parameters. We do not have access to such a variety of models so the one we have must do.

Table 2.3 The market grab scenario. Absolute changes compared to baseline

	2000	2001	2002	2003	2004	2005	2006	2007	2008	2009	2010	2015	2020
OECD demand (mbd.)	0.3	0.6	1.1	1.6	2.0	2.2	2.4	2.5	2.5	2.5	2.4	2.1	2.0
Other market econ.	0.2	0.4	0.8	1.1	1.4	1.7	1.9	2.0	2.1	2.2	2.2	2.1	2.2
World supply (mbd.)	0.4	1.1	1.9	2.7	3.4	3.9	4.3	4.5	4.6	4.7	4.6	4.2	4.2
OPEC	0.9	2.0	3.1	4.1	4.8	5.3	5.6	5.7	5.7	5.6	5.5	5.0	5.0
Market economies	-0.5	-0.9	-1.2	-1.4	-1.4	-1.4	-1.3	-1.2	-1.1	-0.9	-0.9	-0.8	-0.8
Crude oil price	-1.9	-3.3	-4.6	-4.8	-5.0	-4.7	-4.4	-4.0	-3.6	-3.2	-2.9	-2.6	-2.6

An important assumption in the calculations is that OPEC changes its policy in 2000. Due to the importance of oil as a world commodity, higher output and lower oil prices generally affect the world economy. To be consistent we should in principle change our assumptions of GDP growth that drive demand. Given the results in this scenario compared to baseline, these output and price effects will be small and are neglected for simplicity. Table 2.3 presents the effects of this market grab scenario as absolute changes compared to the baseline simulation. Most effects seem to stabilize after approximately ten years and annual results beyond 2010 are not presented.

If we focus on long-term results, we notice that the crude price (both nominal and real) is reduced by some 2.5–3 USD per barrel and OPEC output has expanded by five mbd. in line with capacity. The supply response to lower prices in non-OPEC countries is very small according to our model. In itself this makes it less likely that higher output will be optimal for OPEC according to our theoretical discussion above. One argument in favor of this result and in line with our model is that as long as prices are as high as in both scenarios, operating costs will be covered for most non-OPEC producers. Thus the profit is reduced but it still pays to produce roughly as before, at least on already developed sites.

For OPEC as a whole, gross revenue in 2010 is 897 million USD per day in this scenario as opposed to 888 million USD in the baseline. If we assume that marginal costs in OPEC are two USD per barrel, net revenue in 2010 is slightly higher in the baseline scenario than in this market grab scenario; roughly speaking they are the same in both. However, if marginal production costs are much higher because the increase in OPEC output is spread among many OPEC countries and not those with the lowest costs, it clearly does not pay to expand output according to our model. Beyond 2010, the effect on the crude price is somewhat lower than in 2010 and higher output is then more likely to be beneficial to OPEC. On the other hand, the lower price applies to a higher output as OPEC capacity is assumed to increase beyond 2010. Thus in 2015 the difference in gross revenue is very small between the two scenarios according to our simulation results.

Taken as an investment strategy, any increase in net revenues will have to be discounted against the loss in revenues that comes during the first ten years or so. Notice that the crude price drops considerably during these years, before gradually stabilizing at 2.5–3 USD lower than in baseline. For many years this market grab scenario actually implies a decline in the crude price compared to the average price in 1999 (18 USD). In 2002 and 2003 the crude price is around 16 USD per barrel and the loss in revenues for OPEC is very large in the market grab scenario compared with baseline during the first years. Since the cost of market grab comes early with possible increases in net revenue much later, the market grab scenario does not seem an optimal policy for OPEC as a whole according to our model.

So far, we have discussed the market grab scenario as if it applied to OPEC as a whole. Now suppose that only a few countries within OPEC actually have the potential to increase their crude production considerably. Suppose further that these countries are also low-cost producers. In fact this is the case for countries such as

Iraq and Saudi Arabia. Although it is not clear how fast Iraq can increase its capacity, Saudi Arabia can increase output from around eight mbd., close to present production, to say 14 mbd. by 2010 (assuming growth in baseline with a constant quota within OPEC in addition to 5.4 mbd. according to Table 2.3). In 2010 the baseline Saudi gross revenue is estimated at 234 million USD per day. In the market grab scenario gross revenue would be 318 million USD a day and taking into account a marginal cost of producing the extra 5.4 mbd. at 2 USD a barrel would give a net increase in revenues of 73 million USD a day (318 - 2*5.4 - 234). For Saudi Arabia there would hardly be any short-run costs to this strategy. If Saudi Arabia could increase its production while the rest of OPEC did not, Saudi Arabia would experience considerable economic benefit.

Considering the results for OPEC as a whole, roughly all of the Saudi benefit would be at the expense of other OPEC member countries. OPEC is not likely to survive if such a policy were to be undertaken by Saudi Arabia. Obviously this would also change the whole political scene in the Middle East and for the "Arab nation".

Thus we believe the market grab scenario to be quite unlikely. Consequently we think it is more likely that elements from the policy reform scenario will be chosen. But in order to prove successful, labor supply among Saudis will have to increase to avoid a decline in GDP per capita.

Concluding Remarks

The Saudi economy has not performed well for some time. Negative per capita growth and financial imbalances have been observed for a long time. More or less hidden unemployment is increasing, creating social dissatisfaction. Inflation, on the other hand, has been low and stable. Saudi Arabia has a rapidly growing population and large oil reserves. While the world oil market and OPEC policies limit the potential for oil-based growth, domestic policies and institutions are the main bottleneck for utilizing human resources. We have shown that without any policy reform, the poor performance of the economy is likely to continue. While reforms may increase growth and reduce financial imbalances, tough measures are necessary to improve performance radically. Thus one is tempted to conclude that the stability of the fabric of society is called into question. We also study if the Saudis could benefit from a change in their policy within OPEC leading to significantly increasing Saudi oil production. Our results suggest that this is probably not the case, although we would emphasize that care is needed when interpreting our results. In addition to questioning the economic gains from increasing oil supply, we think the political costs of doing so would be formidable. Such a policy would also run against those policy initiatives that the present leadership in Saudi Arabia has taken. Our conclusion is, therefore, that domestic policy reforms are the most likely option for the present government and that Saudi Arabia will remain loyal to OPEC as long as recent OPEC consensus remains.

However, the collapse of the former Saddam regime in Iraq may change politics in the Arab world and in OPEC. This may change the policy options in Saudi Arabia, including its oil policy and behavior within OPEC. However, we would question the likelihood of a dramatic increase in Iraqi oil production in order to reconstruct the country after the war. First of all there is the problem of political stability that may limit foreign investment. Secondly, any government in Iraq will have to consider what the likely response of Saudi Arabia will be if Iraq increases its production of oil. If OPEC should cease to function as a swing producer, oil prices may fall so much that net revenues for the Iraqi government may not increase much. Thus the kind of reasoning we have carried out above for Saudi Arabia may also be relevant for a future Iraqi government.

References

Bakthiari, A.M.S (1999), "The Price of Crude Oil", *OPEC Review*, Vol. 23, pp. 1–21.

BP Amoco (1999), *Statistical Review of World Energy*, June.

Campbell, C. and Laherrère, J. (1998), "The End of Cheap Oil", *Scientific American*, Vol. 30–36.

Cappelen, Å. and Choudhury, R. (2000), *The Future of the Saudi Arabian Economy*, Reports 2000/7, Statistics Norway, Oslo.

El-Harmassy, E. (1987), "State Building and Regime Performance in the Greater Maghreb", in G. Salamé (ed.), *The Foundation of the Arab States*, Instituto Affari Internazionali, Croom Helm.

Martin, Jean-Marie (1999), "Concerning 'The End of Cheap Oil'", *Energy Policy*, Vol. 27, pp. 69–72.

OPEC (1998), Annual Statistical Bulletin.

Saudi Arabian Monetary Agency (1993), Annual Report, 1412/1413 (1992).

Chapter 3

The Reformist Movement in Iran

Mehrzad Boroujerdi

Introductory Remarks

These are confusing and contentious times in Iran, and analysts are wrangling over how to interpret events there.

Pessimists refer to the intimidation and imprisonment of prominent activists, deputies, editors and publishers, Draconian measures against the press and vigilante violence as evidence that things have changed little since Mohammad Khatami (b. 1943) was elected president in Iran in May 1997.[1] They maintain that the Cabinet and Parliament still lack force, the judiciary and the Guardian Council[2] accountability, the civil service dexterity and the press freedom.

Optimists, on the other hand, insist that we should not interpret the curbing of the belligerent press and the arrest of iconoclastic journalists as anything more than temporary setbacks in Iran's long and arduous march toward a more democratic state. A society where the genie of dissent has been let out of the bottle cannot remain silent in perpetuity, they say, and argue that the demography of a young, urban, educated and politically aware population favors the reform movement.[3] They remind us that, while at the time of the 1979 revolution half of the population lived in urban centers, that figure has now reached over 61 per cent, and more strikingly,

---

1   They have in mind such events as the 1998 serial murders of political dissidents and writers by alleged rogue agents in the Ministry of Intelligence, the assassination of the key theoretician of the reformist movement, the closure of over 90 pro-democracy newspapers and periodicals, the violent crackdown on student demonstrators in July 1999, the trial of numerous intellectuals and activists for taking part in a conference in Berlin or for conducting unflattering public opinion polls, the imprisonment of the most outspoken journalists, scholars and lawyers, and the summoning to court and even jailing of sitting members of the legislature on the grounds that they libeled and slandered the hard-line judiciary during parliamentary speeches.

2   The Guardian Council is a 12-man body of clerics and lawyers which has the mandate of ensuring that all laws passed by Parliament are in accordance with Islamic *shari'a* law and the constitution of Iran. It also has the power to screen and disqualify any candidates contending a national office, on the basis of their ideological and moral qualifications.

3   Iran's population has risen from 33.7 million in 1976–77 to over 65.6 million in 2001. This demographic explosion has meant that in 1996 almost 40 per cent of the country's population was below the age of 15 while only 6.6 per cent were over the age of 60.

during the same time span the literacy rate has skyrocketed from less than 50 per cent to over 83 per cent.[4] The optimists interpret these irreversible demographic trends as harbingers of the revolution of rising expectations that is gaining momentum in the country. Furthermore, they claim that, thanks to the addition of some 21 million new entrants to the ranks of eligible voters since the 1979 revolution, Iranian voters are increasingly asserting their willingness and potential to reshape the sociopolitical and cultural system of their country.[5]

These different readings provide different answers to the following questions:

- Have hard-liners managed to wear the reformist camp down and weaken it in the eyes of voters? Has this movement fallen victim to cynicism, demoralization and dejection – or can it still rejuvenate itself?
- Is it true that President Mohammad Khatami's cautious administration has managed to drive the sensitive to impatience and despair? Will the reformist movement lead a less cautious and syncopated crusade for political liberalization in the years to come?
- Should we interpret the retreats and setbacks of the reformist movement so far as an allegro prelude to a long mournful march towards disillusionment?
- If the reform movement is now battered and beaten, does this mean that political change will now only come from outside the ranks of the regime?

Before we can begin to sort through the answers to these questions, we must ask one that is more fundamental: what have we learned about the nature of political life in post-revolutionary Iran? This chapter will offer the five lessons set out in the following.

Lesson 1: *What has softened the hardness of an Islamic republic born through revolution – and will continue to do so – are the eclectic realities of the political landscape and popular culture of the country.*[6]

The popular reform movement that appeared on the Iranian political radar-screen on May 23, 1997 exposed the fallacy of the argument that we cannot change a *bona fide* theocracy from within. On that momentous day – without having been cajoled by any leader or established political party – over 83 per cent of the voters of Iran took part in the largest-ever turnout for any executive or legislative branch elections

---

4   The above data is based on various editions of *Iran Statistical Yearbook* published by the Statistical Center of Iran and Ashofteh Tehrani (1372/1993).

5   Here we can refer to various sociological studies and polling surveys that indicate that increased literacy has led to a decline in the fertility rate and abandonment of traditional views regarding gender roles and cultural determinism (see Abdi and Goudarzi, 1378/1999). Moreover, analysis of recent electoral data shows that the gap between the political preferences of urban and rural Iranians is narrowing.

6   For discussions of Iranian political and popular culture see Farsoun and Mashayekhi (1992), Khosrokhavar and Roy (1999), Adelkhah (2000) and Yu (2002).

in the country's history and provided the reform candidate, Mohammad Khatami, with a landslide victory. Moreover, in three subsequent elections – the March 1999 village and city council elections, the February 2000 parliamentary elections and the 2001 presidential elections where Khatami was once again a candidate – respectively 64 per cent, 69 per cent and 66 per cent of Iran's voters went to the polling booths and each time overwhelmingly cast their votes for the reformist candidates.[7]

Not only that, but the people demonstrated to themselves as well as the ruling elite that a politically assertive citizenry could tame the conservative clerical establishment by firmly exerting public pressure on it. A brief look at the outcome of the 2000 parliamentary elections demonstrates the truth of these two claims. First, although there were some 1,500 more candidates in 2000 than in the preceding round of general elections, there was a 30 per cent drop in the rate of candidates who were disqualified by the Guardian Council.[8] The voters unseated 73 per cent of the deputies who had served in the outgoing conservative-dominated chamber and handed over 200 seats (out of a total of 290) to reformist candidates.

Once the election results had shown the clear victory of the reformists, influential conservative elements called for the cancellation of the results in Teheran on bogus grounds of election fraud and gerrymandering. Mindful of the possible repeat of the two-week-long student unrest of July 1999 that had rocked the Iranian political establishment, Ayatollah Seyyed Ali Khamenei (b. 1939), the country's Supreme Leader, endorsed the accuracy of the electoral outcome.

The fact that the Emperor has no clothes can be easily observed once one looks at how the percentage of clerics elected to the Iranian parliament has plummeted. The percentage has consistently declined from 49 per cent in 1980 to less than 13 per cent in 2000.[9] A decline of 36 per cent in only 20 years cannot but serve as a powerful reminder to the ruling clerical establishment that power comes with accountability, that trust has an *ad hoc* quality and that loyalty is revocable in light of performance.

Lesson 2: *Demographic and social forces are rapidly transforming the contours of Iranian society from a traditional-authoritarian structure to a modern-democratic one.*

The events of the past few years have made it clear that the members of Iran's 23-million-strong cultural middle class (people with high school diplomas or university degrees) now view themselves not as mere "nationals" but as "citizens". No longer

---

7   For an analysis of the February 18, 2000 parliamentary elections, see Esfandiari and Bertone (2000, pp. 11–45).
8   In 1984, 1988, 1992, 1996 and 2000 respectively 1,584; 2,001; 3,150; 5,365; and 6,856 candidates registered to run for Parliament. In these same years, respectively, 54 per cent, 80 per cent, 65 per cent, 61 per cent and 91 per cent of these candidates were cleared to stand for office by the Council of Guardians.
9   See Baktiari (1996, p. 241) and Islamic Consultative Assembly (1981, p. 199).

interested in hearing pontificators talk about their "patriotic or religious duties", they are increasingly inquiring about their "citizenship rights" (jobs, political and social freedoms). A poised, robust and sober student movement representing over 20 million high school and university students has created a formidable constituency that the state cannot simply absorb, ignore or buy off.[10]

In addition, Iranian journalists and writers have managed to create a substantial, serious and sophisticated media audience as well as an animated court of public opinion which looks doubtfully at the clergy's attempts to present a whitewashed view of the ancient Islamic glory and its own recent heroic past. The number of newspapers, periodicals, books and pamphlets published in Iran has risen dramatically in recent years.[11] This increase has been supplemented with an equally impressive rise in the circulation of books and newspapers as well as the burgeoning of the private-sector press.[12]

These changes are compounded by a fundamental and multi-pronged change-over that society at large is currently undergoing. Emotional and frenzied crowds are giving way to rational actors; populist slogans and ideological appeals (or dictates) are now seen as vain; family structure is becoming more democratic; relationships and expectations better defined; and consumers and purveyors of services better informed. In short, the pace of the transition from a traditional-authoritarian society to a more modern-democratic has intensified. The emerging rifts between ideals and practice, politics and jurisprudence, public discourse and private conduct, and finally, the factual and the "ought to be" (the normative) are responsible for these transformations. The profound cultural, economic and social transformations of the post-revolutionary era have bequeathed to Iranian politics a multi-dimensionality and sophistication previously unimaginable. Today the average Iranian citizen is not politically gullible or subject to flattery, and the polity is not torpid and effete. Indeed, in many ways society has managed to move ahead of politics.[13]

Lesson 3: *In the factional and fluid havoc of Iranian politics, success and failure are often conditional, since gains tend to be marginal and losses temporary.*

Stated positions are rarely inflexible, alliances are hardly enduring, defeat is by no means total, victory is in no way unqualified, grief not at all permanent and political

---

10 In 1996, students constituted some 32 per cent of the total population of Iran.

11 According to the Ministry of Islamic Culture's Director of Domestic Press, more than 57 per cent (927 out of 1,611) of the periodicals published in 2001 were granted a publication permit after the coming to power of President Khatami in 1997 (*Iran Emrooz*, August 23, 2001). The total circulation of daily newspapers, which stood at 1.3 million copies in 1997, increased to 2.7 million in 1999. The reformist newspapers were responsible for most of this increase.

12 In 1986, the total circulation of books and pamphlets published in Iran was 28,112. In 1998, that same statistic stood at 79,402. Non-governmental organizations and individuals were largely responsible for this upsurge.

13 For an interesting eyewitness account of this, see Yaghmaian (2002).

cachet never eternal. One can think of the ministerial interpolations and melo-dramatic public trials of the last few years as an example. While the clerical courts almost always reprimand or find the accused guilty of the offenses with which they are charged, the court of public opinion concurrently bestows upon them the honor of being icons of reform and democracy. Converseley, the February 28, 2003 village-city council elections brought about a crushing electoral defeat for the coalition of the 18 reformist parties that had grown complacent and overconfident about their electoral supremacy. In one of the lowest nationwide voter turnouts in the post-revolutionary period, less than 40 per cent of eligible voters went to the polls and registered their disillusionement with the bitter factional wrangling by electing a slate of largely conservative candidates who were by and large political un-knows.[14]

Lesson 4: *In the overtly polarized, regimented and stilted world of Iranian politics, every action is politically and symbolically significant.*

Even the most innocuous signs (pictures, cartoons, theatrical plays), acts (clapping, dancing, holding hands, whistling, ambiguous language, nostalgic lyrics, anodyne leisure or recreational activity or other manifestations of youthful verve), events (victory or defeat of the national soccer team, temporary loss of water or electricity, factory closures) can cause a serious political crisis, since the state is neither ideologically nor structurally capable of preventing or defusing such escapades. As an advisor to President Khatami has put it, the Iranian regime resembles a tall glass building where voices echo and even the smallest stone that is thrown creates a loud shattering noise.

Lesson 5: *Understanding contemporary Iran is impossible unless we understand the deeply-embedded cultural and political paradoxes that have emerged over the past two and a half decades.*

As Ira Lapidus, a historian of the Middle East, wrote in the pages of the *New York Times*, Iran is "a nation that is open and welcoming but remains hidden and mysterious; a clerical dictatorship but one of the Middle East's liveliest democracies, a puritanical regime but a people who love everyday life; a severe orthodoxy but an expressive cinema and an argumentative press; a revolution that has rejected secularism but a nation heading toward a fusion of Islamic and Persian identities".[15] We can also add the following paradoxes to the list provided by Lapidus:[16]

---

14 In Teheran, less than 12 per cent of eligible voters bothered to vote.
15 Lapidus (2000).
16 I have elaborated on this list of paradoxes in Boroujerdi (2001). See also Hourcade (2002, pp. 99–115).

- a constitution that simultaneously affirms religious and secular principles, democratic and anti-democratic tendencies, as well as populist and elitist predilections[17]
- a society in which many cultural, political and social institutions are Western and modern in pedigree and configuration, yet native and traditional in iconography and nomenclature
- a "hyper-politicized" society that does not benefit from the presence of recognized, legitimate or effective political media such as parties
- a theocracy where religion is an axiom of political life, and yet secular agents, aspirations, ideas, institutions, language and motifs continue to survive and – more importantly – manifest their significance in private and public space
- a society where the eclectic texture of popular culture has made the practicality – let alone desirability – of religiously sanctioned statecraft highly doubtful, in turn leading to a gradual but consistent disillusionment with the belief that Islam is the only [political] solution
- a clerical leadership that has claimed to protect tradition but has amended and broken numerous age-old religious protocols for the sake of state expediency
- a society whose Islamic intellectuals resort to the writings of Western thinkers to validate their own "Islamic" critique of the West
- a citizenry that has come to enjoy sophisticated artistic and intellectual productions despite living under a politically repressive state[18]
- a society where women's rights have been trampled upon, yet where women have continued to make strides into the educational, cultural and professional domains, thereby increasing awareness of women's rights and issues at the social level.[19]

The Future of the Reform Movement

One characteristic of much of contemporary political analysis of Iran is the tendency to equate the future of conservative and reformist factions with the political fortunes of their respective leaders, Supreme Leader Ayatollah Khamenei and President Khatami. I believe we should avoid the pitfall of personalizing politics in Iran, because what we are dealing with is a complex political ambiance that is in constant flux. We should bear in mind that, after Ayatollah Khomeini, *Velayat e Faghih* (Guardianship of the Jurist) is no longer a one-man show but has become a collective institution. The reason Ayatollah Khamenei is becoming less and less of a regal umpire or guru has to do with the fact that he is under intense pressure from

17 See Chehabi (1996) and Schirazi (1997) for discussions of the contradictions inherent in the Iranian constitution and political system.
18 See Tapper (2002).
19 See Mir-Hosseini (1999).

those who have gathered under his mantle and speak in his name – Friday prayer leaders, members of the Experts Assembly, the Council of Guardians, the Expediency Council, judges, leaders' representatives in various ministries, universities, councils, etc. – to safeguard the positions and perquisites that they have become accustomed to.[20]

Nor should we fall for a facile equation of the reform movement with the persona of President Khatami, who increasingly seems to fit Machiavelli's description of an "unarmed prophet" – a man who challenges powerful rivals yet lacks the political muscle to defend himself. Khatami should be viewed simply as a by-product of Iranians' high aspirations, pent-up emotions and tortured hopes. The deep-rooted demands for reform on the part of Iran's young, educated and urban polity indicate that a genuine reformist social movement is quite capable of cutting its umbilical cord to President Khatami, should he fail to keep up with the pace and the turns in the road still ahead. There is even evidence that Khatami's younger and more radical parliamentary allies are becoming more assertive in letting their views be known. As one indicator, we can refer to the confidence votes of President Khatami's two cabinets in 1997 and 2001. In 1997, the conservative-dominated fifth Parliament gave 4,571 positive and 841 negative votes (with 371 abstentions), respectively, to Khatami's cabinet. Then in 2001 the reformist-dominated sixth Parliament, which is more sympathetic to Khatami, gave his ministers a total of 3,690 positive and 1,301 negative votes (with 255 abstentions), respectively.[21] In another move in May 2003, over 130 reformist parliamentarians wrote an open letter to Ayatollah Khamenei asking him to change the course of political events before the entire establishment collapses. This was supplemented by rumors that they will also resign en masse to further discredit the regime.

Even a passing glance at the state of factional fighting in post-1997 Iran would indicate that the squabbling conservatives and reformists will continue to work against each other for the foreseeable future, with rapprochement not presently within reach.[22] And thus, it is likely that the painful and slow process of reform will continue. The conservatives have so far demonstrated their ability to stall, torpedo or dilute any reformist initiative they do not like.[23] In addition, not being worried about how much political capital they have lost, they have not shied away from utilizing the repressive state apparatuses at their disposal. In this way, they have

---

20 One example of such pressure manifested itself on August 6, 2000, when Ayatollah Khamenei directly ordered the newly elected Parliament to drop its plans to pass a more liberal media law. Parliament and the Khatami Administration could do nothing except look on helplessly.

21 Islamic Republic News Agency (August 22, 2001).

22 For accounts of this phenomenon, see Brumberg (2001), Moslem (2002) and Buchta (2000).

23 In May 2003, the conservative Guardians Council rejected two key pieces of legislation which were introduced, with much fanfare, by Khatami and his supporters to enhance presidential powers. Khatami called the action "unacceptable" but, nevertheless, resigned himself to this predicament.

created a situation that can be best described as a political stalemate if not a dead-lock.

Despite all the demographic trends that favor the reformists, prudence dictates that we should not confuse hope with reality. We should be wary of formulations that reduce politics to reflexes of economic processes and social structures. While credit must be given to the reformist camp for maintaining its broad alliance and training its young cadres, we should also recognize that the realization of their goals is neither easy nor imminent. Iran is still a country where the conduct of politics remains non-transparent, where tutelary patronage is a long-established tradition, where elites define interests largely as individual needs and private ends, where politicians are viewed with cynicism, where deliberate political provocations are often effective, where the precipice of mediocrity is hard to ignore, where "free and fair elections" is not synonymous with "democratic governance". It is still a country of "persons" not "laws", a country where the religious-patriarchal state is both able and willing to devour institutions of civil society, where non-governmental organizations cannot act as ombudsmen between civil society and the state, where primordial ties overshadow social obligations, where "trust" as a social capital hardly manages to cut across horizontal family, clan and friendship ties, where social mobility is viewed as based on fortuitous factors, connections or influence-peddling rather than hard work, and where civil society remains under-developed and its shock-absorbing institutions fragile.

On the positive side, however, Iranians are now experiencing perhaps the most serious national debate in their history on such themes as the merits of democracy, tolerance, non-violence, globalization and modernity. Hence, we should be equally skeptical of predictions about the imminent and/or inevitable final victory by either the reformists or the conservatives. This, then, is the nature of factional politics in post-revolutionary Iran.

References

Abdi, Abbas and Goudarzi, Mohsen (1378/1999), *Tahavolat-e Farhangi dar Iran* [Cultural Developments in Iran], Entesharat Ravesh, Teheran.

Adelkhah, Fariba (2000), *Being Modern in Iran*, Columbia University Press, New York and Centre d'Etudes et de Recherches Internationales.

Ashofteh Tehrani, Amir (1372/1993), *Jameashenasi Jameiyat: Nemoneh Iran* [Sociology of Iran's Population], Jahad Daneshgahi, Isfahan.

Baktiari, Bahman (1996), *Parliamentary Politics in Revolutionary Iran*, The University Press of Florida, Gainesville.

Boroujerdi, Mehrzad (2001), "The Paradoxes of Politics in Postrevolutionary Iran", in John Esposito and R.K. Ramazani (eds), *Iran at the Crossroads*, Palgrave, New York, pp. 13–27.

Brumberg, Daniel (2001), *Reinventing Khomeini: The Struggle for Reform in Iran*, University of Chicago Press, Chicago.

Buchta, Wilfried (2000), *Who Rules Iran? The Structure of Power in the Islamic Republic*, Washington Institute for Near East Policy, Washington, DC and the Konrad Adenauer Stiftung.

Chehabi, H.E. (1996), "The Impossible Republic: Contradictions of Iran's Islamic State", *Contention: Debates in Society, Culture, and Science*, Vol. 5, No. 3, pp. 135–54.

Esfandiari, Haleh and Bertone, Andrea (eds) (2000), *Iran Before and After the Elections*, The Middle East Project at the Woodrow Wilson International Center for Scholars, Washington, DC.

Farsoun, Samih K. and Mashayekhi, Mehrdad (eds) (1992), *Iran: Political Culture in the Islamic Republic*, Routledge, London.

Hourcade, Bernard (2002), *Iran: Nouvelles identités d'une république*, Editions Belin, Paris.

Islamic Consultative Assembly (1981), *Ashnaye ba Majlies Shuraye Eslami* [Getting to Know the Islamic Consultative Assembly].

Khosrokhavar, Farhad and Roy, Oliver (1999), *Iran: Comment Sortir d'une Revolution Religieuse*, Editions du Seuil, Paris.

Lapidus, Ira (2000), Review of Elaine Sciolino's *Persian Mirrors: The Elusive Face of Iran*, *The New York Times*, September 27, p. B8.

Mir-Hosseini, Ziba (1999), *Islam and Gender: The Religious Debate in Contemporary Iran*, Princeton University Press, Princeton.

Moslem, Mehdi (2002), *Factional Politics in Post-Khomeini Iran*, Syracuse University Press, Syracuse, New York.

Poya, Maryam (1999), *Women, Work, and Islamism: Ideology and Resistance in Iran*, Zed Books, London.

Schirazi, Asghar (1997), *The Constitution of Iran: Politics and the State in the Islamic Republic*, I.B. Tauris, London.

Tapper, Richard (ed.) (2002), *The New Iranian Cinema: Politics, Representation and Identity*, I.B. Tauris, London.

Yaghmaian, Behzad (2002), *Social Change in Iran: An Eyewitness Account of Dissent, Defiance, and New Movements for Rights*, State University of New York Press, Albany, New York.

Yu, Dal Seung (2002), *The Role of Political Culture in Iranian Political Development*, Ashgate Publishing, Burlington, Vermont.

Chapter 4

The Psychology of Corruption in Azerbaijan and Iran

Daniel Heradstveit and G. Matthew Bonham

Introduction

Societies permeated by corruption, like the Azerbaijani and Iran, enslave their citizens. This is not a matter of winners and losers; the paralyzing culture of corruption affects everybody, and everyone is a victim. Corruption prevents economic growth and development; it erodes respect for the law; and teaches people that honest work is not where the rewards are to be found. Corruption demoralizes people and destroys social cohesion.

If Azerbaijanis and Iranians are to experience a free, modern and stable society, they must break the chains of corruption. Azerbaijan, with its oil wealth and a pre-Communist democratic heritage, and Iran, with the historic hero Mossadeq and substantial oil resources, should be in a position to give their citizens a good standard of living and the rule of law so fundamental to democracy. In present-day Azerbaijan and Iran, on the contrary, corruption is making the rich richer and the poor poorer. We have seen how the political elites that enjoy power are pocketing public funds. This is the kind of thing that destabilizes a country, and makes prospects for the future problematic. When the mass of the people see that they are not getting their rightful share of the oil wealth, they may sooner or later flock to political movements dedicated to revenge against the rulers. This has happened in several of the oil states, for example, in both socialist Algeria and imperial Iran.

This chapter is part of a research effort on the role of Western oil companies in promoting democratic societies. Case studies on Azerbaijan (Heradstveit, 2001a and Heradstveit, 2001b) and Iran (Heradstveit, 2001c) provide an understanding of the cultural context of corruption in each country, while another study provides a comparative perspective of the whole range of issues involved (Heradstveit, 2000d). This research explores the psychology of corruption from a comparative perspective. It was supported by the Norwegian Research Council (Project no.: 144705-510) and the Norwegian Ministry of Foreign Affairs.

To help combat corruption, the international community, including both inter-governmental organizations, like the World Bank, and NGOs like Transparency International, have used a variety of tools such as exposure of corruption through the construction of indexes, incentives for promoting reform and best practices, as well as the development of civil society. Although these tools can be very effective, other approaches, including the cognitive dimension, are often overlooked. An understanding of how people living in societies where dishonesty is pervasive attribute the causes of corruption is a first step toward its solution. If people view corruption as being situational or part of the culture, then they will have little incentive to attempt reform: "This is part of the system and there is nothing to be done about it." If, on the other hand, they attribute corruption to dishonesty on the part of a few officials or individuals in high places, there is the possibility that these individuals could be replaced by persons of integrity.

This chapter describes how elites in Azerbaijan and Iran attribute the causes of corruption in the oil industries of their countries and explain the relationship between the "culture of corruption" and democratization. The research is based on in-depth interviews with 20 oppositional figures in Azerbaijan, including party leaders and political candidates, plus some media, NGO and academic persons, and a similar sample of 32 members of the oppositional elite in Iran.[1] An analysis of the interviews shows that Azerbaijani respondents were more ready to blame the high level of corruption on situational factors. When this is the case, individuals performing the corrupt acts are acquitted, because the problem is seen as coming from the outside forces. This suggests that the Azerbaijani respondents to a higher degree than the Iranian respondents rely on traditional ways of analyzing the problem of corruption as compared to modern secular thinking. Iranian respondents, on the other hand, overwhelmingly provide dispositional explanations for corruption. Dispositional explanations shift the locus of causation to individuals rather than institutions. Therefore, the principal remedy proposed by Iranian respondents is to expose corrupt acts in the modern media and promote transparency as the main ethical code of behavior – for both foreign investors as well as the Iranians, themselves.

The Study of Social Attribution[2]

To help understand how people in Azerbaijan and Iran perceive the causes of corruption, concepts from attribution theory will be utilized. The study of attribution as a separate area within social psychology can be traced back to Heider (1958), who examined the process of "causal attribution in the perception of others". Since the publication of Heider's early work, attribution theorists have studied the efforts

---

1 The survey data are from fieldwork carried out in Azerbaijan in September–October 1999 and Iran in April 2000, March 2002 and April 2002. See list of respondents in Appendices I, II, and III.
2 This section is a revision of the literature review and critique found in Heradstveit and Bonham (1996).

of people to explain and draw inferences from behavior – their own behavior and the behavior of others. The individual, according to this viewpoint, is a "constructive thinker" or "naive scientist" who searches for the causes of events and draws conclusions about people and their circumstances as a basis for action. Often, the search for causal explanation is aided by schemata, or cognitive structures that represent "organized knowledge about a given concept or type of stimulus" (Fisk and Taylor, 1984, p. 140). Schemata include general structures, based either on standard knowledge or an individual's direct prior experience, self-schemata, generalizations about the self that are derived from past experience, and persona, which are representations of the "personal traits and characteristic behavior or particular human types" (Vertzberger, 1990, pp. 156–9).

In the field of international relations, Jervis (1976) has applied attribution theory to foreign policy decision-making, Heradstveit (1979) has studied how Arabs and Israelis perceived the causes of the Middle East conflict, Larson (1985) has used attribution theory to explain the containment policies of the Cold War, and Heradstveit and Bonham (1986) have analyzed the attributions of American and Norwegian policy officials with respect to Soviet activities in northern Norway.

The Fundamental Attribution Error

Jones and Nisbett (1972) have observed that attributors emphasize dispositions (abilities, traits or motives) when explaining the behavior of others, while they use situational factors (external pressures and constraints) to explain their own behavior. Ross and other writers have referred to this phenomenon as "the fundamental attribution error", a tendency in social attribution "to underestimate the impact of situational factors and to overestimate the role of dispositional factors in controlling behaviour" (1977, p. 83).

The persistence of the tendency to ascribe "causal importance to persons at the expense of circumstances" suggests to some that the "fundamental attribution error" may be "deeply rooted in the individual psyche", rather than a consequence of "the complexity and ambiguity of 'reality'" (Renshon, 1993, p. 72). Behavior attributed to the inherent nature of others has the advantage of imposing regularity and predictability, thus enhancing the feeling of control (Miller et al., 1978). This creates a dilemma, however, because the feeling of control provided by dispositional explanations "has to be balanced against other needs, such as the need for veridicality. These other needs may result...in self-serving situational explanations of others' behaviour" (Vertzberger, 1990, p. 162).

Although the "fundamental attribution error" has been confirmed in laboratory research, it has not been found in all situations (Cheng and Novick, 1990, p. 547). Moreover, one can argue that the term "error" is a misnomer. Is an involved actor in a better position to identify the cause of his or her own behavior than that of an uninvolved observer? Monson and Snyder (1977) have stated the case for the actor. First, they argue that actors have knowledge of their own inner states, attitudes and dispositions. Such information is normally not available to observers. Moreover, actors are usually more knowledgeable about their own behavior in other situations and at other times than observers. Their analysis "suggests that the actor's attributions of cause would be more often 'correct' than those of the observer" (Monson and Snyder, 1977, p. 94).

Not all psychologists agree that actors are aware of their higher order mental processes. Nisbett and Wilson (1977) argue convincingly, however, that people, when asked to report how a particular "stimulus" influenced a particular "response", apply or generate "causal theories about the effects of that type of stimulus on that type of response". Sources for these causal theories include the culture or subculture, empirical observation, and shared "networks of connotative relations surrounding the stimulus description and the response description" (Nisbett and Wilson, 1977, p. 248).

Other research emphasizes the importance of the evaluative aspect – the social desirability of behavior – in the attribution process. Taylor and Koivumaki (1976) found that the actor does not generally view his or her behavior more situationally than the behavior of others. Instead, the actor explains his or her *positive* behavior in terms of dispositions (e.g., I won because I'm strong), but dismisses *negative* behavior as being caused by the situation (e.g., I was outnumbered). Likewise, Heradstveit (1979) found little evidence for the "fundamental attribution error" until the evaluative aspect of behavior was taken into account. Arab and Israeli respondents, however, were overwhelmingly dispositional when observing their own good behavior (and their opponent's bad behavior) and situational when attributing their own bad behavior (and their opponent's good behavior). These findings seem to be consistent with motivational or functional approaches to the study of attribution.

Theoretical and Methodological Concerns

Methodological problems have hampered research on social attribution. Findings are based, for the most part, on laboratory experiments in which captive populations, such as college undergraduates, are asked to explain their actions or the behavior of others in hypothetical or trivial situations. Because the generalizability to "real world" settings of many of these experiments is "questionable" (Olson and Ross, 1985, p. 287), "much more empirical work using more naturalistic stimulus materials (rather than or in addition to linguistic materials) to represent social stimuli will be necessary..." (Weary et al., 1989, p. 61). Such research, conducted in natural settings and focusing on complex situations, may reveal that "people do not simply attribute causes and responsibility; they also offer more elaborate accounts and stories" (ibid., p. 194).

Forced-choice, closed-ended scales are almost always used to record attributions, but studies using multitrait-multimethod approaches show a lack of convergence among such scales. This implies "either that the scales are unreliable or that they are measuring different things" (Miller et al., 1981, p. 83).

Research based on the use of free-choice and open-ended scales, on the other hand, which allows respondents to express their own views about cause and blame, is time-consuming and open to coding problems (Howard, 1987, p. 50). Coding is often done on the basis of the form of the response, rather than the content (Van der Plight, 1981). For example, the statement, "John doesn't want to go to the soccer match because of hooliganism", might be coded as a situational attribution. However, the response "John will not go because he is afraid of getting mixed up in a fight" might be coded as a dispositional attribution (Van der Plight, 1981, p. 99).

This coding problem is frequently encountered because the situational-dispositional distinction is "not really a dichotomy. Most situational explanations imply assumptions about relevant dispositions" (Monson and Snyder, 1977, p. 20). "Each covers more than one type of thing, and either can have the same role in some instances" (White, 1991, p. 266). For example, "He did it for the money" can be restated as the dispositional attribution, "He did it because he is money hungry". Hence, the situational-dispositional distinction "may reflect differences in language rather than thought" (Monson and Snyder, 1977, p. 20).

Ross (1977, p. 5) has attempted to solve the problem by formulating the following definitions of situational and dispositional attributions:

Situational Attributions   Those explanations that state or imply no dispositions on the part of the actor beyond those typical of all or most actors.

Dispositional Attributions   Those explanations that state or imply something unique or distinguishing about the actor.

Although the proposal by Ross may not have solved the problem (Lau and Russell, 1980), it does offer some guidance. The situational-dispositional distinction may not represent a dichotomous classification, but we can make judgments and code the perceiver's weighing of the relative importance of each (Monson and Snyder, 1977).

An explanation or attribution is dispositional only when it focuses on the idiosyncratic or the particular. It may be useful to call dispositional attributions "personal" attributions instead, as then the content stands out more clearly. We may thus ask whether the respondent is explaining an event by referring to the personality traits and peculiarities of the actor, or by referring to a response that is thought to be caused by stimuli in the actor's environment.

Research Expectations

The distinction between dispositional and situational explanations in the literature on the "fundamental attribution error" can be used to gain a better understanding of the views of Azerbaijanis and Iranians about corruption in their countries and draw some conclusions about prospects for change. Azerbaijan is often viewed as a typical non-Western oil-producing country, where corruption is endemic, such as Nigeria and the Gulf states. Iran, on the other hand, seems to be different. Not only is Iran more developed and democratic than many of the non-Western oil-producing countries, but also it has witnessed historical events that might have transformed the way in which people view the nature of corruption. For example, the historical events surrounding the overthrow of Mossadeq, the installation of the Shah, and the Iranian revolution may have resulted in a different perspective on the oil industry and the nature of corruption. Rather than blame "the system", Iranian elites may attribute corruption to individuals, who are simply dishonest.

Such differences between elites in Azerbaijan and Iran with respect to attributions of corruption have implications for the prospect of change. In Azerbaijan, like most of the non-Western oil countries, change does not seem very likely. If people attribute corruption to situational factors, they will be less inclined to do anything about it: "This is part of the system, and we can't change it." "We are locked into a culture of corruption that is supported by a set of institutions that are impossible to reform, short of a revolution, which is a highly unlikely prospect." In Iran, on the other hand, there may be hope. "We had our revolution. The fault lies, not in our institutions, but in the individuals who deal with the oil companies and supply them with services. The top leadership is honest. What we need now is a major effort by them (or more energetic leaders) to crack down on the corruption at lower levels."

Empirical Data and the Analysis

Sampling and Interviewing Procedures

For this research the characteristics of the statistical universe are unknown, which makes it difficult, if not impossible, to obtain a "representative" sample. Nobody has yet developed general criteria that can be used to define who is and who is not an elite political actor. Even if the relevant elite groups were clearly defined, it would still be difficult to specify which persons ought to be included in the theoretical universe. Such a specification would require much costly field work and complex analysis merely to delineate the theoretical universe.

Instead, an effort was made to find "leaders of opinion" in the context of corruption – people thought to have a direct or indirect influence on at least the perception of the issue. In other words, the focus is not necessarily on those who occupy a high position, but rather on those people who have a well-articulated point of view.

Samples were drawn from these categories: active politicians, civil servants in the foreign ministry, members of university faculties, and journalists and editors (see list of respondents in the appendices). Two sampling strategies were employed. On the basis of our general knowledge of the two countries involved, a list of people considered influential was constructed. Here experts were consulted such as Raoul Motika of Heidelberg University on Azerbaijan and Mehrzad Boroujerdi of Syracuse University on Iran. Once in the field, a second technique was used. After having interviewed a respondent, he or she was asked for names of others it might be useful to interview. This technique, called "chain selection", was very helpful for obtaining appointments. On the other hand, the persons recommended will probably be those the respondent likes or agrees with, which means that the sample becomes self-selecting. It was therefore important to combine the two methods.

Results

There are a number of possible explanations of corruption. Most discussions operate with a dichotomy – corruption is driven by greed or corruption is driven by the need to survive. The first explanation is a dispositional attribution, because it links the question of "guilt" to the individual. The inherent characteristics of the individual who performs corrupt acts explain why there is corruption. In Azerbaijan, the individual-characteristic explanation is often applied to the elite (except that it is called by the pejorative term, "clique") that sits on the top of the heap and pulls the strings. The political elite is greedy and devoid of any social conscience, and, as long as it remains in power, nothing much can be done. Attributing behavior to the characteristics of the individual in this way mobilizes the observer's emotional reaction – his or her affective structure. Doing this is a vital and powerful motive in all political mobilization and in the rhetoric of revolution or coup. Sometimes this dispositional analysis is generalized to levels below the power elite, with complaints of the moral degeneracy of the Azerbaijani nation.

The other approach is to relate corruption to structural conditions. The observer will then "acquit" the individual; for example, he or she is acting under duress. Here cognitive distancing prevails, and the affective component is repressed. In Azerbaijan, for instance, it may take the form of the assertion that the police are corrupt because the police force is overmanned (by 50 per cent) and therefore underpaid. It is not the individual characteristics of the police that make them corrupt, but the situation that forces them into corruption. The analytic literature identifies many such causes of corruption in structural conditions. Low pay of officials obliges them to take bribes in order to feed their families. Many states still lack an independent judiciary, which means that corrupt judges will not be punished by other branches of government, and potentially honest judges cannot risk the displeasure of the regime. There is no adequate rule of law of which a corruption-hunter could make use. Empirical studies show that there is more corruption in the public than in the private sector. When authoritarian penal methods are abandoned in the drive to democracy, the result is that there is no check on corruption at all. The literature emphasizes the theory that when a culture of corruption has first taken root, the individual is enmeshed in a system which is almost impossible to break since a relationship of mutual dependence develops between the giver and the taker of bribes.

Table 4.1 Causal explanations of corrupt behavior in Azerbaijan*
   (n is the number of causal statements)

Causal explanations of corrupt Azerbaijani behavior		Causal explanations of corrupt Western oil company behavior	
Situational	Dispositional	Situational	Dispositional
41% (7)	59% (10)	44% (19)	56% (24)
n = 17		n = 43	

*Since we have a non-random sample and a relatively low n, no significance tests are reported.

Respondents' Situational Explanations of Corrupt Azerbaijani Behavior

Table 4.1 shows that situational and dispositional explanations of Azerbaijani corruption were divided fairly evenly. In other words, the respondents see corruption as residing partly in human frailty and partly in structural conditions. It was emphasized that in a society where corruption is widespread, the individual will be co-opted into playing the game; he or she will be recruited by being tempted to commit minor irregularities and the leverage thus obtained will be used to compel him or her to do something more serious. If he or she refuses to obey orders, he or she will be threatened with publication of "the file on him or her" and prosecuted for previous corrupt acts. Few dare to speak out against corruption because they fear that the searchlight may then be turned on them.

   Many respondents deny emphatically that corruption is an integral part of Azerbaijani culture. In principle Azerbaijanis are not corrupt, they say, and refer to opinion polls in which everyone is "against corruption". As these respondents see it, the corruption is due to unjust political arrangements through the ages, with the Soviet period as the most recent and worst example. "It was the Russians who brought corruption to Azerbaijan," is an oft-heard refrain. Others reject this and conclude that it is the new epoch that has brought corruption.

Respondents' Dispositional Explanations of Corrupt Azerbaijani Behavior

When respondents make dispositional attributions, the corrupt disposition is attributed to the regime and not to the nation as such. Azerbaijanis are not corrupt, just the people at the top – this is what can be called the "black-top image". Ordinary people are honest and upright, and if they are enmeshed in corrupt behavior, this is against their will. The rulers have little in common with the grass roots as regards mentality and conduct – the "fat cats" have developed a culture of greed, totally devoid of any social conscience or sense of fair play. Some of the respondents talked about the Aliev "clan", since the charmed circle includes his brothers, sons, nephews as well as his friends, but others thought the term misleading, and preferred "network".

The respondents, who are prominent representatives of the political opposition, therefore share the perception that as long as the current regime is in power, the problem of corruption will never be solved. With a corrupt power elite and a government linked to the black economy, it is useless to take up the struggle. Widespread corruption prevents the oil revenues benefiting the country and its people, as the money goes into the pockets of the rulers instead of being productively invested. Azerbaijan can become the "new Nigeria". Some respondents, however, refuse to paint so bleak a picture. Despite everything there are strong democratic forces in Azerbaijan that may be able to break the culture of corruption.

The respondents asserted that foreign investors were shocked at the ability of the rulers to keep financial transactions secret. The lack of transparency is the power base of the culture of corruption. Some claim – but on this point there is no consensus among the respondents – that Western oil companies showing signs of wanting to do something about corruption are compelled to leave the country. There was also disappointment that Western oil companies can make profitable agreements with a dictator who does not hesitate to violate human rights. And, as long as the rulers fail to respect the laws of the land, no one can expect that the ordinary people will do so. Azerbaijan is in a state of moral decline; despite the fact that most people are strongly against corruption, there exists a dominant nihilism.

As an example of the cynicism that characterizes the little clique at the top, the respondents cited the diversion of foreign aid for the poor and marginalized refugees. The "fat cats" have no scruples about helping themselves to this money – most of it disappears into corrupt pockets and little of it reaches the people for whom it was intended.

The above results show that the political gates are not entirely locked, and so there should be a basis for a certain degree of collaboration in the fight against corruption. Some members of the Azerbaijani opposition explain corruption primarily as a result of the greed that animates the ruling clique, but it is also worth noting that they identify structural and situational features of society as being responsible. The political opposition is willing to admit that the problem is complex and has many causes. However, in periods when relations between government and the opposition are polarized and hostile, the regime is given all of the blame for corruption.

Situational Explanations of Western Oil Companies' Attitudes toward Corruption in Azerbaijan

A frequent argument was that collaboration with a corrupt regime is itself corrupting. As an illustration of this, respondents mentioned the bonus money that the companies pay when contracts are signed. It was claimed that this money never appears in the accounts; in other words, it disappears, into the dictator's own pockets. In this context respondents stressed that the oil companies have no moral right to deny that they share responsibility. Aliev and the oil companies have acted in concert, and so both are guilty. It is interesting to note that the opposition is here asserting the same ethical principle as Transparency International: "The donor is as guilty as the recipient. They are in collusion." The argument about bonus money that corruptly disappears is the single assertion that recurs most often in discussions of corruption.

Many others in the sample were willing to moderate the accusations against the Western oil industry's activities in Azerbaijan. They would not go so far as to say that the companies *want* to be corrupt, but when they operate in a country like Azerbaijan, they cannot avoid being caught in the net. They argue that there is a difference between the oil contracts made at government level, which are not corrupt, and contracts for services in the Azerbaijani infrastructure: as soon as the companies enter this arena, they tumble into the culture of corruption and become a part of it. Some would claim that this happens against the companies' own wishes, but that they are powerless. To get the oil out of Azerbaijan, the oil companies are dependent on Azerbaijani infrastructure and other services, which are permeated by corruption. Some assert that the senior managers of the Western oil companies are straight, while others distance themselves even further from the suggestion that the companies were corrupt, by pointing out that the big Western companies have a reputation to protect, and they are exclusively interested in doing business in accordance with ethical principles.

From the general observation that it was difficult to do business in Azerbaijan without paying bribes, the conclusion was often drawn that Western oil companies were not clean, but this suggestion was rarely supported by hard evidence. The oil companies, some respondents said, operate in a culture where it is fully acceptable to take unlawful advantage. Western investors who became involved with the country after the fall of the Soviet Union had raised the corruption level. Some respondents therefore concluded that increased Western activity has increased corruption. Others reasoned differently, but came to the same conclusion, namely that since almost all national income comes from the oil industry and the level of corruption is high, corruption must necessarily be linked to the oil industry.

The ordinary Azerbaijani sees Western oil companies as part of Aliev's corrupt system, and that they are thus helping to maintain that system. Some assert that merely collaborating with a corrupt regime makes the oil companies themselves corrupt. Even if you never pay bribes yourself, you are not innocent of corruption, for you are still operating in a corrupt environment and aiding and abetting a corrupt regime. All Western companies that set up shop in the former Soviet Union sooner or later become involved in corruption. They become part of a culture characterized by secrecy, the cornerstone of corruption. When the dictator tells the oil companies to lie for him, they lie for him. An example of this is the Azerbaijani state oil company, SOCAR: there is no public inspection of SOCAR's accounts –

not even ministers get to see any figures. Nor do Western oil companies reveal what *they* pay to SOCAR, thus helping it to keep its practices secret.

Several of the respondents understand the oil companies' behavior from a situational perspective. They are painted into a corner; they are powerless to deal with the culture of corruption, and they don't know what to do. Nevertheless, for a company that is in principle against corruption, the choice must be between accepting it and leaving the country. By paying the dictator money, which he deposits in his foreign bank accounts, the Western oil companies are institutionalizing Azerbaijani corruption. Solid foreign companies in Azerbaijan that earn money without being corrupt serve as signposts, showing the people that it is not, after all, a law of nature that you have to be corrupt to survive.

Dispositional Explanations of Western Oil Companies' Attitudes toward Corruption in Azerbaijan

The general perception is that Western oil companies are in principle honest and against corruption, but that the country is so corrupt that they are compelled willy-nilly to make fatal compromises. These respondents are thus "acquitting" the oil companies of "guilt" by their intuitive analysis in terms of situational attributions.

However, there was also a school of thought among the respondents saying that the oil companies were indulging in the corrupt practices with open eyes, even that they had been corrupt before setting foot in Azerbaijan.

A form of corruption practiced by the companies quite deliberately is to restrict competition for assignments. Invitations to tender in the oil industry are very often secret, and companies with a record of assignments are favored. The principle of free competition is thus an illusion, which has been extremely destructive for Azerbaijan.

Some people went further than merely hinting that the oil companies make corrupt deals with the government. For example, it was mentioned that in 1998 one million tonnes equivalent of oil disappeared without trace. Even if Western oil companies knew where it went, they refused to say anything. Another recurrent accusation is that the oil companies pay bribes to the dictator for contracts – there is a mutual admiration society between him and the companies. It is usual to pay a bonus on the signing of oil contracts. Accusations of corruption related to these bonuses were the most frequent among the respondents, and ordinary Azerbaijanis are also very concerned about this. It was emphasized that this bonus money vanishes without trace, which surely means that it goes into the fat cats' pockets. This has become a big problem, not only for the dictator, but also for the oil companies, because they are held responsible for the money going astray and yet either cannot or will not say where it ends up. This line of argument entirely brushes aside the oil companies' claims that they don't know what is really going on, for it is their duty to know.

If Western oil companies are, as they claim, against corruption, this must be expressed in a policy of transparency that allows public access, even if this is not what the regime wants. Instead of transparency, however, the oil companies are practicing secrecy, not only about the contracts but also about accidents; they lie about them and keep Azerbaijani specialists at arm's length when corrective action is taken. Much of what Western oil companies get up to does not tolerate the light of day. Unless the oil companies rethink their policy, some say, they risk meeting the same fate as they did in the Iranian revolution, that is, being nationalized. The behavior of the oil companies in Azerbaijan is remarkably like that in the Shah's Iran. Finally, the oil companies show their true colors by never supporting Azerbaijani NGOs working against corruption.

Results from Iran

The following table shows the results of the attributional coding of explanations for corruption proffered by Iranian respondents.

Table 4.2 Causal explanations of corrupt behavior in Iran*
(n is the number of causal statements)

Causal explanations of corrupt Iranian behavior		Causal explanations of corrupt Western oil company behavior	
Situational	Dispositional	Situational	Dispositional
15% (5)	85% (29)	6% (2)	94% (30)
n = 34		n = 32	

*Since we have a non-random sample and a relatively low n, no significance tests are reported.

Respondents' Dispositional Explanations of Corrupt Iranian Behavior

Some of the explanations of the current regime and corruption emphasized Iranian culture. It was said that Iran had always had an autocratic government. This negative tradition is visible in current Iranian political culture, in that people do not see the need for an alternative.

The lack of democracy was attributed to a greater degree to the ideological legacy of the revolution, namely a glorification of religious dictatorship, which, in turn, had paved the way for a culture of corruption by the elites in power. Many of the respondents explained this in terms of the revolution (that they themselves had helped to make) having been hijacked both politically and religiously and ending up at a quite different destination than they had in mind. They had advocated the modernization of Iran. Although the "destructive" aspect of the revolution, the overthrow of the Shah, was a success, it lacked a "constructive" aspect, a vision of what was to be done after the departure of the Shah. In this ideological vacuum, the revolution was taken over by the clergy and the bazaaris and a new ideology was created, this time hostile to democratic development, which could have worked against the corruption inherent in Iranian political culture.

However, some respondents claimed that compared with other countries – and particularly the neighbors in the Persian Gulf – Iran is not very corrupt. Moreover, Iran was much more honest compared to countries like Nigeria and Azerbaijan. Some argued that in addition to an ongoing public debate on corruption, there is effective surveillance, and corrupt individuals risk losing their jobs. The respondents reminded us that the Islamic revolution had an ethical and cultural dimension, not just an economic one. Other respondents strongly disagreed with this, saying that, on the contrary, the culture of corruption is in the process of spreading, even if those on the top are not normally corrupt. The revolution's ethical program has not yet been victorious; the continued existence of the culture of bribery is a defeat for the revolutionary goals of Islamism. In Iran, like Azerbaijan, respondents blamed people at the top (the so-called "black-top image"), but here in Iran a "white-top" image was also encountered. Some Iranian respondents claimed that the people at the very top were honest.

Some argued that Iranian authorities are gradually moving towards more transparency in dealing with foreign oil companies.

It was also emphasized that attempts by the oil industry to tackle the corruption problem by propaganda and pressure, such as sponsoring seminars in Iran, will be counterproductive. One respondent stated that if the oil companies tried to administer anti-corruption pills to the government, it would just spit them out again. All attempts at direct influence will be seen as meddling in domestic Iranian affairs, and this will make life more difficult for the forces within Iran which are actively working against corruption. The oil companies must instead work indirectly by encouraging privatization by placing their orders with private companies. According to some of our respondents, more privatization meant less corruption. Others expressed what could be termed a middle-of-the-road point of view by saying, for example, that conferences on Iranian corruption sponsored by foreign oil companies could be useful – but only if organized outside Iran.

The theme most frequently mentioned by the respondents as a remedy against corruption was support for education. There was great faith that education would make people less corrupt. People in cultures with lower levels of education do not perceive corruption in the same way. One respondent said that in France, for example, if a minister earned 20,000 dollars in an irregular manner, he would be sacked on the spot, but that in Iran this would hardly be seen as a problem. Another respondent said that an indirect way of combating corruption was giving student grants.

Support for education was the best weapon against corruption. In the respondents' opinion, such support – awarding of scholarships, publication subsidies and so forth – would not be perceived as "interference in Iran's internal affairs" in the same way, but would be seen positively by everyone.

Situational Explanations of Corrupt Iranian Behavior

Structural arguments were also offered; for example, the complete dependence on a single external resource (oil) makes it easier for an autocrat to maintain his despotism. The first striking feature of the results generated by this question is the dearth of structural explanations provided by the respondents. However, this does accord with the predictions of social psychology's cognitive attribution models, whereby the roles of persons are magnified and structural causal variables minimized – especially where this offers a chance to "blame" external agents (see above). But as can be seen from Table 4.2 very few (only five) were offered by the Iranian respondents.

Dispositional Explanations of Western Oil Companies' Attitudes to Corruption in Iran

When explaining the reasons for the religious dictatorship and the corruption following in the path of the dictatorial rule in Iran, the single biggest cause cited is foreign meddling, and when we look at the arguments in greater detail, we find the Western oil industry to be the arch-villain. The events of 1953, when Prime Minister Mossadeq, regarded as the foremost exponent of freedom and democracy in Iranian history, was overthrown in a *coup d'état* carried out by the Shah and orchestrated by the CIA, made an indelible impression.

The Iranian perception is that Pahlavi would never have managed it without the aid of the CIA, and that the reason for the coup was the American wish to continue controlling Iranian oil. In 1951 Mossadeq nationalized the considerable British oil interests. The idea that Iran could control its own oil resources in this way was anathema to Western oil companies and Western governments, which regarded it as a serious contravention of the principles of "world order" and global trade. Such a theory was hardly weakened by the fact that the USA was represented in the international consortium formed after the coup to make contracts with the new regime. The West did not care that the coup also strangled Iranian democracy in its cradle: It is better to get one's oil from a tame dictatorship than have to bargain for it with a rambunctious democracy.

The dramatic overthrow of Iran's first democratic leader has defined Iran's attitude to Western oil companies ever since. It is therefore no coincidence that when the American ambassador, in the spring of 2000, made a *démarche* for reconciliation between the two countries, he apologized for the American actions in 1953. Our respondents describe the coup as merely the tip of the iceberg of Western interference in Iran since the discovery of oil. BP, which before Mossadeq nationalized the oil industry had (as Anglo-Iranian Oil) a virtual monopoly, was described in particularly virulent terms. This monopoly was used, in alliance with the Shah, to safeguard its own interests at the expense of democratic institutions. When Mossadeq formulated his slogan, "We must cut off the foreign hand", it was BP he had in mind. Our respondents maintained that BP had operated in classical colonialist style by:

1 Meddling in domestic policy.
2 Appointing its own candidates to lead the Iranian oil administration.
3 Exploiting its position to influence parliamentary elections.
4 Paying for positive media articles about BP.
5 Operating with fake invoices to avoid paying the Iranian government its dues.
6 Promoting corruption within the Iranian government.
7 Preventing Iran influencing the pricing of oil. What Iran received was minimal.

This historical background constitutes the glasses through which our respondents view foreign oil companies even today.

The respondents emphasize that they have no illusions about the oil industry. They reminded us that this industry by and large operates in countries where regimes and cultures alike are permeated by corruption. To win contracts, it is practically essential for the Western oil companies to participate in the culture of corruption and become a part of it. A company that becomes involved in Iran risks this, and it is up to the company itself, if it wants to run this risk. But it was also said that investments by the Western oil companies could reduce corruption: such investments would stimulate the development of private companies that would be independent of the public sector. Respondents clearly regard the private sector as less corrupt than the public, although this naturally does not apply to those companies that are currently private in name, but which in reality are part of the state.

The sharpest distinction drawn by the respondents, however, was that between American and other oil companies – American companies were praised as the standard-bearers of ethical values. European companies, on the other hand, were lumped with the Arab and Japanese, where there is little reluctance to become drawn into the culture of corruption. The big contract with Total was frequently cited as an example of what *not* to do when signing oil deals; there were persistent rumours of corruption, and if true, it means that the little clique that made the contract on the Iranian side will be getting very rich. There was no question here of public access to information, whereas American companies make it very clear to their Iranian partners that transparency is a condition of the contract. It is claimed that the American perspective is accepted in Iran.

The responses sometimes appeared contradictory. The respondents spoke of the absence of corruption at the top, but at the same time, when discussing the contract with Total, they complained of corruption in high places.

It was emphasized that Western oil companies, in order to safeguard their economic privileges, used to actively oppose democracy and human rights. The greatest symbol of this murky past, as already mentioned, is the overthrow of Mossadeq. When some Western oil companies talk about democracy and human rights, therefore, it is because they are forced to do so – this is not a change of heart, not an ethical standpoint, but merely lip service. They are happy to build a hospital here and organize a human-rights conference there, but this is merely window dressing. One respondent said it sounded like a joke when the oil companies were supporting democracy and human rights. Another made the following comment:

> Your description of the oil companies "new thinking" isn't true. There has been no change. We have heard some talk about a new ethics, but we haven't seen any of it. Countries like Saudi Arabia, Kuwait and the UAE demonstrate that the companies are operating in the way they always have. The policies of the British and American companies have undergone minimal change. And it is disgusting to see that the money from the oil industry is spent largely on weapons even today. The companies must contribute to channelling the revenues into more positive projects such as bringing water to a region. There are, it is true, signs that the oil companies are no longer as willing to support the dictatorship, but the change, of course, can only be seen with a microscope.

The oil companies trim to the prevailing winds, it is said; the globalization agenda has its ethical items and the companies cannot simply ignore this, but if anything will come of it is an open question.

However, some respondents believed that Western oil investment in Iran could indirectly promote democracy and human rights. Western investment – which means mostly oil investment – is essential to improve the economy, and a better economy would create better conditions for democracy and human rights and by implication lead to less corruption.

The respondents' main concern is the lack of transparency in the oil industry. They complain that no other industry, domestically or globally, is so unwilling to provide information as the oil industry. Moreover, corrupt despotisms in the countries where the oil industry operates also have an interest in keeping oil matters secret, which makes for a natural alliance, and such a climate in turn fosters the culture of corruption. The recently signed contract with Total was seen as an example of these negative trends in both Total itself and in the Iranian government. They told us that Total has no contact with Iranian civil society, the company insulates itself completely, and it is impossible to extract information about the company's operations. There was no public debate about the Total contract, which was made between a small clique of bureaucrats in the Energy Ministry and a few top politicians including the president. The way in which this was done was subsequently heavily criticized, and it was stated that in future Iranian civil society would demand much more transparency. Some found it reprehensible that the contract was made with ulterior political motives, that it was not the market alone that decided.

It was also stated that if the Western oil industry were to operate effectively as regards Iranian corruption, the companies must stand together and agree on a joint strategy; but there was little faith that this would happen. Western companies' activities in the Persian Gulf clearly show that most companies have no scruples about making corrupt contracts.

Situational Explanations of Western Oil Companies' Attitudes to Corruption in Iran

Hardly any situational explanations were offered by our respondents for the behavior of Western oil companies. This tells us that the affective component of their attitudes towards the companies is very strong. For the oil companies, one excuse is offered for the corruption connected to oil business in the area. Respondents admit that it is almost impossible not to become caught up in the paralyzing culture of corruption, typically for the whole Persian Gulf including Iran, and finally become a part of it. It is easy for the oil companies to see it as normal, natural or, at any rate, inevitable.

Summary

The distinction in attribution theory between situational and dispositional attributions has proved to be a novel and fruitful way of looking at corruption in Azerbaijan and Iran.

Compared to Iran, Azerbaijani respondents are more ready to blame the high level of corruption on situational factors. When this is the case, the individuals performing the corrupt acts are acquitted. They see the solution of the problem as coming from the outside. Azerbaijani behavior is seen as typical and normal. The problem is caused by outside actors. This suggests that the Azerbaijani respondents to a higher degree than Iranian respondents rely on traditional ways of analyzing the problem of corruption as opposed to modern secular thinking. However, many of the Azerbaijani respondents also emphasize the value of transparency in combating the great evil of corruption.

The Iranian respondents, on the other hand, overwhelmingly provide dispositional explanations for corruption. Dispositional explanations shift the locus of causation to individuals rather than institutions. Therefore, the principal remedy proposed by Iranian respondents is to expose corrupt acts in the modern media and promote transparency as the main ethical code of behavior – for both foreign investors as well as the Iranians, themselves. This result is contrary to observations of area studies on Islam, which suggest that people in Islamic countries usually always blame foreigners for the ills of their society. The Iranian respondents say that there are two parties involved in corrupt acts, and both parties are to blame. This is exactly the type of understanding of corruption associated with modern secular democracies.

Implications for the Problem of Corruption

Geopolitical changes and transformations of the global economy after the Cold War have aggravated the problem of corruption worldwide. It is therefore essential to move against corruption and the unhealthy societies it creates. History shows that this fight is not a hopeless one. The American "Foreign Corrupt Practices Act" criminalizes the bribery of foreign officials. That 33 OECD countries and five others in February 1999 approved regulations based on the philosophy of the American legislation was another step in the right direction. General Electric, Shell and Rio Tinto are examples of multinationals that have imposed a strict ethics code. The danger of being mired in corruption has led these companies to withdraw from what could otherwise have been lucrative businesses as when Unilever pulled out of Bulgaria. In Italy, it was not until the big companies resisted paying bribes that the Tangentopoli investigation started. In Seoul, anyone can participate in public procurement over the Internet.

One of the main principles of the American "Foreign Corrupt Practices Act" is the doctrine that the company paying a bribe is as guilty as the person who receives it; this attracted great interest among our sample of respondents, particularly in connection with the bonuses paid by Western oil companies when contracts are signed. Often this money never appears in any official accounts and no one knows where it goes. It is a hopeful sign that many Western oil companies are currently concerned about the problem and interested in doing something about it, even though Western oil companies seem to be far less concerned after September 11.

While ethical codes and laws like the Foreign Corrupt Practices Act can be a positive influence, our research suggests that it is also necessary to move along other paths. To help change the culture of corruption in certain oil-producing countries, the counterproductive cognitive mechanisms that blame everyone else for being dishonest, and therefore nobody, have to be altered. What is needed, instead, is a cognitive transformation that focuses responsibility not on the "system", but on individual actors. Here, Iran can serve as a model for countries like Azerbaijan. Iranian elites for the most part attribute to dishonest individuals who can be removed from power, a viewpoint that is strikingly different from Azerbaijan. An educational program in Azerbaijan that supports forces working for democratization and promotes a model of individual responsibility may help to transform corruption from something that is "normal" to behavior that cannot be tolerated.

Appendix I – List of Respondents in Baku 1999

Politicians

1. **Isa Qambar**, Chairman of the Musavat Party, former Speaker of Parliament, right-wing politician, espouses some liberal and some nationalistic ideas. Historian, former Research Fellow at the Institute of Oriental Studies. Ethnic origin: Azerbaijani Turk.

2. **Abulfaz Elchibey**, Chairman of the Popular Front of Azerbaijan. Former President. Calls himself a right-wing politician, Turkic nationalist. Historian (Oriental Studies), former Senior Research Fellow at the Institute of Manuscripts, Academy of Science. Ethnic origin: Azerbaijani Turk.

3. **Ali Kerimov**, First Deputy Chairman of the Popular Front. Right-wing politician, espouses some liberal and some nationalistic ideas. Leader of informal "Yurd" organization, Member of Parliament. Education: Law. Ethnic origin: Azerbaijani Turk.

4. **Muzaffar Djabrayil-zadeh**, Chairman of the Islam Party (pro-Iranian, in favor of an Islamic Republic).

5. **Leyla Yunusova**, Chairman of the Peace and Democracy Institute. One of the founders of the Popular Front, former Chief of National Army Information Service (in Elchibey's time). Ethnic origin: Azerbaijani Turk.

6. **Ilyas Ismailov**, Co-Chairman of the Democratic Party (shares this position with Rasul Quliyev, now in asylum in the USA). Calls himself a democrat and an adherent of "common sense". Vague political views. Former Prosecutor-General (during the later Soviet years) and former Minister of Justice (in Elchibey's time). Education: Law. Ethnic origin: Azerbaijani Turk.

7. **Zardusht Alizadeh**, Co-Chairman of the Social Democratic Party (shares this position with his brother Araz Alizadeh). One of the founders of the Popular Front Movement, later founded the SDP. Education: Oriental Studies. Advocates good relations with Iran and Russia. Against pan-Turkism, in favor of Mutallibov. Ethnic origin: unknown, calls himself an Azerbaijani.

8. **Nazim Imanov**, Deputy Chairman of the National Independence Party, Member of Parliament, Doctor of Economics. Right-wing politician, liberal-minded, in favor of a free market model. Ethnic origin: Azerbaijani Turk.

9. **Dr Firidun Jalilov**, Speaker of the Assembly, National Independence Party, former Minister of Education (in Elchibey's time). Strong Turkic nationalist. Ethnic origin: Azerbaijani Turk.

10. **Tahir Kerimly**, Chairman of the Vahdat (Unity) Party, former Chief Justice (in Elchibey's time), Education: Law. Calls himself a democrat, not in favor of pan-Turkism. Ethnic origin: Azerbaijani Turk.

11. **Etibar Mamedov**, Chairman of the National Independence Party, Member of Parliament, historian. Right-wing politician, strong nationalist, in favor of "Order and Stability". Ethnic origin: Azerbaijani Turk.

12. **Sabit Bagirov**, President of the Far Centre research institution. One of the founders of the Popular Front, former Chairman of the State Oil Company (in Elchibey's time). Member of the Musavat Party, economist, liberal-minded. In favor of the Baku-Iran-Turkey pipeline. Ethnic origin: Azerbaijani Turk.

13. **Panah Husseynov**, Chairman of the People's Party, former Prime Minister (in Elchibey's time), One of the founders of the Popular Front, historian. Espouses liberal, nationalistic, social-democratic and populist ideas. Ethnic origin: Azerbaijani Turk.

14. **Ramiz Axmedov**, Chairman of the Azerbaijan Communist Party, philologist, journalist, First Secretary of the Communist Party in the Gabala and Evlakh regions under the USSR, former Editor-in-Chief of the Communist Newspaper (main governmental paper in the former USSR). Pro-Russian and anti-Western. Has good links with the Russian Communist Party. Ethnic origin: unknown.

Intellectuals, NGOs and Massmedia Magnates

15. **Dr Hasan Guliyev**, Chief Analyst, *Turan Information Agency*, Doctor of Philosophy, liberal-minded. Ethnic origin: Azerbaijani Turk.

16. **Rauf Arifoglu**, Editor-in-Chief of the most popular newspaper in Azerbaijan, *Turkic nationalist*. Ethnic origin: Azerbaijani Turk.

17. **Hadjy Azer Samedov**, Chairman of the independent "Islam Ittihad" religious community. Moderate Shi'i Islamist, in favor of good Azerbaijani–Iranian Relations. Ethnic origin: Azerbaijani Turk.

18. **Rauf Talishinski**, Editor-in-Chief of *Zerkalo*, the most popular Russian-language newspaper in Azerbaijan. Liberal-minded. Ethnic origin: unknown.

19. **Vagif Sefikhanov**, Professor at Baku State University, CEO of RISK Computer Software Company. Liberal-minded. Ethnic Origin: Azerbaijani Turk.

20. **Hikmet Hadjy-zadeh**, Vice-President of the Far Centre research institution, Member of the Board and Head of the Analytical Department of the Musavat Party. Liberal-minded. Ethnic origin: Azerbaijani Turk.

Appendix II – List of Respondents in Teheran 2000

1. **Dr Shahriar Rohani**, political activist and adviser to President Seyyed Mohammad Khatami. Shahriar Rohani served as the spokesman for the committee that, after the Islamic Revolution, took over all Iran diplomatic and consular functions in the US, including at the UN. Rohani held this position for about 13 months, after which he moved back home to become the Editor-in-Chief of *Keyhan* (Universe). At the time of the Revolution, *Keyhan* was the most popular daily with a circulation of about 400,000, which is still a record. Just before the Islamic Revolution, the paper was bought by a revolutionary businessman, and it became a supporter of the Revolution and the Freedom Movement (*Nehzate Azadi*). The Freedom Movement was a party founded after Mohammad Mossadeq's fall in 1953 by Mehdi Bazargan and other veteran members of the National Front (*Jebheie Melli*), Mossadeq's party. After the Revolution, disagreements with the clergy pushed them into opposition, where they still are, 20 years later.

2. **Dr Hamid Zaheri**, an oil expert. General Manager for International Affairs of the National Petrochemical Company (*Sherkate Mellie Petroshimi*). OPEC spokesman from 1974 to 1983.

3. **Dr Alireza Tabibian**, Associate Professor at Teheran University and member of "The Institute for Research in Development and Planning", a semi-governmental organization. The architect of the second five-year economic plan under Ali Akbar Hashemi Bahremani (better known as Rafsanjani, which refers to the city he comes from, Rafsanjan).

4. **Dr Morteza Mardiha**, an intellectual and writer. Political journalist on the daily *Asre Azadegan* (The Time of Liberals). This paper, which was shut down by the conservatives in April 2000, was the successor of two dailies shut down one after the other, *Jame-e* (Society) and *Neshat* (Happiness). All three dailies, with the same editorial board, advocated the establishment and development of public, non-governmental media as the forth pillar of democratic society. Dr Mardiha is known for a pragmatic rather than an idealistic approach.

5. **Dr Abdelkarim Soroush**, formerly a Professor of Philosophy at Teheran University, and a member of the Iranian Philosophical Society (*Anjomane Hekmat va Falsafeie Iran*). Regarded by many as the leading intellectual and theorist of the reformist movement. He is now suspended from his professor-

ship. His doctrine of compatibility between democracy and Islam, and his intellectual struggle against vulgar/ritualistic interpretations of the Muslim religion, have made him the bugbear of the conservative clergy. *Time Magazine* has offered the following description of him: 'Abdelkarim Soroush, the 52-year-old philosopher who has emerged, reluctantly, as the Islamic republic's most dangerous dissident. Soroush poses such a challenge to Iran's powerful religious establishment that his situation is unlikely to be eased by the recent election as President of Mohammed Khatami, who promised more openness and freedom. Soroush's sin, in the eyes of the mullahs, is to question the central tenet of the late Ayatollah Khomeini's notion of Islamic government: that Iran's holy men have a God-given right to rule. That appears to go too far even for Khatami." (*Time*, June 23, 1997, Vol. 149, No. 25.)

Though he is not himself a politician, his writings are inevitably interpreted in a highly political way in Iran.

6. **Dr Alireza Rajaiee**, newly elected member for the 6th Parliament. In a very controversial decision the Council of Guardians (*Shoraie Negahban*) declared his election invalid. Head of the political writers of the pro-democracy daily *Asre Azadegan* (The Time of Liberals). Although not officially a member of any party, his candidacy for parliament was supported by a wide range of pro-democracy groups including student organizations.

7. **Mr Mohammad Torkaman**, a political historian, writer and journalist interested particularly in oil-related events. Pro democracy and human rights. Close to the Freedom Movement (*Nehzate Azadi*).

8. **Mr Ali Akbar Moeenfar**, former minister of oil during the Bazargan government. Now an oil consultant. A political activist since Mossadeq's time as a member of the National Front (*Jebheie Melli*). After the fall of Mossadeq he joined the Freedom Movement (*Nehzate Azadi*) of which he is currently one of the leaders. He also joined the Islamic Society of Engineers (*Anjomane Eslamie Mohandesin*). He was elected from Teheran to the first post-revolutionary Parliament, where he became a member of the group opposing clerical rule.

9. **Dr Ghassem Salehkhoo**, international financial consultant, pro democracy and human rights. Iran's ambassador to Japan, Tunisia, Algeria, Morocco and Afghanistan and its representative to the IMF.

10. **Dr Morteza Nasiri**, lawyer, expert on international contract law, now with an office in both Teheran and the USA, politically close to the Freedom Movement (*Nehzate Azadi*). He has represented some Iranian national companies such as IranKhodro (the biggest automobile factory in Iran) as well as private industries in international contexts. Acted as an adviser to the Bazargan government.

11. **Dr Mohsen Sazegara**, consultant to the President. Political activist and writer (journalist). One of the founders of the Revolutionary Guards (*Sepahe Pasdaran*), now a radical reformist. A member of the committee established by Khomeini during his exile in France. It is interesting to note that almost all the members of that committee are now either executed, like Sadegh Ghotbzadeh (the former minister of foreign affairs), or exiled, like Abolhassan Banisadr (the former president, now living in Paris), or belonging to the present opposition in Iran (Sazegara himself). The function of the Paris-based committee was to translate Khomeini's speeches and thoughts for Western media and more generally to the entire world. In addition the committee designed many revolutionary policies and approaches. Dr Sazegara was later one of the founders of the now closed daily *Jame-e* (Society) and is still very active in pro-democracy activities like managing meetings and writing critical articles in the daily press.

12. **Dr Parviz Varjavand**, leader of the National Front (*Jebheie Melli*) and minister of culture in the Bazargan government. The party goes back to Dr Mossadeq, who was famous for his struggle with the oil companies, particularly BP. He is also a political writer and Professor at universities such as Islamic Azad University.

13. **Dr Hossein Zaiem**, oil industry management and marketing expert, member of the National Front (*Jebheie Melli*), the party established by Dr Mossadeq as an umbrella organization for all modernizers. The main item on the agenda was to nationalize Iran's oil industry. The National Front's days of glory ended with the coup of 1953, and it now lives mostly on its history and its heroes.

14. **Dr Mohammad Hosein Bani-Asadi**, engineer. Consultant at Iran Industrial Foundation Co. Member of the central committee of the Freedom Movement (*Nehzate Azadi*). The Freedom Movement is the only overt opposition group in Iran that dates back to Khomeini's day. The Movement was against the continuation of the war with Iraq and the totalitarianism of the clergy (*Rohaniiat*). (*Rohaniiat* is used as the proper name for the conservative body of clergy belonging to the establishment as opposed to *Rohaniioon*, which has the same dictionary meaning as *Rohaniiat* but in political usage stands for the more reformist part of that establishment. Khatami, for example, belongs to the *Rohaniioon* but Rafsanjani to the *Rohaniiat*.)

Dr Bani-Asadi is the son-in-law of ex-Prime Minister Bazargan and was his special adviser. He is also the founder of the *Bassij* militia, founded at the beginning of the Revolution. (*Bassij* is the name of the organization and *Bassiji* refers to a member.)

Appendix III – List of Respondents in Teheran 2002

1. **Bahman Farmanara**: b. 1942. Went to England at the age of 16 and studied acting and then to the US where he studied film-making at USC. He returned to Iran to work in Iranian TV. Returned to the US and Canada from 1980–1990 where he ran several film companies. He has made five feature films, the most recent of which are Smell of Camphor, Scent of Jasmine, and House Built on Water.

2. **Sadegh Ziba Kalam**: b. 1948. Studied engineering in London and obtained a PhD in Bradford, UK on the Iranian Revolution. He is a Professor of Political Science at the Faculty of Law and Political Science, Teheran University.

3. **Farhad Ataie**: b. 1953. PhD in Near Eastern Studies from U.C. Berkeley. Professor of Economics at Imam Sadegh University.

4. **Naghmeh Samini**: b. 1973. PhD candidate in Teachers College in Art and Theater. She is a playwright and teaches in Teheran's Azad University in Dramatic Literature. She is also a theater and cinema critic.

5. **Abadollah Molaei**: Director of Euro-American Studies at The Institute for Political and International Studies, Teheran, Iran.

6. **Seyed Kazem Sajjadpour**: PhD from the US. Director General of The Institute for Political and International Studies, Teheran, Iran.

7. **Mahmoud Sarioghlam**: Educated in the United States, he is a Professor at the Faculty of Economics and Political Science, Shahid Beheshti University and Head of the Center for Scientific Research and Strategic Studies of the Middle East.

8. **Hamid Reza Jalaiepour**: One of the most active reformist journalists, he was involved with most of the now-closed newspapers, including *Jame-e* and most recently *Bonyan*.

9. **Farshid Farzin**: b. 1967. He is an MA candidate at the Faculty of Law and Political Science of Teheran University, working on his thesis on International Laws and Satellite Legislation. He is also a consultant to Atieh Bahar Consulting Firm.

10. **Amir Mohebian**: No biography. He is a columnist for the conservative newspaper *Resalat* and is considered to be the most vocal spokesperson for the conservative side.

11. **Mohammad Ali Najafi**: b.1945. He holds an MA in architecture. He has also directed several films and television series. His architectural firm is responsible for designing a mosque and a cultural center in Teheran.

12. **Siamak Namazi**: b. 1971. He received his MA from Rutgers University in Urban Planning and has lived in Iran since 1999. He is the Risk and Strategic Management Director at Atieh Bahar Consulting in Teheran.

13. **Dr Hadi Semati**: b. 1960. He received his PhD in Political Science from the University of Tennessee in Knoxville. 1978–80 in the United States, returned to Iran and did his military service and worked for the Foreign Ministry. He spent the years 1985–1993 in the US and currently teaches at the University of Teheran, Faculty of Law and Political Science.

14. **Hatam Ghaderi**: Professor of Political Philosophy at Teheran's Teacher Training University.

15. **Ahmad Zeydabadi**: b. 1965. PhD candidate in Teheran University's Faculty of Law and Political Science. His dissertation is on Religion and State in Israel. He works as a journalist at the Foreign Desk of *Hamshahri Newspaper* and for various other newspapers. He was in prison for 7 months in 2001 and was recently sentenced to 23 months plus a 5-year prohibition from journalistic activity.

16. **Farhad Firouzi**: Previous editor of the weekly journal *Karnami*. Independent writer, author.

17. **Ibrahim Asgharzadeh**: b. 1955. Studied Electrical Engineering in Sharif University and became part of the student movement before the Revolution. He was one of the main US hostage-takers and was an MP in the third Parliament. He is currently an elected member of Teheran's City Council and an outspoken reformist.

18. **Seyyed Ibrahim Nabavi**: b. 1958 He is Iran's most popular satirist whose newspaper columns appear regularly in the mainstream and reformist press. He was imprisoned for his writings and currently runs his popular website nabavionline.com.

References

Cheng, P.W. and Novick, L.R. (1990), "A Probabilistic Contrast Model of Causal Induction", *Journal of Personality and Social Psychology*, Vol. 58, pp. 545–67.

Fisk, S. T. and Taylor, S.E. (1984), *Social Cognition*, Addison-Wesley, Reading, Massachusetts.

Heider, F. (1958), *The Psychology of Interpersonal Relations*, Wiley, New York.

Heradstveit, D. (1979), *The Arab-Israeli Conflict: Psychological Obstacles to Peace*, Norwegian University Press, Oslo.

Heradstveit, D. (2001a), *Democracy and Oil: The Case of Azerbaijan*, Reichert Verlag, Wiesbaden.

Heradstveit, D. (2001b), "Democratic Development in Azerbaijan and the Role of the Western Oil Industry", *Central Asian Survey*, Vol. 20, No. 3.

Heradstveit, D. (2001c), "Elite Perceptions of Ethical Problems Facing the Western Oil Industry in Iran", *Journal of Iranian Research and Analysis*, Vol. 17, No. 2.

Heradstveit, D. (2001d), "Local Elites Meet Foreign Corporations. The Examples of Iran and Azerbaijan", *Cahiers d'études sur la Méditerranée orientale et le monde turco-iranien*, No 32.

Heradstveit, D. and Bonham, G.M. (1986), "Decision-making in the Face of Uncertainty: Attributions of Norwegian and American Officials", *Journal of Peace Research*, Vol. 23, pp. 339–56.

Heradstveit, D. and Bonham, G.M. (1996), "The Fundamental Attribution Error and Arab Images of the the Gulf War", *Political Psychology*, No. 2.

Howard, J.A. (1987), "The Conceptualization and Measurement of Attributions", *Journal of Experimental Social Psychology*, Vol. 23, pp. 32–58.

Jervis, R. (1976), *Perception and Misperception in International Politics*, Princeton University Press, Princeton, New Jersey.

Jones, E.E. and Nisbett, R. E. (1972), *The Actor and the Observer: Divergent Perceptions of the Causes of Behavior*, General Learning Press, Morristown, New Jersey.

Larson, D.W. (1985), *Origins of Containment: a Psychological Explanation*, Princeton University Press, Princeton, New Jersey.

Lau, R.R. and Russell, D. (1980), "Attributions in the Sports Pages", *Journal of Personality and Social Psychology*, Vol. 39, pp. 29–38.

Miller, D.T., Norman, S.A. and Wright, E. (1978), "Distortion in Person Perception as a Consequence of the Need for Effective Control", *Journal of Personality and Social Psychology*, Vol. 36, pp. 598–607.

Miller, F.D., Smith, E.R. and Uleman, J. (1981), "Measurement and Interpretation of Situational and Dispositional Attributions", *Journal of Experimental Social Psychology*, Vol. 17, pp. 80–95.

Monson, T.C. and Snyder, M. (1977), "Actors, Observers, and the Attribution Process", *Journal of Experimental Social Psychology*, Vol. 13, pp. 89–111.

Nisbett, R. and Wilson, T.D. (1977), "Telling More than we can Know: Verbal Reports on Mental Processes", *Psychological Review*, Vol. 84, 231–59.

Olson, J.M. and Ross, M. (1985), "Attribution Research: Past Contributions, Current Trends, and Future Prospects", in J.H. Harvey and G. Weary (eds), *Attribution; Basic Issues and Applications*, Academic Press, Orlando, pp. 283–311.

Renshon, S.A. (1993), "Good Judgment, and the Lack Thereof, in the Gulf War: a Preliminary Psychological Model with Some Applications", in S.A. Renshon (ed.), *The Political Psychology of the Gulf War*, University of Pittsburgh Press, Pittsburgh.

Ross, L. (1977), "The Intuitive Psychologist and his Shortcomings: Distortions in the Attribution Process", in L. Berkowitz (ed.), *Advances in Experimental Social Psychology*, 10, Academic Press, New York.

Taylor, S.E. and Koivumaki, J.H. (1976), "The Perception of Self and Others; Acquaintanceship, Affect, and Actor-Observer Differences", *Journal of Personality and Social Psychology*, Vol. 33, pp. 403-408.

Van der Plight, J. (1981), "Actors' and Observers' Explanations: Divergent Perspectives or Divergent Evaluations?", in C. Antaki (ed.), *Psychology of Ordinary Explanation of Social Behavior*, Academic Press, London.

Vertzberger, Y. (1990), *The World in their Minds. Information Processing, Cognition, and Perception in Foreign Policy Decision Making*, Stanford University Press, Stanford.

Weary, G., Stanley, M.A. and Harvey, J.H. (1989), *Attribution*, Springer Verlag, New York.

White, P.A. (1991), "Ambiguity in the Internal/External Distinction in Causal Attribution", *Journal of Experimental Social Psychology*, Vol. 27, pp. 259-70.

Chapter 5

Energy Supply as Terrorist Targets? Patterns of "Petroleum Terrorism" 1968–99

Brynjar Lia and Åshild Kjøk

Introduction

Most current assessments of the threat of terrorism to petroleum infrastructure in low-risk countries tend to focus on existing physical vulnerabilities and hence on windows of opportunity for a prospective adversary.[1] There have been few studies of terrorist target strategies, based on historical patterns of terrorist and rebel attacks on petroleum-related targets.[2] This study is meant to fill that gap. It is primarily a survey study, drawing upon terrorist incidents recorded in ITERATE, a comprehensive database of transnational terrorism.[3] From this database of more than 5,000 incidents, there are 262 incidents in which petroleum infrastructure or personnel have been targeted.[4] Drawing upon these data, the general patterns of "petroleum terrorism" are analyzed with regard to methods, targeting strategies, ideological orientation and motivations. Special attention is devoted to terrorist attacks against petroleum targets on the Arab Peninsula and the Greater Middle East region.

---

1   This chapter is a shortened and updated version of a research report (Kjøk and Lia, 2001) originally published by the *Terrorism and Asymmetric Warfare Project* at the Norwegian Defence Research Establishment (FFI).
2   One general study of terrorist targeting strategies is Drake (1998). Two Norwegian scholars (Bjørgo, 1990 and Heradstveit, 1992) have written on the threat of terrorism to Norwegian petroleum infrastructure. These studies were written a decade ago, however, and none of them systematically analyzed data derived from empirical chronologies of terrorism.
3   ITERATE covers in principle the period from 1922 to 1999, but the collection of data for the pre-1968 period is not systematic.
4   The great majority of the incidents in this survey thus occurred in the period from 1968 to 1999, and 14 happened between 1922 and 1968.

Definitions and Methodological Problems

There is no universally accepted definition of terrorism (Schmid and Jongman, 1988; Hoffman, 1998). In this study ITERATE's definition is used, which focuses on acts of political violence committed by non-state groups with some degree of transnational ramifications.[5] Wherever a distinction is made between "rebel" and "terrorist" groups, it is primarily to indicate the scale of the armed conflict with the state (rebel movements operating in a civil war environment), and does not reflect any judgment on the legitimacy of acts of political violence.

For the purpose of this study, "petroleum infrastructure" is defined to include the following:

- production facilities, such as petroleum fields, wells, platforms and rigs
- refineries and gas processing plants
- transportation facilities including pipelines and pumping stations, terminals and tank ships
- oil and gas depots
- administration buildings
- distribution centers/petrol stations
- all personnel on or employed at these installations.

"Petroleum terrorism" is defined simply as attacks by terrorist or rebel groups directed against, or significantly affecting, petroleum infrastructure (Kjøk and Lia, 2001: 42–5).

Any statistics which draw heavily upon databases on terrorism are subject to great uncertainty, partly because of the absence of a generally accepted definition of terrorism, and partly because existing databases give unequal coverage of various geographical areas. A second problem with using statistical data on terrorism is that a statistical approach tends to accord equal importance to incidents of very different nature and gravity. Qualitative assessments may offset this bias partly, but not entirely. A third difficulty is that even though ITERATE is a comprehensive database, it is not complete.[6] For example, threats are greatly underreported in ITERATE, which is why this study excludes threats.

---

5 The complete definition is "the use, or threat of use, of anxiety-inducing, extra-normal violence for political purposes by any individual or group, whether acting for or in opposition to established governmental authority, when such action is intended to influence the attitudes and behavior of a target group wider than the immediate victims and when, through the nationality or foreign ties of its perpetrators, its location, the nature of its institutional or human victims, or the mechanics of its resolution, its ramifications transcend national boundaries".

6 For example, we have been able to identify 26 additional incidents (excluding threats) from other sources (Anderson and Sloan, 1995; Bjørgo, 1990; Heradstveit, 1992). These additional incidents have not been included in the empirical basis of the study, as most of these additional sources focus on particular types of attacks and specific sectors of the petroleum industry. The inclusion of these incidents in the statistical overview could

ITERATE, and hence this study, covers only international and transnational terrorism. This means that a number of terrorist attacks and incidents involving petroleum infrastructure have been omitted. However, as the petroleum industry is predominantly international, this should not invalidate the conclusions of this survey. The great majority of strikes against petroleum installations will have "ramifications that transcend national boundaries", as specified in the ITERATE definition. Indeed, many if not most recorded incidents are clearly linked to domestic terrorist or rebel groups. One may therefore assume that ITERATE's underreporting of domestic terrorism is significantly less with regard to attacks on petroleum infrastructure than regarding attacks on other targets. Another possible source of under-representation may result from some petroleum companies attempting to conceal or at least downplay minor terrorist incidents against their installations, for fear of losing market confidence. However, it is impossible to estimate the extent of such practices.

A final methodological problem is related to the fact that a few countries have been disproportionately exposed to attacks against their petroleum installations, and this may distort the overall picture. These countries are Colombia, Yemen, Nigeria and Israel, all of which have also suffered from protracted internal violent conflicts. One therefore runs the risk of presenting petroleum terrorism mainly as a reflection of the nature of political violence and terrorism in these four countries, while important aspects of target selection strategies of terrorist and rebel groups might be ignored. Partly for this reason, one subsection will be devoted to the patterns of petroleum terrorism in states that are without internal violent conflicts and that are ruled by democratic governments. A final subsection is devoted to terrorism in the Arab peninsula and the new terrorist threats associated with the al-Qaida network.

Given the limitations of existing databases with regard to the recording of terrorist incidents and the above-mentioned methodological problems, our results should not be interpreted as scientifically accurate findings. What this study offers are suggestive and tentative results. Further research work is needed, especially towards generating more and qualitatively better data, in order to enable more scientific conclusions. Nonetheless, given the poor state of the art, the present study hopefully makes a good start at describing and outlining the basic patterns of petroleum terrorism.

---

therefore introduce an additional source of error. However, these incidents have been included in the qualitative assessments wherever relevant. Bomb threats are also under-reported. For example, Norwegian petroleum companies received at least 13 bomb threats between 1989 and 1998, but none of these are registered in the database. These threats are not among the 26 additional incidents mentioned above.

Manifestations of "Petroleum Terrorism"

Between 1968 and 1999, a total of only 262 incidents of petroleum terrorism were reported. This would indicate that petroleum installations are not a particularly attractive target for terrorist and rebel groups. Terrorist strikes against petroleum installations have represented only about two per cent of international terrorist incidents in recent decades. There was an average of eight terrorist strikes per year from 1968 to 1988, with a certain increase over time – from an annual average of six in the early 1970s to ten by the late 1990s. However, one should not read too much into this increase, as the number of incidents has remained quite small. It probably reflects the global expansion of the petroleum industry and hence the number of targets rather than any significant shift in terrorist strategies of target selection.

The 262 incidents registered occurred in 59 different countries. Many of these countries do not produce oil or gas themselves, but have experienced attacks against traversing pipelines, depots, petrol stations, etc. Conversely, only 29 of the world's 56 petroleum-producing countries have experienced serious terrorist strikes against their installations, and 13 out of this group have suffered only one or two strikes. Terrorist and rebel attacks on petroleum infrastructure are not necessarily very serious. Only about 11 per cent of the recorded attacks led to temporary shutdowns. About 16 per cent of the attacks resulted in casualties: 25 incidents led to one or two casualties, 13 caused from three to six casualties and only five attacks (out of the total of 262) involved between 10 and 100 deaths.

Terrorist target selection is a complex process involving political, ideological and tactical considerations. When terrorist and insurgent groups choose to target petroleum infrastructure, key determinants appear to be tactical factors such as access to location and available escape routes. Attacks on difficult-to-protect targets such as pipelines and personnel account for more than half of all incidents of petroleum terrorism.

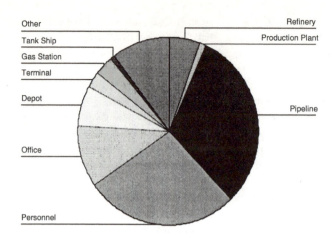

Figure 5.1 Distribution of physical targets[7]

Blasting and Sabotage of Pipelines

Blasting of pipelines is the commonest kind of attack; it has also caused by far the greatest number of closedowns. If one includes incidents involving sabotage, arson and armed attacks directed against pipelines and /or pipeline personnel, such strikes are responsible for nearly 60 per cent (16 out of 28) of all closedowns resulting from terrorist or rebel attacks as recorded in the ITERATE database.

One incident from the Middle East may serve as an illustrative example of attacks causing closedowns of pipelines, as well as ecological damage. On May 30, 1969, a leftist Palestinian group, the Popular Front for the Liberation of Palestine (PFLP), placed an explosive charge in the Baniyas River, heavily damaging a section of the Trans-Arabian Pipeline on the Israeli-occupied Golan Heights. The flow of oil through the 1,000-mile pipeline, which connected Dhahran in Saudi Arabia to Sidon in Lebanon, was blocked due to the resultant fire, although Israeli authorities managed to contain the blaze after 14 hours. This pipeline had been providing millions of dollars in royalties and transit fees to Saudi Arabia, Jordan, Syria and Lebanon. A PFLP spokesman stated that his group had intended to pollute the water supplied to Israeli settlements and fisheries in the Hutch Valley. Oil was reported to be seeping into the northern part of the Sea of Galilee, and oil slicks were seen on the Jordan River. In recent years, there have been a number of small-scale pipeline attacks and threats to petroleum infrastructure in North Africa. In late

---

7   As a result of two protracted bombing campaigns in Colombia which single-handedly represented at least 307 incidents, we have for methodological reasons registered these campaigns as two incidents only in the ITERATE database (Kjøk and Lia, 2001).

2001, the Algerian Salafist Group for Preaching and Combat (SGPC), a group closely associated with al-Qaida and Usama bin Laden, made serious threats against the trans-Mediterranean pipelines from North Africa to Europe.[8] The organization said it intended to attack the pipelines carrying liquid gas from Algeria to Spain via Morocco and to Italy via Tunisia, alongside Algeria's giant refineries on the Mediterranean ports of Arzew and Skikda (Nash, 2001).

Blasting of pipelines has caused the third largest number of incidents that have resulted in deaths (five out of 43 lethal attacks). In some cases, single pipeline bombings or acts of sabotage have killed a large number of people. Several incidents illustrate the potential lethality of this kind of attack. An extremely bloody incident took place in October 1998 in Nigeria, when more than 1,000 people burned to death after a ruptured pipeline caught fire (Anderson, 1998). Most of the victims of the inferno had been trying to collect leaking oil when there was an explosion, apparently set off by a spark from either a cigarette or a motorbike engine. According to the pipeline company, the fuel leak itself had been caused by sabotage. This and other incidents demonstrate the potential lethality and the ecological consequences of sabotage attacks against pipelines.[9] Fortunately, such highly lethal attacks represent exceptions rather than the rule: 39 out of 44 pipeline bombings did not cause any injuries.

The reason why pipeline blasting is a common type of petroleum terrorism is probably tactical. It is easy to carry out, as there are long stretches of unguarded pipelines; since pipelines are relatively easy to repair, oil companies have often invested little in their protection. It should be noted that none of the registered attacks have targeted *offshore* pipelines. Technically, such operations would have been more difficult. Although all continents have experienced attacks against their pipelines, some regions have been more exposed than others. It is probably no surprise that a considerable portion of the incidents recorded have taken place in the Middle East, many as a result of the Israeli–Palestinian conflict. Also Colombia has been extremely exposed, as a result of the civil war between the government and radical leftist guerrillas. More surprisingly, Western Europe has also suffered a significant number of pipeline attacks (12 incidents), mainly from radical domestic leftist

---

8 The threat was issued by SGPC leader Hasan Hattab, following the arrest in late September 2001 in Spain of six SGPC members after a British intelligence tip-off, for their role in a plot to blow up the US embassy in Paris. The message sent to the Algerian media named France, Germany, Britain and Belgium as the "European countries that persecute Islamists and cooperate with the US in their struggle against Bin Laden". Hasan Hattab attended a recent meeting in Kuala Lumpur, Malaysia, with associates of Mr bin Laden, and one of the suspected September 11 hijackers, according to a CIA video of the meeting (Nash, 2001).

9 Another example: On October 18, 1998, over 70 persons died and more than 100 were injured when a Colombian rebel group, The National Liberation Army (ELN), bombed the Ocensa crude oil pipeline. The powerful bomb caused major damage when the oil spills caught fire and set ablaze houses and part of the conduit in Machuca, near Segovia in the Antioquia Province. Between 20,000 and 40,000 barrels of crude oil were spilled in the attack.

groups. The statistics for Western Europe reflect the large number of active terrorist groups over the past decades, the relative density of petroleum production and transportation infrastructure in Europe, and perhaps also an over-representation of anti-Western attacks in the ITERATE database.

Sabotage against pipelines (excluding blasting) is far less common than blasting, accounting for only 13 incidents. The number of such strikes decreased somewhat in the course of the 1990s. None of the attacks have caused any injuries, but as many as four resulted in closedowns and another four involved considerable economic losses. In Europe, the only recorded incident of pipeline sabotage other than blasting took place in Germany on February 22, 1972, when the radical Palestinian group Black September sabotaged an ESSO pipeline near Hamburg, accusing the company of aiding Israel. In the Gulf region, pipeline blasting and sabotage have occurred perhaps most commonly in Yemen, primarily by tribesmen protesting against the negligence of the central government.

Kidnappings and Armed Attacks on Petroleum Company Personnel

Kidnapping has become increasingly widespread in recent decades, and petroleum company personnel have suffered to a substantial degree from this. Like pipeline blasting, kidnapping is usually easier than direct attacks on well-guarded petroleum production plants, refineries and terminals. This may account for the high frequency of this type of action. Kidnappings of petroleum company personnel are not necessarily fatal, however. Hostages have often been released without physical injuries, usually after a relatively short time, although at least eight cases of kidnapping fatalities have been recorded. Employees have usually been abducted from their workplace or during work journeys. By and large, kidnapping has been geographically confined to a handful of countries, in particular Yemen, Nigeria and Colombia. During the 1990s there were several hundred incidents of kidnapping and carjacking annually in Yemen. A small number of these incidents involved foreign petroleum company employees.

A typical incident was the abduction of Steve Carpenter by al-Sha'if tribesmen near the Yemeni capital of Sanaa on October 30, 1997. Carpenter was the American director of a Yemeni company that subcontracts to the US-based Hunt Oil. The tribesmen demanded the release of two fellow tribesmen who had been arrested on smuggling charges. The group also demanded that several public works projects allegedly promised to them by the government should commence. Carpenter was freed unharmed on November 27. In most other countries, however, the most important motivation is probably ransom, not demands for more government spending on public works.

In line with the increase in kidnappings, armed assaults on petroleum company personnel became more common during the 1990s, although far less frequent than abductions.[10] Such attacks are by their very nature extremely dangerous, and not surprisingly, all attacks except one resulted in casualties. Rebel movements operating in civil war situations have carried out most of the armed attacks on petroleum company personnel, obviously as part of their wider insurgent strategy to weaken the economic basis of the central government.

With regard to the assailants' ideology, the predominance of Islamist insurgent and terrorist groups is significant. Islamist groups have probably been responsible for more than half of the recorded armed attacks on personnel – which also indicates that terrorist or insurgent groups motivated by religion are often far more lethal than their secular counterparts. Many of these attacks have taken place in the context of the Algerian civil war, which has been extremely brutal, with the Armed Islamic Group (GIA) employing assassinations and massacres of civilians as a major mode of operation.[11] Its insurgent strategy seems to have been linked to the particular conditions of the Algerian civil war in the mid-1990s, when the disruption of all foreign support for the Algerian regime was seen as a critical precondition for victory on the battlefield (Lia and Kjøk, 2001). The physical petroleum infrastructure, however, does not seem to have been singled out as a particularly favored target, perhaps due to its remote and well-protected location.

Bombing of Petroleum Company Offices

Bombing of petroleum company offices is the third most frequent type of attack, accounting for 25 incidents alone. Such incidents have occurred throughout the period, but were especially common during the 1980s.[12] Only one incident caused very serious material damage, however. Offices are usually easy to attack, as they are often located in city centers.[13] The commonest way of attacking is simply to

---

10 The 11 incidents coded as armed attacks on personnel consisted of direct attacks on people. However, it is often difficult to determine whether an attack is directed specifically at personnel, material infrastructure or vehicles. Personnel can be targeted indirectly, for instance through an attack on their transport vehicles. Some rebel groups have proved capable of bringing down helicopters and aircraft. One such attack happened on March 8, 1995 in Burma, when three military helicopters carrying French and Burmese employees working on a pipeline project were shot down by the separatist Karen National Union (KNU). Five people were killed and 11 were injured.

11 A typical incident took place in Algeria on July 11, 1994, when four Russians and one Romanian were shot dead in a morning attack near the Oued Ouchayeh tunnel, east of Algiers. They were shot after Islamist gunmen at a fake roadblock had stopped their state-owned Sonatrach Oil Company bus.

12 12 attacks in the 1980s, as compared to five attacks in the 1990s and seven in the 1970s, plus one in 1968.

13 Two examples: On May 8, 1989, the offices of three foreign oil companies in Angola, ESSO, French company Petromar and the Japanese Sumitomo Corporation, suffered severe damage by a bomb that exploded during the night. The local Sumitomo Corporation Director was slightly wounded. Another incident occurred in Cyprus on March 14, 1985, when a midnight bomb explosion occurred in front of the ESSO oil company of-

place a bomb in front of the office entrance. The reason for targeting petroleum company offices is most likely that they are important symbols of such companies, as well as of the countries and interests they represent. Political terrorist groups tend to see violence as a means of political communication, a form of "armed propaganda" where targets are chosen for their symbolic value rather than their military significance. Many petroleum office bombings have occurred at night, probably indicating that these are deliberate attempts to inflict material damage without causing human casualties.

That attacks on symbolic targets such as offices rank third after pipeline attacks and kidnapping may suggest that attacks on petroleum infrastructure are normally the work of insurgent and rebel groups, while political terrorists lacking well-defined territorial or military objectives are inclined to avoid such targets. This conclusion is partly supported by the observation that attacks on petroleum infrastructure are far more common in countries that are already involved in armed conflicts. By contrast, attacks on offices have occurred relatively more frequently in Western countries, which host a large share of the world's terrorist groups but have had very few militarily strong rebel movements in recent decades.[14]

Attacks on Depots, Refineries and Petrol Stations

The remaining types of attacks – bombing of oil and gas depots, refineries and petrol stations and hijacking or seizure – have been far less common. Only 13 incidents of bombing of oil and gas depots have been recorded. Half of these had no serious material consequences, and only two resulted in casualties. Still, oil depots and liquefied gas tankers can cause extremely serious material damage and extract heavy human tolls if set ablaze by a terrorist group determined to cause maximum damage. Separatist groups were accountable for nearly half the attacks on depots.[15] Six of the depot bombings took place in Western Europe and three in the Middle East. One recent incident involving Palestinian militants in Palestine/Israel illustrates the potential destructiveness of such attacks. An explosive device was successfully planted on a diesel cargo tank vehicle during the course of its daily delivery route. The device was detonated by remote control while the driver was taking on a load at the country's largest fuel terminal, the Pi Glilot gas storage facility just north of Ramat Aviv, outside Tel Aviv. The resultant fire was brought under con-

---

fice on Grivas Dhyianis Avenue in Nicosia, damaging the entrance to the office and breaking windows in nearby buildings, but injuring nobody.

14 Western Europe and the USA have suffered six bombings each, while the figures for other regions are Asia (6), Southern America (4), Middle East (2) and Africa (1). The Philippines is a special case in this regard, with as many as four attacks alone.

15 The IRA carried out between two and four strikes against petroleum depots in England, and two attacks on terminals. The IRA also claimed credit for a February 1993 attack when three bombs were set off, destroying two huge natural gas tanks in Warrington, 15 miles west of Manchester. No injuries were reported, but about 100 people were evacuated from their homes.

trol without injury, but the attack could have caused massive casualties, had the above-ground natural gas tanks exploded. Analysts suggested the explosion would have equaled that of a small nuclear device. In addition, the disruption of fuel supply would have been very serious (*Jane's Terrorism & Security Monitor*, 2003; Sinai, 2003).

Bombings of refineries have also occurred relatively infrequently: 12 recorded incidents, only two of which were during the 1990s. Moreover, two-thirds of these involved insignificant material damages and no casualties. Guerrilla or rebel groups fighting their national government were responsible for at least five of the bomb attacks against refineries. Refineries are likely to be more tempting targets than pipelines, but since they are usually better protected and more difficult to attack, only groups with a certain level of sophistication and resources can hope to succeed in carrying out such attacks. The reasons for targeting oil/gas depots and refineries may vary. Perhaps some depots have been easily accessible; or they may have been attractive targets because they represent large economic assets. Moreover, bombing oil depots makes for spectacular explosions – which guarantee a return on investment in terms of media coverage. Economic motives cannot be discounted. One incident from the USA involved extortion: on September 28, 1982, officials of the Gulf Oil Company petrochemical plant in Cedar Bayou, Texas, received a letter threatening that ten bombs would be set off unless the extortionists were paid US$10 million. The police later found five bombs at the site.[16]

Bombings of petrol stations have not been very common, according to ITERATE: only eight incidents have been recorded, nearly all occurring in countries suffering from violent internal conflicts.[17] It is very likely, however, that attacks on petrol stations are greatly under-represented in the database, since such incidents rarely have international ramifications like the series of low-scale incidents during the 1980s of incendiary bomb attacks against petrol stations of oil companies which continued to trade with South Africa under apartheid.[18] More recently, information from documents recovered in Afghanistan and from interrogation of senior al-Qaida operatives suggest that priority plans were made for attacking petrol stations in New York and Washington, using fuel tankers as weapons.

---

16 The seven-page letter indicated where one of the bombs was and said four others were easily found. Police detonated one of the bombs harmlessly by firing a water cannon at it and found the other four bombs. The last five bombs were found when the Federal Bureau of Investigation (FBI) agreed to free a suspect's wife in return for information as to their location.

17 Colombia, India, Iraq, Israel, Mozambique, Namibia, Singapore and South Africa. The ninth country was Poland. One example: a bomb explosion occurred in Jerusalem on August 24, 1980, when a bomb hidden in a trashcan exploded at a Jerusalem gas station, killing a station attendant and wounding several tourists. The Palestine Liberation Organization was blamed for the attack.

18 One example from Europe: On June 16, 1986, anti-apartheid militants, critical of Shell's ties to South Africa, firebombed three Shell petrol pump stations in Amsterdam during the night. Damage was estimated at US$ 420,000. Several other stations were also damaged in Groningen.

These operations were initially meant to be part of the 9/11 attacks, but al-Qaida reportedly returned to these plans in 2002 (*Newsweek*, 2003).

ITERATE has recorded ten instances of seizure of petroleum infrastructure facilities, accompanied by hostage-taking. These incidents include hijackings of helicopters, seizure of production plants, a flow station, an office, a housing complex and other oil company facilities. These are usually serious attacks with grave consequences.[19] Such seizures bear a certain resemblance to kidnappings, with three countries – Nigeria, Colombia and Yemen – accounting for most attacks. Motivations are also similar, with ransom and political-economic concessions from the central government being most common. Since such incidents involve the capture of a potentially large number of people, and enable the terrorists to control the petroleum facilities, they tend to generate more media attention. On the other hand, hijackings and seizures are quite difficult to accomplish and offer few escape opportunities. These are probably the reasons why this form of terrorism is so infrequent.

Attacks against oil platforms, oil tankers, and offshore installations have been exceptionally rare – good news for producer countries whose petroleum production facilities are situated largely offshore. There have been only a few attacks on oil platforms, nearly all of them in Nigeria, and very few incidents of seizures of offshore oil installations, again in Nigeria.[20] This pattern may well shift, as new terrorist organizations have emerged with greater capabilities and more ambitious targets than were previously associated with terrorism.

Petroleum Terrorism on the Arab Peninsula: Recent Developments

Regarding terrorist threats to the oil industry in Saudi Arabia, there have long been recurrent, minor incidents of attacks and sabotage of oil facilities, primarily in the Eastern Province, and mostly attributed to elements from the disaffected Shi'i minority in the country (Cordesman, 2001, pp. 43, 65). These and other incidents of political violence and unrest in the Saudi Kingdom are usually shrouded in secrecy. According to one study, "a large number of Saudi attacks on Saudi and Saudi targets, both by Sunni extremists and Saudi Shiites, go unreported" (ibid., p. 59). Hence, very few incidents have been recorded in the ITERATE chronology, which

---

19 Half of them resulted in closedowns, and two, possibly three, incidents had important material consequences. Casualties have fortunately been low: one hostage has been killed, while at least 11 have been injured.

20 For example, on June 27, 1999, four heavily armed youths stormed a platform in Port Harcourt in the Niger Delta Region, inflicting damage to the platform, hijacking a helicopter and kidnapping three employees, who were released for ransom after 19 days. On July 31, 2000, 35 armed young men from Bayela village used a rowboat to reach two oil platforms off the coast. They managed to board the rigs and take 165 oil workers (including 20 foreigners) hostage. They demanded that Shell employ more Nigerians and that it pay a fee to the local community for exploiting its petroleum resources. Shell made a deal with the hostage-takers, and the employees were released after four days.

is based on open sources. While terrorist groups have targeted the US military presence in Saudi Arabia (US office at the Saudi National Guard in November 1995 and the Khobar Towers in June 1996) and representatives of the regime, oil facilities and foreign civilian workers appear to have become a more important target over the last few years. For example, the Saudi Kingdom has recently witnessed a number of car bombings and armed attacks targeting Western foreigners. In 2000–2002, there was a spate of attacks on Western citizens mainly in Riyadh and al-Khobar, killing at least five and injuring more than a dozen, by late October 2002 (*Stratfor.com*, 2002). Official Saudi statements, underpinned by reportedly forced confessions by several detained suspects, that the incidents stemmed from "turf wars" involving the illicit liquor trade, have been deemed not credible. More likely, the perpetrators were Islamic militants, enjoying the protection of powerful patrons in Saudi society. Al-Qaida has a significant following in Saudi Arabia. 15 of the 19 hijackers on September 11 were Saudi citizens. Some 125 Saudis were among the approximately 650 detainees at Guantánamo Bay.

Recently, there have been credible reports of al-Qaida plots against the sprawling Ras Tanura complex, probably the world's largest oil facility. A vital artery for global oil exports, Ras Tanura daily transfers five million barrels of oil to tankers, more than six per cent of the 76 million barrels produced worldwide each day. During the summer of 2002 the planned terrorist strike on the terminal complex, as well as pipelines that serve it, was averted by a series of arrests in the Kingdom. Subsequent media investigation into the plans revealed that several employees with access to the sites had been involved. The discovery of al-Qaida sympathizers inside Saudi Aramco, the world's largest oil company, was a worrisome trend. According to an assessment by US officials in early 2003, al-Qaida sympathizers "are sprinkled throughout the Saudi government" (*The New York Times*, 2003). In February 2003, media sources reported fresh intelligence suggesting that al-Qaida would make new attempts at striking Ras Tanura and other key oil facilities in the Saudi Kingdom as well as Kuwait. A devastating attack on the Saudi oil industry would serve a dual purpose. It would undermine the Saudi monarchy, and it would directly affect the United States because of the tight oil market and its dependence on Saudi oil exports (*ABCNews.com*, 2003; *The New York Times*, 2003; *Associated Press*, 2002).

Until mid-2002 al-Qaida had specifically refrained from attacking petroleum facilities in the Gulf region. By decree, bin Laden had banned any assaults on oil, stating it is the heritage of the Arab nations. The planned assault on Ras Tanura and the attack on the *Limburg* oil tanker (see below), therefore, signalled a shift in al-Qaida target selection strategy whereby economic targets would receive higher priority.

Given the relative rarity of terrorist assaults (not piracy) on maritime commercial traffic, the terrorist attack on the French-registered oil tanker *Limburg*, carrying nearly 400,000 barrels of crude oil off the south-eastern coast of Yemen in early October 2002, represented a new development. There had been several forewarnings of such attacks after the US warship *USS Cole* was hit by seaborne suicide bombers in Aden in October 2000 and following the arrest of an al-Qaida cell in Morocco, planning attacks on US and British warships in the Straits of Gibraltar. The terrorist weapon used against *Limburg* was a small fishing vessel, filled with explosives and directed by a 23-year-old Yemeni suicide attacker. It blew a hole in the new, double-hulled ship, causing a fire in which one Bulgarian crew member was killed and 12 others were hospitalized. The incident caused 50,000 barrels of crude oil to seep into the sea. An al-Qaida affiliated group, the Aden-Abyan Islamic Group, claimed responsibility for the operation, stating that *Limburg* was targeted because of its mission "to supply the 5th Fleet [based in Bahrain] for striking the brothers in Iraq" (*Washington Times*, 2002). The attack was meant to be supplemented by a simultaneous car bomb attack against a hotel in al-Sanaa, used by US military and intelligence officials.

A bin Laden audio tape published shortly after the attack hailed the *Limburg* bombers and promised more attacks:

> We congratulate the Muslim nation for the daring and heroic jihad (holy war) operations which our brave sons conducted in Yemen against the Christian oil tanker and in Kuwait against the American occupation and aggression forces. [...] By striking the oil tanker in Yemen with explosives, the attackers struck at the umbilical cord of the Christians, re-minding the enemy of the bloody price they have to pay for continuing their aggression against our nation [...] (*Reuters*, 2002).

The investigation into the Limburg attack revealed the existence of a network of al-Qaida supporters and operatives encompassing Kuwait, Saudi Arabia and Yemen, involved in various aspects of the operation (*The New York Times*, 2002).

Who are the "Petroleum Terrorists"?

The Predominance of Domestic Groups

According to our data, domestic groups have been responsible for most terrorist strikes against petroleum infrastructure. Foreign groups ("foreign" in terms of the dominant nationality of the perpetrating group members) have carried out only six per cent of the attacks recorded.[21] Moreover, throughout most of the period 1968–99 there has been a significant increase in the number of attacks performed by domestic groups. This reflects the gradual expansion of the petroleum industry into regions hosting active rebel and terrorist groups. Recall that ITERATE is a database that focuses on terrorist attacks with *international* ramifications, so that the actual predominance of domestic groups is likely to be even greater than the data indicate. This is an important finding, as it suggests that countries with little or no

---

21 The terrorists' nationality was unknown in 15 per cent of the incidents. However, in most of the uncertain cases, the perpetrators were probably domestic groups, judging by circumstances and available information about these strikes.

domestic terrorism are unlikely to be exposed to attacks on their petroleum instal-lations. On the other hand, it has also been suggested that globalization has led to a process of *transnationalizing terrorism,* in which terrorist groups – their ideas, weapons, funds and personnel – move across national borders more easily now than in the past. However, our survey tends to indicate the converse: there was in fact a decrease in strikes committed by foreign groups in 1970–94, albeit with a slight rise in 1995–99 (see Figure 5.2 below).[22] The number of attacks perpetrated by foreign groups is small, and alterations over time may be caused simply by coincidence or changes in the strategy of a few groups. For example, Palestinian groups perpetrated nearly all recorded "petroleum" attacks by foreign groups in the early 1970s; after 1995, Colombian guerrillas operating across the borders into neighboring countries were responsible for three out of four foreign attacks targeting petroleum infrastructure and personnel. Islamist groups have also carried out attacks on petroleum infrastructure outside their home country, whereas, to our knowledge, this has never been the case with right-wing extremists and militant environmental groups.

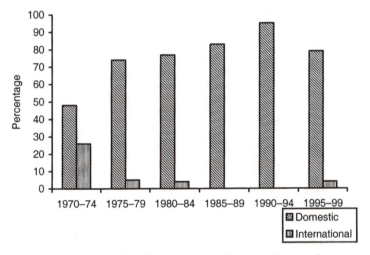

Figure 5.2 Domestic and foreign group involvement in petroleum terrorism

As to target selection and methods, there are some differences between domestic and foreign groups. Domestic groups have targeted personnel more often than have foreign groups, while the latter have shown a greater propensity to attack refineries. Indeed, our data show that refineries and personnel are the most common targets

---

22 In 1970–74, domestic and international groups were responsible for 48 per cent and 26 per cent of the strikes respectively, whereas in 1990–94, the figures were 95 per cent and 0 per cent.

for foreign groups.[23] This might indicate a preference for high-profile strategic targets on the part of foreign groups. On the other hand, this study has found no attacks on depots and production plants by foreign groups. For other targets, there are only minor differences between domestic and foreign groups. One may also discern differences between foreign and domestic groups regarding methods of attack. Foreign groups seem to prefer blasting (61 per cent), and have never carried out any armed attacks. This may indicate that foreign groups have a smaller range of capabilities and operational modes than have domestic groups. Importantly, foreign groups have thus far never succeeded in carrying out any seizures or armed attacks on petroleum installations, nor have their attacks ever caused any closedowns. This trend is probably about to change. As already alluded to, the rise of al-Qaida and its network of affiliated Islamist groups has contributed to increasing the possibility of spectacular attacks on a global scale, using new and innovative methods of attack.

Ideological Orientation

Terrorist and rebel groups that have been involved in strikes against petroleum infrastructure belong primarily to one of two ideological trends: either nationalist with separatist goals, or some variant of leftist Marxist-Maoist ideologies.

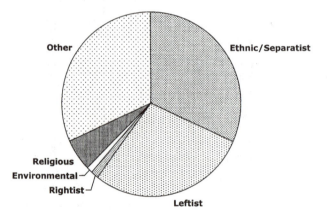

Figure 5.3 Distribution of groups responsible for terrorist attacks

Religious "fundamentalist" groups have carried out six per cent of the incidents, nearly all of which can be ascribed to militant Islamists (15 incidents in total – 14 by Islamists). By contrast, attacks by militant environmentalists and right-wing extremists account for one and two attacks respectively from the total of 262 incidents. The remaining strikes can be attributed to mentally disturbed individuals, criminals or unknown groups, although circumstances surrounding the "unknown

---

23 Each represents 22 per cent of the attacks from foreign groups.

actor" incidents indicate that most of them were also probably the work of leftist and ethno-separatist groups.

Naturally enough, the general ideological orientations of "petroleum terrorists" have changed over time, reflecting the evolution of old terrorist and insurgent movements and the emergence of new groups. In the 1970s many attacks were attributed to Palestinian and Arab groups, who alone accounted for 16 attacks; then the level of petroleum attacks by these groups declined during the 1980s, reflecting the transformation of the PLO to a major political non-state actor. The 1990s witnessed a considerable rise in ethno-separatist strikes against petroleum infrastructure, caused by the upsurge of inter-tribal conflicts in Yemen and Nigeria, in addition to a certain increase in other ethno-separatist attacks that reflected the general upsurge of intra-state ethno-nationalist conflicts in the early post-Cold War period. This was caused partly by the collapse or weakening of former Soviet client regimes around the world.

With regard to the predominant role of leftist groups in petroleum terrorism during the 1980s, most of these incidents occurred during the civil war in Colombia (19 out of 32 attacks). But even if one excludes the Colombian incidents, one finds a notable increase in leftist attacks from the 1970s to the 1980s and 1990s.[24] A few Western European Communist or left-wing groups were particularly active in targeting petroleum infrastructure during the mid-1980s, accomplishing as many as ten out of the 13 attacks carried out by non-Colombian groups, including several attacks on NATO oil pipelines in Europe. This might be explained by increased Soviet support for Communist revolutionary groups in the West, following the collapse of the *détente* of the 1970s, President Reagan's "Star War" program, his "Evil Empire" rhetoric, and importantly, the US Administration's covert and overt support of anti-Communist rebel and terrorist organizations in Nicaragua, Afghanistan and elsewhere.

Since 1979 there has been greater involvement of Islamist organizations in petroleum terrorism. This seems to be a by-product of the Islamic Revolution in Iran, and the Iranian regime's commitment to exporting the revolution and supporting radical Islamist, and in particular Shi'i, groups abroad. Most Islamist attacks have occurred during armed conflicts in which Islamist groups were one of the belligerent parties. Only three out of a total of 14 recorded Islamist attacks happened in countries not involved in internal armed conflicts or inter-state war.[25] This trend will probably change as militant Islamist groups increasingly subscribe to al-Qaida's doctrines of a global *jihad*.

The remarkably low number of incidents involving environmentalist and right-wing groups is an interesting finding that clearly demonstrates the relative margin-

---

24 1970s: eight strikes, 1980s: 13 strikes, 1990s: 12 strikes.

25 The figures are uncertain due to the number of incidents by the "unknown" groups. At least two or three of the attacks committed by "unknown" groups during peacetime appear to have been perpetrated by Islamist groups.

ality of "Green terrorism"[26] and right-wing extremists[27] as a threat to petroleum production facilities. This "inactivity" on the part of militant environmentalists may
well stem from a fear of inflicting additional environmental damage, a major risk
when attacking petroleum infrastructure.

With regard to target selection strategies, methods and capabilities, one finds
that ideological orientation does make a difference.[28] Our statistical results suggest
that attacks by ethnic-separatist groups cause more material and economic damage
than those of leftist groups. This may have ideological causes. Leftist radicals have
often used terrorism as a kind of "armed propaganda", a theater conveying a political message to the government and a wider audience. Ethno-separatists, however,
seek to weaken the physical and military capability of the central government as a
step towards independence. Islamists distinguish themselves from other groups by
the lethality of their attacks, using armed attacks on personnel as their primary
method. Islamist groups have also been involved in blowing up a refinery and a
terminal, and in one instance setting fire to an entire complex in Kuwait, containing
an oil well, a plant and a terminal. Almost half of their attacks have resulted in
casualties, and nearly a quarter of the attacks have had other major impacts on human beings such as injuries or loss of freedom. On the other hand, none of their attacks led to closedowns and few of them had important economic effects.

The inclination on the part of many leftist groups and, to a lesser degree, separatist movements to avoid large casualties, relatively speaking, as compared to
Islamist groups, may be explained by differences in ideology. Militant Islamists
tend to seek religious justification of their attacks by obtaining a *fatwa* from a religious authority, whereas leftist and separatist groups are often more dependent on

---

26 Militant environmentalists have barely been involved in attacks on oil and gas facilities,
    according to our data, although a thorough survey of domestic incidents during the past
    decades would probably yield more events. The only recorded incident that can be re-
    lated to an environmentalist cause occurred in Ecuador in 1998, when an Indian group
    kidnapped three employees from an oil company as a protest against environmental
    damage to their land, caused by the oil companies. The hostages were released un-
    harmed.

27 Two examples of right-wing involvement in petroleum terrorism: a right-wing group
    occupied a production plant in Bolivia in 1981. The occupation lasted for three days,
    during which time 52 employees were kept hostage. Another right-wing extremist group
    planned to blow up a refinery in the USA in 1997. The plan was uncovered by police in
    advance, and was never carried out. In addition to blowing up the refinery, the group
    probably intended to cause the release of lethal gas, thereby killing rescue workers, first
    response teams, policemen, etc, and possibly even neighbors. The group had provided
    their own family members with gas masks.

28 It is difficult to determine why terrorist groups of different ideological trends choose
    different target types when they attack petroleum infrastructure. Tactical security con-
    siderations are important when planning and carrying out attacks on petroleum targets,
    and since the security environment differs from one group to another, the targeting pat-
    tern will also differ. It is therefore impossible to ascribe different targeting patterns to
    ideological differences alone.

maintaining a level of popular support from a local or regional constituency (Hoffman, 1998, p. 196ff).

Motivations: Why do Terrorists Attack Petroleum Infrastructure?

Terrorist and rebel groups do not necessarily state their intentions and goals, and it may be difficult to understand their motives. A list of the motivations and demands most commonly put forward by the groups themselves cannot therefore be entirely exhaustive.

- Economic motives are the most frequently stated reason. Demands for ransom, blackmail and also outright robbery have occurred in 21 incidents altogether. Fund-raising is extremely important for rebel and terrorist organizations, especially with the decline in state sponsorship after the end of the Cold War. In several cases, rebel groups have degenerated into profit-hungry warlords and criminal organizations, abandoning their erstwhile political-ideological goals.
- Opposition to the national government has been stated as a reason in 13 cases of attacks; demands for a greater share in the government's revenues have been put forward in four recorded incidents.
- Opposition to foreign oil companies' exploitation of national petroleum resources has been quoted in seven cases.
- Other common reasons include protest against the involvement of multinational companies in Third World countries, and also the policies of Western governments towards these countries.
- Part of efforts to negotiate the release of imprisoned group members and labor conflicts were cited as group motivation in four to six incidents.

The above are the motives explicitly stated by the terrorist or rebel groups. If one turns to the implicit reasons, then, judging by available information on the groups involved, the most common motivation seems to be opposition to the national government and foreign petroleum companies, followed by economic motives.

The Impact of Political Regime and Armed Conflict

It has been noted that terrorist attacks on petroleum infrastructure seem to be undertaken more often by insurgent and rebel groups involved in armed conflict with their national government rather than by political terrorists who are operating in peaceful democracies and who lack well-defined territorial or military objectives. The Colombian civil war, which has raged since 1984, strengthens this assertion. Control over the flow of oil revenues has been a key issue between the contending parties – the national government, and a conglomerate of leftist guerrillas, partly in alliance with drug-trafficking mafias. Over the years, the two main guerrilla organizations, the National Liberation Army (ELN) and the Revolutionary Armed Forces of Colombia (FARC), have perpetrated numerous attacks on a wide range of petroleum installations and personnel, seriously disrupting production and export (*Associated Press*, 2001).

A similar example is Yemen. Although it was ravaged by a civil war in the early 1990s, the country is today more affected by its fragility as a state than by an ongoing insurgency. Violence in Yemen is the product of continuous tribal conflicts, proliferation of small arms, and extremely weak government control outside the main cities. While kidnappings of foreign personnel and sabotage against oil pipelines primarily have been the work of disaffected tribal elements demanding a greater share of the state's resources, recent events suggest that new motivations, Islamic militancy in particular, are becoming a more important factor. In addition, younger members of tribes, for whom ancient codes of honor and protection of visitors count less than the need for immediate financial returns, have become more involved in the kidnapping-for-ransom business. This seems to lead to more bloody outcomes of the traditionally non-violent Yemeni hostage situations (International Crisis Group, 2003).

Rebel and Insurgent Attacks on Petroleum Targets during Armed Conflict

In order to study how the patterns of petroleum terrorism may vary depending on the presence of internal armed conflicts, one may divide incidents into two main categories: strikes in countries in armed conflict, and strikes in countries at peace.[29] Not surprisingly, one finds that both the presence and the intensity of the armed conflict are significant in accounting for the level of petroleum terrorism. The analysis of incidents occurring in countries in armed conflict indicates that while methods and targeting patterns in these countries chiefly follow the general pattern, with blasting of pipelines and kidnapping as the most frequent methods of attack,

---

29 When defining countries at peace and at armed conflict, Wallensteen and Sollenberg's table of armed conflicts has been used (Wallensteen and Sollenberg, 1999). It covers the period 1989–98. The table covers wars (defined as conflicts causing more than 1,000 deaths a year), intermediate armed conflicts (more than 1,000 deaths during the conflict, but less than 1,000 a year) and minor armed conflicts (less than 1,000 deaths during the entire conflict). No table of wars covering the entire period (1922–99) was found. As the number of incidents is relatively small for 1989–99 (54 incidents), we decided to review them by sorting the events from the pre-1989 period using *Correlates of War and Peace* (Singer and Small, 2001), which covers the entire period from 1816 to 1992 (although with a higher threshold for casualties). This yielded some 80 incidents, and the general pattern of targeting corresponded to our previous results, using Wallensteen and Sollenberg's table. The disadvantage of using *Correlates of War and Peace* is that it operates with a much higher threshold for armed conflict than Wallensteen and Sollenberg's table, and hence, it does not cover minor and intermediate armed conflicts.

armed attacks on petroleum industry personnel are far more common and more lethal than otherwise.[30]

Petroleum Terrorism in Peaceful Democracies?

For threat assessment purposes, one is more interested in patterns of petroleum terrorism in democracies without internal armed conflict. Drawing upon various sources on armed conflicts and democracy performance (in particular *Freedom House*, which rates countries as "free", "partly free" and "not free"),[31] one obtains the following results:

Table 5.1 Political regime and the occurrence of petroleum terrorism 1972–99

Incidents in "free" countries	90	Incidents in "partly free" countries	91
Incidents in "not free" countries	48	Total	229

It is indicative of the relationship between political regime and the level of terrorism that "not free" countries – which were quite numerous during most of this period, and which also hosted much of the petroleum industry – had a relatively small share of the attacks. This underlines the common observation that highly authoritarian and totalitarian regimes rarely experience high levels of terrorism (Lia and Skjølberg, 2000). In "free" countries without internal armed conflicts, one finds that out of a total of 229 incidents of petroleum terrorism between 1972 and 1999, there were only 53 recorded incidents (or 23 per cent).[32] It also appears that while the number of attacks on petroleum installations worldwide has remained relatively constant over the past 20 years, in peaceful democracies the number of attacks has decreased in the past decade.[33]

---

30 When looking at the entire 1922–98 period, combining Wallensteen and Sollenberg's table and the *Correlates of War and Peace*, one finds that all recorded lethal terrorist attacks against pipelines had occurred during armed conflict, and that four or five of these attacks had caused more than 124 casualties.

31 In order to determine which countries can be classified as "peaceful democracies", we have drawn upon data from various sources (Singer and Small, 2001; Wallensteen and Sollenberg, 1999; Ayres, 2000, pp. 107–17). Data from *Freedom House*, http://www.freedomhouse.org have also been used. The latter regularly rates countries as "free", "partly free" and "not free".

32 Eight incidents that have occurred in England are not included in this overview, as a result of the Northern Ireland conflict. Between five and seven of these incidents were indeed carried out by the IRA, and mainly targeted depots (2–4) and terminals (2). However, an unknown group (possibly Islamists) bombed the offices of Kuwait Oil in London in 1980.

33 The total figures of incidents are 1972–79: 37, 1980–89: 99, 1990–99: 95 and in peaceful democracies: 1972–79: 19, 1980–89: 21, 1990–99: 10.

As to methods and targeting, one finds that bombing of offices is relatively more common in peaceful democracies than elsewhere – almost twice as frequent as in countries in armed conflict. Refineries have also been targeted in peaceful democracies, but ITERATE has recorded no armed attacks on petroleum industry personnel, and kidnappings have been rare, confined largely to Latin American democracies. The only armed terrorist assault that has been recorded – the Armed Communist Fraction attack on the Italian President of Chevron Oil on April 21, 1976 – did not result in any casualties. Moreover, apart from a PFLP attack at an OPEC meeting in Vienna in 1975, one finds no hijacking or seizure operations against petroleum targets in peaceful democracies. Let us take a look at one of the most serious campaigns of petroleum terrorism in democracies at peace.

Several European leftist groups launched a series of attacks on petroleum targets in Europe in the mid-1980s, protesting against "the Americanization of Europe", capitalism and the NATO alliance. The Belgian leftist group Combatant Communist Cells (CCC) briefly formed an alliance – the "Anti-Imperialist Armed Front" – with the German Red Army Faction (RAF) and the French Action Directe (AD), to co-ordinate their actions against NATO member governments.[34] This new organization carried out an extensive bombing campaign against NATO pipelines in Europe in 1984–85. Its German branch, the RAF, bombed six NATO pipelines going through Germany, and probably also a pumping station in an attack where nobody claimed responsibility. On December 11, 1984, the Belgian CCC bombed six unguarded pumping stations along the 3700-mile NATO oil pipeline that runs across Belgium, the Netherlands, Luxembourg, Germany and France. Fires resulting from the blasts were quickly brought under control, but nevertheless caused a 48-hour shutdown to the pipeline. In the following year, the CCC attempted to repeat the campaign by placing a bomb in a NATO pipeline pumping control room in Ghent. In France, AD bombed the offices of the Elf-Aquitaine Petroleum Company in Paris on December 10, 1984.

The campaign against NATO pipelines by European leftist terrorist groups was definitely a nuisance, but not a strategic threat. Also the targeting pattern demonstrated that symbolic violence, not maximum death and destruction, was the underlying theme. The Anti-Imperialist Armed Front does not seem to have perpetrated any kidnappings or armed attacks on personnel from the petroleum sector, apparently due to the CCC's ideological disinclination to excessive bloodshed. Looking at the overall effects of petroleum terrorism in democracies at peace, one finds that closedowns have been remarkably rare (only one out of 53 incidents). There have also been fewer casualties per incident in peaceful democracies.

Thus it seems clear that the main causes of petroleum terrorism in peaceful democracies are either ideological – with the perpetrators usually domestic groups

---

34 Unlike RAF and AD, however, the CCC "tended to pick symbolic and strategic targets for bombings and to target property rather than human life, using the terrorist event as 'armed propaganda' for publicizing their own specific issues or causes rather than as direct military tactics to achieve revolution" (Anderson and Sloan, 1995, pp. 70–71).

motivated by leftist ideologies, often claiming to act on behalf of the oppressed masses in the Third World – or spillover attacks from nearby civil war zones.[35] The Gulf War in 1991 also caused a temporary upsurge in attacks on petroleum targets in Western Europe. For example, on January 29, 1991 a Greek leftist group, the November 17 Organization, fired rockets at the British Petroleum office in Athens, causing serious damage, in protest at "the barbarous Western assault" on Iraq. Attacks on military pipelines were also reported in Germany and Spain during the Gulf War.[36]

In democracies at peace, foreign groups seem to have been responsible for a relatively larger share of petroleum terrorism than elsewhere, accounting for between 7 and 11 of a total of 53 incidents.[37] Attacks by non-domestic groups on petroleum targets in peaceful democracies in 1972–99 can be ascribed to mainly two sets of groups – Palestinian and Colombian organizations. Among the domestic groups, leftists are the predominant actors.

Concluding Observations

Historical patterns do not repeat themselves endlessly. Nor should they be seen as a guarantee for the future absence of serious petroleum terrorism. Although historical patterns underline the importance of symbolic-ideological considerations rather than strategic-military goals when terrorist groups target petroleum infrastructure, this need not be the case in the future. Globalization, transnational migration, spread of new technology and expertise and the diminishing importance of distance and space contribute to blur the distinctions between domestic and international terrorism, and to lower the walls between the zones of peace and zones of turmoil.

Recent years have witnessed the rise of illegal non-state actors who have, or had at certain periods, de facto control over territory, thousands of trained members and impressive financial resources. Examples include al-Qaida and its affiliated groups, the Colombian FARC and the Sri Lankan Tamil Tigers (LTTE), all of whom have

---

35 A rough estimate of the 53 incidents indicates that export of conflict was the cause in 10–12 strikes, ideology in 23 strikes and ideology combined with export in seven strikes (the motivation is uncertain for 11–13 strikes).

36 The missile was launched from a nearby construction site. It broke two adjacent windows on the second floor of the BP building, pierced two wooden partitions, and exploded in a large office housing the firm's distribution department. No injuries were reported. Two other incidents of petroleum terrorism in Western Europe during the Gulf War: on February 21, 1991, a Spanish left-wing group, October First Anti-Fascist Resistance Groups (GRAPO), assumed responsibility for a bomb attack which caused limited damage to an oil pipeline supplying a joint US-Spanish naval base at Rota in southern Spain. On March 18, 1991, a bomb slightly damaged a military fuel pipeline near the German town of Emstek, supplying two German Air Force units that were stationed in Turkey during the Gulf War. The blast caused 300 cubic feet of aviation fuel to leak. No one claimed responsibility.

37 The perpetrators could not be determined in all cases.

proven capable of launching devastating and sophisticated terrorist attack campaigns. Particularly disturbing is al-Qaida's capacity to stage mass casualty attacks with suicide activists and its search for unconventional weaponry, as these introduce an entirely new dimension in the terrorist threat environment. A far less dramatic development has been the recent upsurge of extreme leftist and anarchist groups rallying around an anti-globalization banner. They may prove to be the harbingers of a new era of left-wing violent activism, one in which the capitalist, powerful and global petroleum industry will stand out as a preferred target (Lee, 1996; *Stratfor.com*, 2001).

For the Persian Gulf region, recent years have witnessed a number of events which appear to stimulate the growth of militancy and Islamic extremism in the area, enhancing the probability of terrorist and sabotage attacks against the petroleum industry, the economic mainstay of the regimes. Internal developments such as increasing youth unemployment, economic recession and delays of promised political reforms fuel resentment. External developments add to local grievances. The outbreak of the al-Aqsa Intifada in September 2000, the 9/11 attacks in New York and Washington, the subsequent war in Afghanistan and the US-led invasion of Iraq in March 2003, have exacerbated the dual grievances of US "colonial" hegemony and the impotence of Arab regimes in defending Arab and Islamic causes. While al-Qaida as an organizational entity is weakened, the support for its ideological message and ideas have undoubtedly been strengthened, while the new Iraq has emerged as yet another battleground for al-Qaida-affiliated fighters.

In terms of tactics and modes of terrorist operations against petroleum-related targets in the Gulf region, one would be ill-advised to exclude the possibility of terrorist innovations. The innovative dimension of contemporary terrorism has long been overlooked. 9/11 is only one of many examples of the untapped potential for mass casualty terrorism without having to resort to exotic non-conventional weapons. In this perspective, oil and gas facilities, in particular large liquefied gas tankers, stand out as potential targets for mass casualty terrorism. The kind of attacks and plots which al-Qaida and its affiliated groups are known to have planned, would have appeared very unlikely to most observers a decade ago. 9/11 demonstrated fully how terrorists were able to convert civilian aircrafts into huge cruise missiles. Earlier al-Qaida plots have also involved the use of small explosive-laden aircrafts or helicopters to hit well-protected targets such as the G8 summit in Genoa and the US embassy in Paris. New modes of maritime terrorism also seem likely. Undertaking large-scale offshore attacks requires resources and capabilities that most non-state groups do not have. However, the recent discovery of a submarine vessel construction program among Colombian guerrillas and drug-trafficking mafia, apparently aided by Russian expertise, and among the Moro Islamic Liberation Front, the largest Islamist insurgent group in the Philippines, tells us that new modes of operations, including underwater terrorist attacks, cannot be excluded (al-Sharq al-Awsat, 2000; *Stratfor.com*, 2003). The LTTE's development of speedboats with "stealth" capacity also illustrates the rapidly growing technological range of today's terrorist organizations in the realm of maritime operations (Gunaratna, 2001). Terrorist groups learn quickly from each other and new modes of terrorist operations will certainly be part of the new threat environment.

References

Aas, J., Rutledal, F. and Sandvik, T. (2000), *Beskyttelse av olje- og gassinstallasjoner offshore – FOKS-prosjekt*, FFI/Rapport–2000/05047 (restricted circulation).

ABCNews.com (2003), "Al Qaeda Oil Plot Could Cripple U.S. Economy", February 13.

al-Sharq al-Awsat (2000), "Seizure of Submarine Which Was Being Built by Colombian Drug Traffickers" (in Arabic), September 8.

Anderson, H. (1998), "Nigeria Inferno Survivors Sabotage Oil Pipes", *BBC World News,* November 24.

Anderson, S. and Sloan, S. (1995), *Historical Dictionary of Terrorism*, Scarecrow Press, London.

Associated Press (2001), "Colombia Rebels Threaten Sabotage", July 13.

Associated Press (2002), "U.S. Worried Al-Qaida Targeting Oil", October 17.

Ayres, W. R. (2000), "A World Flying Apart? Violent Nationalist Conflict and the End of the Cold War", *Journal of Peace Research*, Vol. 37, No. 1, pp. 105–117.

Bjørgo, T. (1990), *Maritim terrorisme: En trussel mot norsk skipsfart og oljevirksomhet?* NUPI Report No. 146, June, Oslo.

Cordesman, A. (2001), *Saudi Arabia Enters the 21st Century: Politics and Internal Stability*, Center for Strategic and International Studies, Washington.

Drake, C. J. M. (1998), *Terrorists' Target Selection*, Macmillan, Basingstoke, Hampshire.

Engene, J. O. (1998), *Patterns of Terrorism in Western Europe 1950—1995*, PhD dissertation, Department of Comparative Politics, University of Bergen, Norway.

Gunaratna, R. (2001), "Sea Tiger Success Threatens the Spread of Copycat Tactics", *Jane's Intelligence Review*, March, pp. 12–16.

Heradstveit, D. (1992), "Terrorism Threat in the North Sea – Norwegian Oil Industry as a Target for Arabic Terrorism", *Norwegian Oil Review*, No.7.

Hoffman, B. (1998), *Inside Terrorism*, Colombia University Press, New York.

International Crisis Group (2003), "Yemen: Coping with Terrorism and Violence in a Fragile State", *ICG Middle East Report*, No.8.

Jane's Terrorism & Security Monitor (2003), "Terrorism Threats to Infrastructure Security: Special Report", January 1.

Johansen, I. and Otterley, J. (1994), *En vurdering av trusselen mot norske olje- og gassinstallasjoner*, FFI/Rapport-94/03398 (restricted circulation).

Kaplan, J. (1997), "Leaderless Resistance", *Terrorism and Political Violence*, Vol. 9, No. 3.

Kjøk, Å. and Lia, B. (2001), *Terrorism and Oil – An Explosive Mixture? A Survey of Terrorist and Rebel Attacks on Petroleum Infrastructure 1968–1999*, FFI/Rapport–2001/04031, Kjeller: Norwegian Defence Research Establishment (FFI), www.mil.no/multimedia/archive/00002/Kjok-R-2001-04031_2140a.pdf

Lee, M. (1996), "Violence and the Environment: The Case of 'Earth First'", in M. Barkun (ed.), *Millennialism and Violence*, Frank Cass, London.

Lia, B. (2000), *Er sivil infrastruktur sannsynlege mål for terrorgrupper i fredstid? Nokre førebelse konklusjonar om terrorisme som tryggingspolitisk utfordring i Norge*, FFI/Rapport-2000/01703, Norwegian Defence Research Establishment (FFI), Kjeller, www.mil.no/multimedia/archive/00004/Lia-R-2000-01703_4935a.pdf

Lia, B. (2001), *Militære installasjonar som terrormål i fredstid? Ein gjennomgang av faktiske terroranslag mot militære installasjonar på 1990-talet*, FFI/Rapport–2001/03419, Norwegian Defence Research Establishment (FFI), Kjeller, www.mil.no/multimedia/archive/00002/Lia-R-2001-03419_2133a.pdf

Lia, B. (2003), *Terror mot transport: En revurdering av terrortrusselen mot transportrelaterte mål i lys av 11.september*, FFI/Rapport–2003/00731, Norwegian Defence Research Establishment (FFI), Kjeller.

Lia, B. and Hansen, A.S. (2002), *Globalisation and the Future of Terrorism: Patterns and Predictions*, Frank Cass, London.

Lia, B. and Kjøk, Å. (2001), *Islamist Insurgencies, Diasporic Support Networks, and Their Host States: The Case of the Algerian GIA in Europe 1993–2000*, FFI/Rapport–2001/003789, Norwegian Defence Research Establishment (FFI), Kjeller, www.mil.no/multimedia/archive/00002/Lia-R-2001-03789_2134a.pdf

Lia, B. and Skjølberg, K. (2000), *Why Terrorism Occurs: A Survey of Theories and Hypotheses on the Causes of Terrorism*, FFI/Rapport–2000/02769, Norwegian Defence Research Establishment (FFI), Kjeller, www.mil.no/multimedia/archive/00004/Lia-R-2000-02769_4938a.pdf

Mickolus, E. (1980), *Transnational Terrorism: A Chronology of Events 1968–1980*, Aldwych, London.

Nash, E. (2001), "Extremists Target European Gas Pipelines; Algerian Threat", *The Independent*, September 30, p. 2.

Newsweek (2003), "The Biggest Catch Yet: Khalid Shaikh Mohammed, a.k.a. 'The Brain', Was Planning Horrific New Attacks on the United States", March 10.

Olje- og Energidepartementet (2000), *Faktaheftet 2000 Norsk Petroleumsvirksomhet*, Ch. 4, http://odin.dep.no/oed/norsk/publ/

Reuters (2002), "Bin Laden Hails 'Heroic' Anti-Western Attacks – Text", October 14.

Schmid, A. P. and Jongman, A. J. (1988), *Political Terrorism: A New Guide to Actors, Authors, Concepts, Data Bases, Theories and Literature*, SWIDOC, Amsterdam.

Sinai J. (2003), "How to Forecast Intentions, Capabilities and Likelihood of Terrorist Groups Resorting to Low Impact Catastrophic Warfare", *The Journal of Counterterrorism*, Vol. 9, No. 1, pp. 19–22.

Singer, D. and Small, M. (2001), *Correlates of War and Peace*, http://www.umich.edu/~cowproj

Stratfor.com (2001), "WTO: Splinter Groups Breed as Activists Fracture", November 8.

Stratfor.com (2002), "Saudi Arabia: Vulnerable Expatriates and a Fragile Regime", October 14.

Stratfor.com (2003), "Philippines: New Concerns Arise With Rebel Submarine Plan", March 14.

Sviland, M. K. (1999), *Eksterne forhold som kan medføre en storulykke ved Shell-Raffineriet på Sola med hovedvekt på sabotasje*, MA thesis, Høgskulen i Stavanger, Stavanger, Norway.

The New York Times (2002), "Al Qaeda Member Arrested in Kuwait", November 17.

The New York Times (2003), "Pro-Qaeda Oil Workers a Sabotage Risk for Saudis", February 13.

Wallensteen P. and Sollenberg, M. (1999), "Armed Conflict, 1989–98", *Journal of Peace Research*, Vol. 36, No. 5, pp. 593–606.

Washington Times (2002), "Maritime Terrorism Next?" October 20.

Chapter 6

Shi'i Perspectives on a Federal Iraq: Territory, Community and Ideology in Conceptions of a New Polity

Reidar Visser

As debate over the future of Iraq intensified during 2002 and the first months of 2003, one concept which came to the fore as a possible key feature of a new, post-Ba'th political order was federalism. The present chapter seeks to analyze how religious opposition parties from Iraq's majority Shi'i population interacted with this concept in the period between George W. Bush's State of the Union address on January 29, 2002 (when Iraq was identified as part of the "axis of evil") until the collapse of the Ba'th regime in Baghdad on April 9, 2003. In the final part of the chapter, some observations are made on the emerging power struggle between various Shi'i factions during the first weeks of the US-led occupation, until mid-May 2003 when Iraqi politics clearly entered a new phase with the emergence of a free press, the formation of new political organizations and the return of most of the exiled opposition leaders. The primary focus will be on parties and persons who work with the aim of ultimately establishing an Islamic state, but also currents which seek to further Islamic values within a secular state system will be discussed to some extent.[1] Non-religious parties, a sizeable element of the Shi'i political scene, are outside the scope of the chapter.

The Shi'is and State Power

Any analysis of attitudes to federalism among Shi'is working on an Islamic platform will have to take into account some overarching questions about the relationship between believers, clergy and state power that arise from certain main premises of Shi'i theology. Ever since the emergence of Shi'ism as a distinctive religious

---

1   The concept "Shi'i Islamist" may seem inappropriate for certain movements whose declared aim is to transcend sectarianism, but is used for the sake of convenience in this discussion to denote political parties which are firmly rooted in Shi'i religious and social institutions and which may or may not pursue more universalistic forms of Islamism.

denomination, a central point of controversy among Shi'i religious thinkers has been how to organize society politically in an age when the legitimate ruler – the Twelfth Imam according to Shi'i belief – is absent, in a state of occultation (*ghayba*). This situation has persisted since AD 874, leaving a power vacuum in which temporal rule is fundamentally problematic as it may theoretically constitute a usurpation of the powers of the Hidden Imam.[2]

In practice, Shi'i doctrines have developed in the direction of accepting a sub-stantial societal role for the clergy. The Shi'i ulama identified a task for themselves as the general representative (*na'ib al-'amm*) of the Hidden Imam, with responsi-bility for leading Friday prayers, collecting religious taxes and exercising judicial authority. A significant stratification of Shi'i society and a bolstering of the position of the ulama resulted from the 'Usuli victory over the Akhbaris (who promoted a more egalitarian vision of the community of believers) in the eighteenth century. This consolidated a division of the Shi'is into those who have the necessary quali-fications for interpreting Islamic law (*mujtahids*) and those who do not possess these skills (*muqallids*) and therefore must imitate the jurisprudents. In the nine-teenth century, the hierarchical nature of this system was further strengthened as the concept of a single, pre-eminent source of emulation (*marja' al-taqlid*) – the most learned among the ulama – increasingly gained favor, and theoretically left this leading cleric as the ultimate legal authority for the Shi'is. In practice, there have since been long periods when several *mujtahids* have competed for recognition as the paramount Shi'i cleric.

The question of the political role of the ulama in the age of the *ghayba* has been much more controversial. Historically, regimes whose sovereigns were themselves Shi'is have appeared in many countries, but the Shi'i clergy have often shown con-siderable reluctance towards interacting with and extending legitimacy to these po-litical entities. While rulers in Iran and India had patronized Shi'i ulama and ac-tively sought their co-operation for centuries, many leading clerics in these areas remained aloof from the state and adopted a quietist stand instead.[3] It was not until the early twentieth century that a Shi'i theory for the political involvement of the *mujtahids* in worldly affairs became widespread, when a segment of the ulama entered the debate over a new Iranian constitution and outlined a state model in which they would have an active supervisory role to ensure that legislation passed by the national assembly harmonized with Islamic law.[4] The final step towards political power for the clerics was spearheaded by Ayatollah Khomeini through the concept of the rule of the jurisprudent (*wilayat al-faqih*), according to which a just ruler qualified in matters of Islamic law and possessing the required insight in temporal affairs can legitimately exercise political power in the absence of the

---

2   For a summary of some of the main aspects of this issue, see Moojan Momen, *An Intro-duction to Shi'i Islam* (New Haven, 1985), pp. 189–199.

3   For some less well-known Indian examples, see J.R.I. Cole, *Roots of North Indian Shi'ism in Iran and Iraq* (Berkeley, 1989), pp. 22–24.

4   Abdul-Hadi Hairi, *Shi'ism and Constitutionalism in Iran* (Leiden, 1977), pp. 193–197.

Hidden Imam. This doctrine was implemented in Iran after the Islamic revolution in 1979.

Although it first appeared to be the logical conclusion of a linear process towards an increasingly intimate association between the Shi'i clergy and state power, Khomeini's theory of government has aroused much internal controversy among the Shi'is, and discussions about its validity have therefore taken center stage in Shi'i debates on state power. Many clerics with a more traditional orientation have maintained their skepticism to the close ties between ulama and state structures as manifested in the Islamic Republic of Iran, voicing support for a more limited role for the clergy through the traditional assignments of the *mujtahids*. This controversy has intensified after Khomeini's death, because the qualifications of his successor in traditional religious terms have been disputed by ulama who have a preference for a less politicized clergy.[5] In the early twenty-first century, the world of Shi'ism is therefore characterized by two systems which are often in direct competition: the traditional system of *mujtahids* who struggle for pre-eminence as jurists in an order which is essentially internationalist and less focused on temporal states, their borders, or their administrative subdivisions; and the system of the Shi'i Islamist movements that favor an expression of Shi'ism in the political sphere – some on the basis of Khomeini's thinking, others with reference to ideas which have more in common with theories developed at the time of the Iranian constitutional revolution.[6]

In this context, where the framework of the Islamic state itself remains a matter of dispute, there has been less focus on questions of devolution. Initially, the Islamic revolution in Iran was accompanied by a drive to proliferate the new ideas abroad in order to transcend the established state order,[7] but subsequent political developments and the failure to export the revolution directed much of the intellectual energy of Shi'i Islamist thinkers back to more basic questions about the relevance of political activism on the part of the clergy, or the validity of *wilayat al-faqih*. Problems with affinity to the question of federalism – such as radical decentralization of existing political structures within a specifically Islamic framework – received less attention, and the discussions over administrative decentralization which did materialize frequently turned into local replicas of the more fundamental national debates.[8] By 2003, the idea of comprehensive devolution as a way of solving internal political problems had failed to find large bodies of enthusiastic adherents among Shi'i Islamists in key countries such as Lebanon and Iran. This relative vacuum in the field of political theory may also have had an impact on the emerging debate on federalism among the Shi'is of Iraq.

---

5   Wilfried Buchta, "Die Islamische Republik Iran und die religiös-politische Kontroverse um die *marja'iyat*", *Orient*, vol. 36, no. 3 (1995), pp. 449–474.
6   For a discussion of the political implications of Shi'i internationalism, see Chibli Mallat, *The Middle East into the 21st Century* (Reading, 1997), pp. 154–160.
7   Waddah Sharara, *Dawlat hizb allah* (Beirut, 1996), pp. 313–315.
8   See for instance Kian Tajbakhsh, "Political Decentralization and the Creation of Local Government in Iran", *Social Research*, vol. 67, no. 2 (2000), pp. 377–404.

The Shi'is, the Territorial Integrity of Iraq and the Concept of Federalism

As discussions about federalism in Iraq often involve scenarios of further fragmentation and partition which some fear will result from decentralization, a few observations will be made initially on how the religious forces among the Shi'is have related to the territorial make-up of the modern state of Iraq historically. Outside observers have frequently accused the Shi'is of harboring ambitions of secession or schemes for a merger with Iran.[9] However, analyses of the behavior of the Shi'is during the most critical phases of Iraq's political history call into question the validity of these contentions. The rebellion in 1920 was mainly anti-British and did not propose any territorial alternative to the Iraqi state which was being established;[10] the Iraqi army with its majority of Shi'i soldiers fought an eight-year-long war with Iran without collapsing internally;[11] and the 1991 uprising in the wake of the Gulf War aimed at political control of the Iraqi state as a whole, and did not suggest any redrawing of its borders.[12]

It is noteworthy too that even in the few instances where a separatist option was in fact given some consideration in Shi'i circles, calls for separation did not receive much popular support among the members of the community. The foremost example of this occurred in 1927 during a sectarian conflict between the Shi'is and the Sunnis. As Shi'is complained about discrimination in the educational system of the country and were wary about the prospects of universal conscription being imple-

---

9   A separatist motive is frequently taken for granted and used as a premise in entire analyses, see for instance Daniel L. Byman, "Divided They Stand: Lessons about Partition from Iraq and Lebanon", *Security Studies*, vol. 7, no. 1 (1997), pp. 1–29, and Masoud Kazemzadeh, "Thinking the Unthinkable: Solving the Problem of Saddam Hussein for Good", *Middle East Policy*, vol. 6, no. 1 (1998), pp. 77–78.

10 Claims about Shi'i separatism in 1920 have sometimes been made on the basis of a quotation from Elie Kedourie which appeared in Amal Vinogradov, "The 1920 Revolt in Iraq Reconsidered", *International Journal of Middle East Studies*, vol. 3 (1972), p. 124, referring to "the establishment of a Shi'a state independent from the rest of Iraq". This is a problematic interpretation, for the original source in fact renders no territorial specificity to the revolt at all, Kedourie limiting his remarks in "Réflexions sur l'histoire du Royaume d'Irak", *Der Orient*, vol. 11 (1959), p. 62, to a demand for a "theocratic government", incidentally based upon an easily available British report. For some examples of how the territorial concept of Iraq was reiterated in proclamations from leading ulama in the early 1920s, see textual excerpts in 'Ali al-Wardi, *Lamahat ijtima'iyya min ta'rikh al-'iraq al-hadith* (Baghdad, 1992 repr.), vol. 6, pp. 201–203. On the other hand, the separatism that did later materialize in the south, to which Kedourie also alluded, was mainly Sunni in origin and of a secular orientation, see Baghdad High Commission Files in the National Archives of India (BHCF) 7/15/3, Abstract of Intelligence, June 25, 1921; Muhammad 'Abd al-Husayn, *Dhikra faysal al-awwal* (Baghdad, 1933), pp. 16–17.

11 Marion Farouk-Sluglett and Peter Sluglett, *Iraq Since 1958. From Revolution to Dictatorship* (London, 1990, paperback edition), p. 258.

12 Yitzhak Nakash, *The Shi'is of Iraq* (Princeton, 1994), pp. 277–278. In many areas in Iraq, suggestions of links to Iran were angrily rejected by Shi'i rebels, see Najib al-Salihi, *Al-zilzal* (London, 1998), pp. 118–120.

mented, a few of their politicians suggested measures of radical devolution or partition as possible ways out of the crisis.[13] Tribal leaders made demands for a reduction of the influence of the state through decentralization (*lamarkaziyya*),[14] ulama of the lower ranks developed their preaching in a pronouncedly sectarian direction, and young intellectuals and religious students endeavored to revive the historical heritage of districts with a Shi'i majority.[15] However, the separatist movement never managed to get off the ground. For years, the traditional religious and universalistic aspects of Shi'i rituals such as Muharram celebrations and re-enactments of the battle of Karbala had managed to capture the public imagination, but the novel phenomenon of sectarian propaganda focusing on a particular territory in central and southern Iraq never became any great success. Equally important, the upper strata of the Shi'i religious clergy remained aloof from the project, some apparently because of their wish to stay out of politics altogether, whereas others disapproved of the sectarian character of the separatist proceedings.[16] As a result, no specifically Islamic justification for the separatist enterprise emerged. One year after its appearance, the project had vanished, largely for lack of popular support. For much of the rest of the twentieth century, separatism among the Shi'is was something which outsiders and the Sunni regimes occasionally would hint about, but little activity of this nature materialized among the Shi'is themselves. To the extent that alternative state models were discussed among the Shi'is, what appeared were new ideological visions (communist, later Islamist) for the established territorial framework of Iraq.

---

13 For a summary of the main events, see Colonial Office, *Report on the Administration of Iraq* (1927), pp. 16–21. This episode has been treated as a parenthesis by the few Shi'i writers who have ventured to mention it at all, such as 'Abd al-Razzaq al-Hasani, who dismissed it as "nonsense" in his *Ta'rikh al-wizarat al-'iraqiyya* (Baghdad, seventh impr., 1988), vol. 2, p. 116. Standard Shi'i accounts of the history of the community in the early twentieth century tend to focus on the anti-British uprising in 1920, as well as the campaign to boycott the elections in the early 1920s, before the onset of a period of "political passivity" is described, see for instance 'Abd al-Halim al-Ruhaymi, *Ta'rikh al-haraka al-islamiyya fi al-'iraq* (Beirut, 1985), pp. 282–283.

14 BHCF 7/15/3, Abstract of Intelligence, July 2, 1927. In addition to the British sources which confirm the picture of an administration highly distrustful of the Shi'is, the most convincing piece of evidence indicating that the new Shi'i approach was not some imperialist intrigue was this appearance of an indigenous term for decentralization.

15 For the background of one of the young participants in this project, see Ja'far al-Khalili, *Hakadha 'araftuhum* (Baghdad, 1963), vol. 2, pp. 51–84.

16 An example of the division between the middle ranking (and politically active) ulama and the paramount *mujtahids* who refrained from intervening in politics in this period is given in BHCF 7/15/3, Abstract of Intelligence, February 18 18, 1928. One of the clerics who refused to get involved with the movement advocating decentralization also warned against certain popular rituals with strong communitarian connotations, see al-Khalili, *Hakadha*, vol. 1, p. 210 and vol. 2, pp. 20–21. For an example of how allegiances to the quietist ulama could become politically relevant, see Werner Ende, "The flagellations of Muharram and the Shi'ite 'ulama' ", *Der Islam*, vol. 55 (1978), pp. 33–34.

Shi'i Views on Federalism during the Build-up to War, 2002–2003

Throughout the 1990s, Kurdish political organizations had formed the most vocal alliance advocating a federal system for a future Iraq. Although some Shi'is – primarily individuals not directly affiliated with any of the main Islamist parties – made certain significant contributions, even pro-federalist Shi'is tend to describe this political vision as something that emerged from Kurdish circles and was subsequently and gradually embraced by other members of the opposition.[17] The Kurdish demand for a two-state federation had been one of several issues which had made the Islamists uneasy with the Iraq National Congress (INC) established in 1992,[18] and it was mainly through this increasingly marginalized organization that the scheme for a federal Iraq survived at all during the 1990s, although certain external figures (including King Husayn of Jordan) played a part in developing a new variant consisting of three rather than two federal units.[19]

However, with the INC's comeback in 2002 as a powerful player in the Iraqi opposition with newly acquired support from conservative decision-makers and think tanks in Washington, the concept of a federal Iraq enjoyed a swift revival. In April, Kurdish factions and US representatives expressed agreement on federalism as a key principle to be applied in a future Iraq,[20] and in the autumn, during a succession of opposition meetings, the slogan of a "democratic, pluralistic and federal Iraq" was cultivated to such an extent that very few speeches devoid of these words were made at the final convention in London.[21] Still, not every school of thought within Iraqi Shi'i Islamism was represented at those conferences: in the following, five main currents among the Shi'i religious parties in relation to a federal Iraq will be identified.

Skepticism towards Federalism

Given the historically marginal position of federalism within Shi'i political debate, it is not surprising that some Shi'i Islamists held strong reservations against the concept as it resurfaced in oppositional circles in 2002, initially in the form of familiar schemes based upon two or three federal units. In April that year, when confronted with a question about "federalism for the north of Iraq", the Iraqi Islamist 'Abd al-Karim al-'Anizi first replied that the Kurds had the right to ask for anything that would enable them to live peacefully within a unified Iraq. However, he also observed that the tendency in the world today was towards integration not towards division, adding that the coexistence between Kurds and Arabs in Iraq was "deep-rooted" and that to propose federalism at the present time would be unsuitable, as

---

17 Information from Muhannad Eshaiker, chairman of a working committee on federalism set up by the exiled opposition in September 2002.
18 *Al-Hayat*, October 29, 1992, p. 6.
19 "Hussein: Divide Iraq along ethnic lines", *Jerusalem Post*, November 1, 1995.
20 "US envoy discusses Iraq in Turkey after talks with Iraqi Kurds", *AFP*, April 5, 2002.
21 "Problems of representation", *Al-Ahram Weekly*, December 19, 2002.

the concept remained in many ways undefined and that present circumstances in Iraq would not allow a proper discussion to take place.[22] Writing in *al-Jihad*, the mouthpiece of the Islamic Da'wa party, Ra'd Ghalib in May 2002 attacked the alleged US policy of "dividing Iraq into three separate entities (*kiyanat munfasila*)" in order to acquire full political control over the country, by attracting office-seekers from the ranks of the opposition to join the project.[23] In June, as a group of Shi'is based in London prepared a declaration of political goals which included decentralization to be applied to the whole country, the same newspaper warned in an editorial against any proposal that would create sectarian or ethnic cantons (*kantunat ta'ifiyya aw qawmiyya*) in Iraq.[24] At the same time, a rival branch of the Da'wa party led by Qasim al-Sahlani reportedly dismissed the federalist scheme as a US-imposed project which lacked legitimacy.[25]

A similar attitude persisted in some quarters as the activities of the Iraqi opposition intensified during the autumn. In November, one writer sympathetic to the Iraqi cleric Sadiq al-Shirazi noted that sections of the opposition were hostile to the project of federalism "which would lead to the division of Iraq into cantons", and thought that all questions concerning decentralization should be postponed until an interim, post-Ba'th administration had been established.[26] The leading article in the newspaper of the Da'wa for December focused on warnings against international forces treating Iraq as a "cake" which they could divide among themselves, splitting it into small zones.[27] Shortly after the opposition conference in London later that month, an article in *al-Mawqif* (also a publication of the Da'wa) referred to federalism as one of the "time bombs" which the US had placed before the Iraqi opposition in order to keep them divided over the many unresolved issues (such as the geographical basis for decentralization, or the degree of decentralization) lurking behind the label of federalism.[28] Uneasiness with the concept of federalism was also evident in the way this term was conspicuously absent in the numerous declarations of aims from circles boycotting the US-sponsored conferences in this period. They used vaguer terms instead, calling for "a suitable political structure for resolving the Kurdish problem" and suggesting the extension of local government to all Iraqi provinces (*muhafazat*, a terminology which corresponded to the administrative units within the existing state structure).[29]

Some protests were evidently connected with the image of federalism as a US-backed project, and as such it was refuted by the considerable segments of the

---

22 Interview published at www.islamicdawaparty.org, around April 2002.
23 *Al-Jihad*, May 27, 2002, p. 2.
24 *Al-Jihad*, June 24, 2002, p. 1.
25 "Mukhattat amriki ja'l al-'iraq jumhuriyya fidiraliyya", www.ebaa.net, May 23, 2002.
26 "Adwa' wa-mulahazat 'ala mu'tamar al-mu'arada...", www.iraq.net, November 11, 2002.
27 *Al-Jihad*, December 2, 2002, p. 1.
28 *Al-Mawqif*, January 2, 2003, p. 3.
29 See for instance the declaration of a splinter group of the Islamic Da'wa dated November 6, 2002, published in *al-Da'wa* no. 1, March, 2003, p. 4.

Islamist opposition which were at variance with the very idea of conferences under foreign, non-Muslim auspices. But also the concept of federalism in itself had been treated with caution by many Islamists throughout the 1990s, and more elaborate and specifically Islamic arguments for this attitude had occasionally emerged. Aversion to federalism had been one element in the list of objections which had led the Da'wa party to issue protests against the INC framework in 1992 and withdraw from the alliance altogether the next year, citing the INC's "confirmation" or "consecration" (*takris*) of sectarian divisions as one of their main grievances.[30] The party had earlier proposed "genuine self-government" (*al-hukm al-dhati al-haqiqi*) as a way of addressing the Kurdish issue,[31] but whatever this undefined term meant, it was evidently something different from the Kurdish plan for federalism that was subsequently presented. Similarly, in 1993, the Shi'i Islamist Sa'id al-Samarra'i had strongly rejected federalism as a future model of government for Iraq because, in his view, this administrative arrangement implied the presence of a fundamental problem of coexistence between the various sects or ethnic groups in Iraq. Samarra'i dismissed this interpretation, and attributed any manifestations of sectarian friction in the country to the manipulations of the regime.[32]

This sort of argument also re-emerged in 2002. The very idea that racial or sectarian divisions should constitute almost insurmountable problems for an Islamic regime requiring special administrative arrangements appeared distasteful to some Islamists, among them Jawad al-'Adhari, who in an interview before the war in 2003 maintained that "there is really no racial or national diversity (*ta'addud 'irqi wa-qawmi*) in Iraq, because everyone belongs to Islam".[33] Motives about Islamic unity also led others to denounce as too overtly sectarian a list of Shi'i political demands (including decentralization) which was prepared during the summer and autumn of 2002.[34]

Given this antipathy for divisions within the Islamic community, many Islamist writers have discouraged decentralization on an ethnic basis, implicitly at least: all Muslims should follow the same rules and regulations (linguistic minorities being provided with the right to use their own language), whereas non-Muslims should be accorded a degree of non-territorial autonomy in community and personal affairs.[35] Sectarian differences, if acknowledged at all, should not be further accentuated by

---

30 *Sawt al-Da'wa*, October 15, 1992, pp. 1–2, December 1, 1992, pp. 2–3 and September 1, 1993, pp. 1 and 3.

31 Hizb al-Da'wa al-Islamiyya, *Barnamajuna* (1992). The term used was the same (minus the modifier "genuine") as the one which designated the autonomy formally conceded to the Kurds by the Ba'th regime.

32 Sa'id al-Samarra'i, *Al-ta'ifiyya fi al-'iraq* (London, 1993), pp. 369–370.

33 Undated interview, www.islamicdawaparty.org.

34 Interview with Muhammad Baqir al-Nasiri in *al-Jihad*, September 23, 2002, p. 4.

35 See for instance Muhammad Mahdi al-Shirazi, *Idha qama al-islam fi al-'iraq* (Kuwait, 1999). It is noteworthy that Shirazi in fact had developed a theory of decentralized government, but did not apply it to this study of Iraq and apparently considered it primarily as a model for a larger, pan-Islamic state, see idem, *Al-fiqh. Kitab al-idara* (Internet edition from www.alshirazi.com), second part, third chapter.

becoming enshrined in the administrative apparatus of the state. Instead, it is sometimes suggested that such differences should be scrutinized by leading clerics of the
various schools of Islamic jurisprudence (*madhhabs*) with a view to resolving them
for the sake of greater unity.[36] Supporters of a process of clerical vetting of all
legislation to ensure conformity with Islamic law may see an additional problem
with a high degree of decentralization, as the suggestion that some local disputes
should require special legislation beyond the capabilities of the leading ulama could
appear antithetical to certain central premises in Shi'i 'Usuli doctrine. When the
universal dichotomy of *mujtahid* versus *muqallid* is the point of departure, there
often follow state models where local government has an essentially administrative,
rather than legislative, character.[37]

But in addition to these distinctively Islamic arguments, Shi'i Islamists critical
to the concept of federalism have frequently resorted to a slogan whose religious
connections are far less obvious. The "unity (*wahda*) of Iraq" has often been presented as an antonym to federalism (and the "division" this term is seen to con-
note), occasionally supported with references to the historic continuity of the country back to the ancient, pre-Islamic civilizations of Mesopotamia (*bilad al-
rafidayn*).[38] Earlier in the 1990s, Shi'i Islamists had used this kind of argument to
reject the idea of erecting a Shi'i entity in the south as a scheme to weaken the Iraqi
regime, claiming that "Iraq as an entity and society has been known for its harmony
and cohesiveness for hundreds of years".[39] In many instances, the focus on an Iraqi
separateness for the Shi'is is accompanied by an assertion of their Arabness,
sometimes to the point where it explicitly excludes connections to non-Arab
influences.[40]

Also the common notion among many Iraqi Islamists that the Iraqi scene may
require special political strategies and solutions because of its religious complexity[41] ultimately takes as its point of departure (and serves to reiterate the legitimacy
of) the territorial framework of the modern state. For, despite the several areas
where Sunnis and Shi'is coexist in local communities, it is really the operation of
endorsing the framework in itself that creates complexity on the macro level and
makes Iraq unique and different from, for instance, Iran. As such, this is an expression of an Islamic solidarity which evidently transcends sectarian borders through
its extension to Sunni Arabs and Kurds, but at the same time it implies a limitation

---

36 'Adil Ra'uf, *Hizb al-da'wa al-islamiyya* (Beirut, 1999), p. 19.
37 For some examples from Iran, see Tajbakhsh, "Political Decentralization", pp. 384–386.
38 *Al-Jihad*, May 27, 2002, p. 2. There are also sometimes references to *bilad al-sawad*
(the name of one of the first Islamic provinces in the area), but in this case the
connection to the particular territorial configuration of modern Iraq is less obvious, as
its core area covered a significantly smaller territory than the contemporary state, with
separate governorates to the north of it for long periods, joined together in a vast Islamic
empire extending far beyond Iraq.
39 *Al-Milaff al-'Iraqi* no. 75 (1998), p. 72.
40 Mustafa Jamal al-Din, *Mihnat al-ahwar wa-al-samt al-'arabi* (London, 1993), pp. 15–
16 and 24–25.
41 Fu'ad Ibrahim, *Al-faqih wa-al-dawla* (Beirut, 1998), p. 356.

of the community, pointing to special relationships between Iraqi Muslims which can form the basis of a separate political scene within the greater Islamic community. Throughout the twentieth century, this current of thought emphatically refused to assume the divisive, sectarian and oil-grabbing role assigned to the Shi'is in certain pessimistic scenarios for Iraqi politics, and instead expressed a degree of pride in Iraq's ethno-religious complexity.

At first, it may seem surprising that Islamists should embrace so much of the rhetoric of their adversaries in Baghdad on this particular issue – for however one chooses to interpret the emergence of modern Iraq, it is difficult to see precisely where the Islamic legitimacy of the particular territorial configuration of the contemporary state derives from. Whereas Iraq as a geographical region was well known in the early twentieth century, it usually connoted an area considerably smaller than the modern state, roughly covering the Ottoman provinces of Basra and Baghdad only,[42] and with a history of subdivision into discrete administrative units also before the Ottomans. An emerging group of Iraqi nationalists, on the other hand, laid claim to a much wider area, extending to Dayr al-Zur (in present-day Syria) and to Diyarbakir (in modern Turkey).[43] Most of the actions which led to the creation of a medium-sized state fitting neither of these two visions exactly are usually attributed to British and French political officers.[44] Although Shi'i Iraqi historiography in the twentieth century did establish the notion of the Shi'is themselves as the "founders of the Iraqi state" by virtue of their role in the 1920 anti-British uprising,[45] the strong attachment to this particular territorial structure among Shi'i Islamists remains quite remarkable.[46]

In some contexts, the recourse to the label of unity has the appearance of a tactic to avoid criticism from a repressive regime that would otherwise be seen by international actors as the sole guarantor of regional stability.[47] In other cases, the defense of the established state seems to be a result of a dose of nationalism having entered the Islamist thinking in the shape of essentialist notions of "the Iraqi people" – as when it is claimed (in the context of Iranian interference in Shi'i Iraqi af-

---

42 *Lughat al-'Arab*, vol. 2 (1912–13), pp. 4–5. The objective here is not to reiterate the misleading idea that "Iraq" as a geographical concept was somehow absent from the vocabulary of the region in the early twentieth century, merely to suggest that the area it connoted was usually seen to be somewhat smaller than the state which eventually emerged under this designation. Contemporary Shi'i authors also used the name, see for instance entry no. 1086 for 'Adnan Shubbar al-Musawi in Muhammad Muhsin Aga Buzurg, *Al-dhari'a ila tasanif al-shi'a* (Internet edition from www.ahl-ul-bayt.org), vol. 8.

43 *King-Crane Commission Report*, August 28, 1919, section on "Mesopotamia".

44 The less well-known aspect of this process, the demarcation of the border between Syria and Iraq, is covered in Eliezer Tauber, *The Formation of Modern Syria and Iraq* (Ilford, 1995).

45 See for instance Faysal al-Khazraji, "Al-'iraq. Al-madhabiyya wa-da'awa al-taqsim", *al-Mawsim*, vol. 14 (1993), pp. 9–10.

46 There is an interesting parallel in the Lebanese Hizbullah's preoccupation with the Shaba'a farms.

47 *Al-Jihad*, May 27, 2002, p. 2.

fairs) that "the nature of the Iraqi mind rejects any intervention or supervision in Iraqi matters".[48] However, during the course of the twentieth century, several Shi'i thinkers developed different theoretical frameworks which in various ways lend support to the established state system in specifically religious terms. Many of these emerged historically as resistance to larger, pan-Islamic schemes, but in practice they may have contributed to the marked preoccupation with the "unity" of the existing states.

One example of this is 'Adil Ra'uf's theory of local leadership and the "bonds of the leader to the locality" (*'alaqat al-qa'id bi-al-makan*).[49] Ra'uf (who writes in sympathetic terms about the Da'wa movement) ascribes positive Islamic values to both local leadership and nationalism. Life-long connections with a particular territory will give an individual – the "son of the place" (*ibn al-makan*) – a special sort of attachment to the people of this area and their problems, a factor especially important in the context of modern nation-states and the conditions they impose on the work of the ulama. Iraq is seen as being particularly affected by this historical situation: its holy cities remain a center for the traditional internationalist Shi'i order, and some of the foremost clerics therefore pay more attention to matters concerning their followers elsewhere in the world, leaving the country as a sort of giant capital district in this international system without any leadership specifically devoted to itself. But while the point of departure for several writers quoted by Ra'uf is respect for the merits of attachment to a particular clan or tribe or even locality, the conclusion relates to the (established) national level; that there is a need for Iraqi Islamists to stress their national (Iraqi) identity, and the leadership of ulama hailing from "outside Iraq" (in this case, Iran) is criticized. In this manner, legitimacy is bestowed upon an Islamic leadership model that would replicate and perpetuate the existing state system, rather than challenge it.

Also some leading ulama highly respected by the Da'wa have published theoretical works and made public statements which tend to sanction not only the existing state system, but also the unitary structure of the established political entities. In the writings of Muhammad Husayn Fadl Allah (a Lebanese cleric born in Iraq), the pan-Islamic state belongs to a distant future, and the focus is on finding legitimate arrangements for the present situation. Fadl Allah subscribes to a pluralistic variant of the system of *wilayat al-faqih*, allowing for the emergence of multiple *fuqaha'* (plural of *faqih*) as individual representatives of the Hidden Imam (by inferring from the fact that the imams had numerous representatives before the age of the *ghayba*), and views the competition between several sources of spiritual emulation as something which can have a distinctively positive and vitalizing effect on the Islamic community.[50] Although his discussions of political leadership do not

---

48 Fa'iq al-Shaykh 'Ali, *Ightiyal sha'b* (London, 2000), p. 335.

49 'Adil Ra'uf, *'Iraq bi-la qiyada* (Damascus, 2002), pp. 413–427.

50 Salah al-Khurasan, *Hizb al-da'wa al-islamiyya* (Damascus, 1999), p. 420; Muhammad al-Husayni, "Al-takyif al-dusturi li-shakl al-dawla al-islamiyya", *al-Fikr al-Jadid*, vol. 11–12 (1996); Keiko Sakai, "Modernity and Tradition in the Islamic Movements of Iraq", *Arab Studies Quarterly,* vol. 23, no. 1 (2001), p. 43.

explicitly attribute any particular significance to the existing state system, Fadl Allah's statements on issues such as federalism and decentralization, both in Lebanese and in Iraqi contexts, indicate that it is precisely the Middle Eastern states which emerged after the First World War that stand to profit from his pluralistic views. In the early 1990s, when some politicians advocated radical decentralization as a way of solving the political crisis of Lebanon, Fadl Allah lauded those who worked against federalism and the "partition" he saw as its logical conclusion.[51] Again, on the eve of the Iraq War in 2003, he expressed misgivings about a future federal system for the post-Ba'th era. Equating it with partition, he warned against instability that would follow Kurdish separatism, rejected the idea of introducing sectarian divisions, and denounced supporters of the project as "the opposition of exiles".[52]

Several of the Shi'i thinkers quoted so far in this section belong to a common current within Shi'i Islamism. Many are or have been members of the Da'wa party or its splinter factions.[53] Originally a pan-Islamic movement with members in countries from Lebanon to the Gulf, the Da'wa acquired a specifically Iraqi character during the 1980s after a failed Iranian attempt to establish full political control of the organization and its large number of adherents now living in exile in the Islamic Republic.[54] Disagreements about the validity and the correct interpretation of the concept of *wilayat al-faqih* were a key source of dissent and gave rise to some of the early divisions of the party.[55] Debate about the extent to which the Da'wa should be incorporated into Iranian governmental structures continued in the 1990s, and new defections followed in 1998 as a branch based in Europe emerged victorious in a power struggle against circles favoring closer links with Teheran.[56]

The activist Iraqi cleric Muhammad Baqir al-Sadr, executed by the Ba'th regime in 1980, is represented by the members of this movement (many of whom are themselves laymen) as the ideal religious leader for the Shi'is, a figure with the ability to direct the community through active interference in politics. The leadership gap created by Sadr's assassination was exacerbated by the fact that some potential successors left the movement in the 1980s over controversies of *wilayat al-faqih*, an issue on which Sadr had taken an intermediate position stressing the idea of the accountability of the *faqih* and contemplating the prospect for collec-

---

51 Interview in *Monday Morning*, May 13, 1991, p. 15.
52 Interview in *al-Shira'*, March 17, 2003, and transcript of interview from al-'Arabiyya Television, March 23, 2003, www.bayynat.org.lb.
53 Sadiq al-Shirazi, another individual mentioned above, remained independent in organizational terms. On this cleric and his better-known brother, the late Muhammad al-Shirazi, see "Al-marja'iyya al-shi'iyya ba'da rahil al-shirazi", *al-Sharq al-Awsat*, December 27, 2001.
54 Abdul-Halim al-Ruhaimi, "The Da'wa Islamic Party: Origins, Actors and Ideology", in Faleh Abdul-Jabar (ed.), *Ayatollahs, Sufis and Ideologues* (London, 2002), p. 159.
55 Al-Khurasan, *Hizb al-da'wa*, pp. 409–423.
56 *Al-Milaff al-'Iraqi* no. 77 (1998), p. 51 and no. 81 (1998), pp. 44–45.

tive religious leadership.[57] In the 1990s, when many Iraq-based clerics followed a quietist line, substantial numbers of Da'wa members began to look to the above-mentioned Fadl Allah in Beirut for guidance instead.[58] The main Da'wa faction boycotted the US-sponsored conferences during 2002, but, as will be seen in the subsequent sections, some of its leading members tentatively started to grapple with the issue of federalism in a more conciliatory fashion towards the end of the year. The party's apparent uneasiness with the concept of *wilayat al-faqih*[59] should in theory make them more receptive to some sort of pluralistic arrangement in Iraq, but there is also much to suggest that many in this camp remained reluctant to contemplate any scheme that might be seen as constituting a threat to the "unity of Iraq".

Federalism as a Matter outside the Domain of the Ulama

Another important school of thought within Shi'ism was much less explicit with regard to the federalism project in the period under investigation. However, by virtue of their silence on the issue, and the conservatism of the few public statements they made that related to the state structure of Iraq, they effectively withheld the support of a significant body of Shi'i opinion from the federalist project.

In general, the more traditionalist ulama among the Shi'is tend to devote their attention to matters less directly connected with the particular structures of the modern state. For instance, one issue which brought the grand *mujtahid* 'Ali al-Sistani into the public limelight to some extent in 2002 was the question of which date to be reckoned as the first of the holy month of Ramadan – a decision based upon the lunar calendar and the appearance of the crescent moon. Because of controversies regarding the means of establishing the first appearance of the crescent moon (visual sightings by the unaided eye versus astronomical calculations) as well as the fact that the timing will differ according to the geographical location of the observer, different dates for commencing the fast sometimes occur in different countries. In 2002, Sistani declared November 6 to be the first day of Ramadan, while Iranian authorities officially announced that the fast should start on November 7. Despite the differences, Sistani issued a public statement through his spokesman in Teheran, and many of his *muqallids* in Iran heeded the advice and started the fast one day earlier than the Iranian regime had recommended.[60]

On the other hand, Sistani's public pronouncements with regard to the war in Iraq in 2003 were far more guarded. Both a declaration in support of the Ba'th re-

---

57 For slightly different interpretations of Sadr's emphasis, see Joyce N. Wiley, *The Islamic Movement of Iraqi Shi'as* (Boulder, 1992), pp. 125–128, 132–135, and 'Ali al-Mu'min, *Sanawat al-jamr. Masirat al-haraka al-islamiyya fi al-'iraq, 1957–1986* (London, 1993), pp. 380–381.

58 On Fadl Allah's influence, see Sakai, "Modernity".

59 *Iraqi Issues*, vol. 2, no. 2 (1994), p. 2.

60 "Al-iraniyyun yasumuna al-khamis", www.islamonline.net, November 6, 2002.

gime attributed to Sistani but read out by a little known cleric,[61] as well as subsequent US attempts to claim that the coalition forces had some sort of backing from Sistani have been questioned or repudiated by his supporters.[62] The few public statements Sistani made during the war were of a cautious and conservative nature, for instance when he essentially reiterated the existing administrative map of Iraq in its smallest detail when he called for the establishment of committees to take care of public affairs "in every province (*muhafaza*), district (*qada'*) and subdistrict (*nahiyya*)" of the country.[63] His traditionalism was also evident in warnings to the Shi'is against trying to alter the sectarian map of Iraq in territorial terms through forcefully taking control of Sunni mosques.[64] Later, one of Sistani's representatives publicly referred to the *mujtahid*'s intention not to interfere in the process of devising a post-Ba'th regime,[65] and Sistani advised other members of the clergy against taking up government positions, outlining a more limited role for the ulama where any forays into politics should be confined to advisory functions of a more general nature.[66]

A similar attitude to state power could be discerned in some of the statements of the late 'Abd al-Majid al-Khu'i, a son of the former grand *marja'* Abu al-Qasim al-Khu'i, although the son, as will be seen later, had a rather more complex attitude to politics than the father. In an interview in November 2002, he sidestepped the federalism debate by declaring that the question of whether the state should be unitary or decentralized was of secondary importance only. In his opinion, the issues that mattered most were to safeguard the traditional autonomy of the religious institutions as well as the right of Shi'is everywhere to be able to take matters relating to personal status law to Shi'i courts – both clearly demands of an intrinsically non-territorial character.[67] Khu'i also made it clear that not even "a Shi'i government" should have the right to interfere with the religious colleges and places of worship. On this particular occasion he thus reproduced much of the spirit of his father, who had also been Sistani's teacher. But when the political struggle in Najaf intensified in April 2003 as the Iraqi regime disintegrated, Khu'i became deeply involved in local administrative affairs and it was Sistani who maintained the quietist position, in the words of one local cleric, "closing the door behind himself and refusing to talk to the people".[68] Just as in 1927, a significant figure in the religious hierarchy thus made himself unavailable for others who were seeking religious legitimacy for altering the existing state structures.

The theoretical foundation for this rather apolitical position and the unwillingness to interfere directly in formulating the structures of government

---

61 "Shi'at al-'iraq yarfiduna al-ghazw", *al-Nahar*, March 26, 2003.
62 Declaration (*bayan*), www.seestani.com, April 2, 2003; *al-Hayat*, April 4, 2003, p. 1.
63 *Al-Hayat*, April 20, 2003, p. 3.
64 "Al-sistani yuharrimu intiza' al-jawami' ", *al-Sharq al-Awsat*, May 3, 2003.
65 *Al-Wifaq*, May 10, 2003, p.1.
66 "Al-sistani fi fatwa jadida – tahdid dawr al-'ulama' ", *al-Zaman*, June 1, 2003.
67 Interview, *al-Zaman*, November 28, 2002.
68 *Al-Hayat*, April 11, 2003, p. 6.

relates to the basic problem of legitimacy in the age of the *ghayba* noted above. In this regard it is of considerable significance that Sistani, as the scholarly heir to Khu'i, refrained from offering public support for the federalist project during the crucial transitional period in the spring of 2003. In the early 1990s, several individuals affiliated with or working through the media channels of the Khu'i Foundation in London had pioneered schemes for an Iraqi federation in Shi'i circles, and there has been some speculation about Khu'i himself having been a supporter of a new, more activist orientation, possibly also involving a greater emphasis on the Shi'i heartland in a territorial sense.[69] Whatever the reality was with respect to the association of Khu'i with these initiatives, Sistani subsequently directed the quietist camp back into a more non-interventionist position, which it maintained during the first weeks of the US occupation of Iraq.[70] Reports of friction between the foundation and Sistani over the past years may corroborate the interpretation of a growing political divergence between the two.[71]

In early 2003, 'Ali al-Sistani was considered to be the *marja'* with the largest numbers of followers worldwide, with many of the *muqallid*s of the former grand *marja'* Khu'i (who died in 1992) having transferred their allegiance to him during the 1990s.[72] The traditionalist trend he represents and its refusal to extend support to Khomeini's theory of government had been a problem for the Islamic Republic throughout the 1990s, especially after 1994 when 'Ali Khamenei tried to gain influence as a *marja'* by officially announcing his candidature but failed to prevail in competition with Sistani. Despite harsh measures against him by the Iraqi authorities, Sistani managed to stay on in Najaf, and maintained his status as the pre-eminent *mujtahid*. Given his ascendancy to this level within the Shi'i hierarchy, it is natural that Sistani's priorities have taken on a markedly internationalist character, where the aim has been to facilitate contacts with his vast number of *muqallid*s in different countries rather than engage in work to change or overturn the governing structures in any of the states his followers live in. The 'Usuli tradition has historically established itself as a powerful *modus operandi* for the most eminent ulama, enabling this sort of progress without forcing them to enter into intimate relationships with the existing state structures. From this position, they have, according to one Shi'i cleric, "what the states do not have – the rule over the hearts".[73]

As a consequence of his growing number of supporters, Sistani also established offices staffed by personal representatives in major cities worldwide, including

---

69 For an interesting interpretation along such lines see Jens-Uwe Rahe, "Irakische Schiiten im Londoner Exil", *al-Rafidayn*, vol. 4 (1996), pp. 119–134 (particularly p. 127) and p. 148.

70 As will be seen in the final part of the chapter, some interesting (and potentially highly significant) tendencies to increased activism on the part of Sistani materialized in the late spring of 2003.

71 "Maqtal al-khu'i", www.aljazeera.net, April 16, 2003; report from *al-Ra'y al-'Amm*, April 11, 2003, published by Foreign Broadcast Information Service (FBIS).

72 "Hawzat al-najaf tatahaffazu li-isti'adat dawriha al-marja'i", *al-Hayat*, February 4, 2003.

73 "Hal yumkinu li-rijal al-din hukm al-'iraq", *al-Sharq al-Awsat*, April 18, 2003.

Teheran, Beirut, London and Damascus. Despite the problems he posed for the Iranian regime by showing no enthusiasm for *wilayat al-faqih,* he was able to expand his institutional presence in Qum and other parts of Iran throughout the 1990s, where his popular influence was too strong to be ignored completely by the regime.[74] In Iraq, he had an institutional base in schools considered close to him (such as the Religious University of Najaf)[75] and reportedly enjoyed a high standing among several of the important Shi'i tribes. By contrast, Sistani's position among the urban masses appeared less consolidated, and when his personal safety was threatened by hostile armed gangs after the breakdown of government authority in Najaf in April 2003, it was reportedly tribesmen from areas along the Euphrates who intervened to guarantee the security of the grand *mujtahid.*[76] Ever since the murder of Muhammad Baqir al-Sadr, there have been calls from more radical Shi'i opinion in Iraq for some of the ulama to step in to take up his political agenda, but for Sistani both doctrinal convictions as well as the prospect of his religious prestige worldwide becoming tarnished by too much politics may have discouraged him from following Sadr's path or from engaging in the battle over spoils in a future, post-Ba'th Iraq. The supporters of federalism are another Shi'i group who failed to benefit from his public support in the first half of 2003.

"Administrative" Federalism

For most of the 1990s, the debate about a future federal Iraq focused on federalism as a device to address "the Kurdish issue" in Iraqi politics. Among the INC, the prevailing view was that radical decentralization was offered as a "concession" to the Kurds to ensure their participation in the opposition effort.[77] During the same period, the leading Shi'i Islamist parties remained on the sidelines of the INC platform, with federalism forming one of the principles they were critical about, and only a few leading clerics (among them Muhammad 'Ali Bahr al-'Ulum) became regular participants in the INC's political work.[78]

However, among exiles in London, a new current of thought gradually started to emerge, emphasizing federalism as an arrangement which all segments of the Iraqi

---

74 For examples of his activities in Iran, see the booklet *Lamha 'an nashat maktab samahat ayat allah al-'uzma al-sayyid al-sistani* (published by 'Ali al-Dabbagh, n.d.). Several Iran-based Internet sites, such as www.rafed.net, contributed to spreading Sistani's scholarship and legal opinions. Even Iranian diplomatic missions abroad extended a degree of recognition to Sistani by listing him as one of the clerics whose legal rulings could be consulted through reference to Iranian embassies, such as the one in Canada (website at www.salamiran.org).

75 "Centuries on, Shiites still Divided about Role in Political Life", *AFP*, May 3, 2003. For the history of this institution, see 'Ali Ahmad al-Bahadli, *Al-hawza al-'ilmiyya fi al-najaf* (Beirut, 1993), pp. 337–341 and pp. 356–357.

76 *Al-Hayat*, April 15, 2003, p. 3 and April 24, 2003, p. 3.

77 See for instance INC, "The Democratic Opposition Reaffirms the Fight against Saddam", statement by Ahmad Chalabi, March 10, 1997.

78 Chibli Mallat, "Muhammad Bahr al-'Ulum", *Orient*, vol. 34, no. 3 (1993), pp. 342–345.

community (including the Shi'is themselves) could profit from. This group, some of whose members had connections to religious institutions and also Islamist circles, attributed inherently positive qualities to federalism instead of viewing it as an obstacle to Islamic unity or a prelude to the partition of Iraq. The Khu'i Foundation (whose leading figure himself often tended to eschew the debate over the particular shape of a future Iraqi government, as discussed above) offered space in their publications to thinkers who envisioned a post-Ba'th Iraq where federalism would be applied to the entire country, not only the Kurdish north. A distinctive feature of most of these proposals was the emphasis on an "administrative" form of federalism, a term used in slightly different ways by different writers but almost invariably stressing that ethno-religious geography should not form the basis for demarcating the constituent units in a future federal system.[79] Moreover, this regime should be applied to the whole of Iraq on an equal basis, thus roughly corresponding to the notions of "congruous" or "symmetric" federalism sometimes used in political theory literature. Again, the prospect of a comprehensive devolution of powers to local authorities – in one of the schemes encompassing almost every sphere of government except foreign policy – meant that these schemes were highly consistent with (and to a certain degree probably inspired by) principles of federalism in the traditions of Western political thought.

It was this second model of federalism which received increased interest also among Shi'i Islamists in 2002. In a declaration of the political goals of the Shi'is of Iraq, several Islamists, including some who had explicitly warned against federalism previously, now joined a cross-political Shi'i alliance to call for decentralization (*lamarkaziyya*) to be applied in any new system of government for Iraq.[80] The signatories of the document highlighted decentralization as a means to prevent the concentration of power and public services in the capital, and referred to it as a mechanism for devolving considerable powers in the legislative, executive and judicial branches of government to the provinces. As in the case of the early federalist initiatives outlined above, the willingness to cede sovereignty from the central to the provincial level in a number of administrative spheres indicated a wish to carry out to the letter the "federal" dimension (this term was used in the authorized English translation), although the Arabic word *lamarkaziyya* is more multi-vocal and historically has been used also to describe local government in systems which according to Western criteria would appear to be unitary in essence (including Egypt, Morocco and Qatar).[81] Finally, the initiators also pointed out that

---

79 *Dialogue* (February 1992), pp. 2–3; *Iraqi Issues*, vol. 1, no. 4 (1992), pp. 4–6; Ali Allawi, "Federalism" in Fran Hazelton (ed.), *Iraq Since the Gulf War* (London, 1994), pp. 211–222; Laith Kubba, *The Plight of the Shi'a of Iraq* (London, n.d.). "Administrative federalism" is thus employed in this context in a manner which differs somewhat from the specialized usage of the term often encountered in political science studies.

80 "I'lan shi'at al-'iraq", www.iraqishia.com, December 17, 2002.

81 Arab writers sometimes distinguish between political (*siyasi*) and administrative (*idari*) decentralization, and these two terms often correspond to the dichotomy between a federal and a unitary state structure as employed in Western terminology. The use of terms

the basis for drawing new provincial borders should not be "sectarian" criteria ("which could be the first step towards a partition of Iraq into small statelets") but rather "demographic, administrative, and geographical" characteristics.

A similar attitude prevailed among the few Shi'i Islamists who participated in the US-backed symposia held in the autumn of 2002 to address issues related to a transition to a new regime in Iraq. Only one Shi'i with a background as an active front figure in the Islamist movement, Muhammad 'Abd al-Jabbar, participated in the workshop devoted to federalism issues, but another Islamist, former Da'wa member and now independent Muwaffaq al-Rubay'i, also made a contribution to the discussions on the subject. Their visions for federalism coincided roughly with the views of other Shi'is in this forum: generally agreeing on federalism for the entire country as well as a medium number of provinces (five to seven), they managed to prevent a reiteration of the traditional, tripartite projection of Iraq and the concomitant accusations of sectarianism and separatism.[82] Some of the Islamist proponents of federalism had earlier written theoretical pieces which emphasized the necessity of the state for the Shi'is, and the virtues of establishing a "humanistic state" (*dawlat al-insan*) as an improvement over an authoritarian regime in a context when political circumstances prevent the creation of an Islamic state.[83] Nevertheless, arguments directly stemming from Islamist political theory apparently did not come to the forefront in this debate.

In addition to Muhammad Bahr al-'Ulum, who had already embraced a federalist vision through his association with the INC in the 1990s, several exiled clerics (including such central figures of Shi'i milieus in London as Husayn al-Sadr and

---

such as "administrative federalism/decentralization" (*al-fidiraliyya/al-lamarkaziyya al-idariyya*) can therefore potentially give rise to different interpretations, as the emphasis on "administrative" used by some writers to underline the "non-political" criteria for demarcating the federal units rather than to qualify the degree of devolution, can by others be seen as a concession to a state logic which is essentially unitary in spirit.

82 Majmu'at 'Amal al-Mabadi' al-Dimuqratiyya, *Taqrir 'an al-tahawwul ila al-dimuqratiyya fi al-'iraq* (2002), p. 3, n. 1, appendix, pp. 118 and 184–195; Muhammad 'Abd al-Jabbar, "Al-mu'arada al-'iraqiyya", www.aljazeera.net, January 3, 2003; *al-Nahar*, November 9, 2002, p. 10.

83 See for instance Muhammad 'Abd al-Jabbar, "Afkar awwaliyya hawla al-dawla... wa-al-dawla-al-islamiyya", *Qadaya 'Iraqiyya*, vol. 1, no. 11 (1993), pp. 12–15. In this contribution, the problem of political legitimacy in the age of *ghayba* is de-emphasized, and the specifically Shi'i arguments for the necessity of the state and the basis for its ideal form are to a large extent drawn from the Islamic experience prior to the disappearance of the Twelfth Imam, in addition to eclectic quotations from Muhammad Baqir al-Sadr in which the principle of consultation (*shura*) more generally is highlighted, with less attention to the controversy over the clerical role in government. 'Abd al-Jabbar had also suggested in the 1990s that decentralization "and possibly federalism" might become relevant in a new state structure for Iraq, (in this context presented without elaborations on Islamic political theory), "Min ajl hall watani dimuqrati shamil li-mushkilat al-shi'a fi al-'iraq", *al-Mawsim*, vol. 14 (1993), pp. 45–47.

Husayn al-Shami) joined this body of opinion during the course of 2002.[84] Many had attained influential positions among Iraqi Shi'is in exile, but they did not have the same number of followers as the leading *mujtahid*s of the holy cities of Iraq or Iran.[85] The pronouncedly more active political approach during the final months before the war in 2003 of 'Abd al-Majid al-Khu'i, whose position is also discussed in the previous section, drew him and the Khu'i Foundation closer to this group, and his participation in the opposition meetings gave the impression of acquiescence, at least, with regard to the concept of federalism.[86] A number of the Islamists who joined the calls for administrative decentralization in 2002 were professionals with a secular education who had been members of the Da'wa but later left the organization, including a former member of the political leadership of the party, Sami al-'Askari. Now styling themselves "independent Islamists", many subsequently developed closer links with the INC, joined the follow-up committee to the London conference, and signaled an interest in participating in the new governmental structures that would emerge in a future Iraq.[87]

It is significant that, despite the objections already discussed, some active members of the main branch of the Da'wa also began to express more interest in the federalism concept towards the end of 2002. In an Iranian television interview in December, Abu Bilal al-Adib described federalism as "acceptable" but warned against decentralization in a "nationalist, geographic" sense (*al-fidiraliyya bi-al-ma'na al-qawmi al-jughrafi*) as this would serve Israel's interest by creating divisions and small and weak statelets, unable to defend themselves, "just like the Gulf states".[88] Another Da'wa leader indicated that they might agree to federalism in the future, but that the main issue was to avoid any administrative arrangement that would threaten "the unity of the country".[89] Like many proponents of the theory of "administrative" federalism, these Da'wa leaders refrained from elaborating on explicitly Islamic arguments in favor of this model of government and did not venture to incorporate it directly into a more fully-fledged vision of an Islamic political system. On the other hand, some of the other new enthusiasts for federalism who emerged among the Iraqi Islamists in 2002 had earlier developed detailed

---

84 "Madha yuridu shi'at al-'iraq min mu'tamar al-mu'arada al-'iraqiyya?" and "Khalil zadah yu'akkidu: al-'iraq satataharrraru...", www.iraq.net, December 12 and 15, 2002 respectively.

85 For Shami, see Rahe, "Irakische Schiiten", pp. 64–66.

86 It is important in this regard to stress the essential difference between Khu'i the grand *mujtahid* and, by the time of his death in 1992, the *marja'* of a majority of the world's Shi'is, and the Khu'i Foundation, led by his son who never approximated his father's standing from the point of view of religious learning, and was in any circumstances far too young to aspire to such a position which requires decades of scholarly study and practice.

87 "22 mu'aridan 'iraqiyyan yahtalluna manasib istishariyya fi al-mu'aqqata" from *al-Watan* (Kuwait), published at www.nahrain.com, April 16, 2003.

88 Interview with Iran 2 Television, December 2002, transcript from www.daawaparty.com.

89 Jawad al-Maliki interview, Sahr Television, December 24, 2002, www.daawaparty.com.

paradigms for Islamic government where decentralization might fit in, although these ideas had originally been formed in an altogether different context.

Federalism as an Element in Larger Islamist Schemes

A gradual reversal in attitude towards federalism seemed manifest in the public statements of the Supreme Council for the Islamic Revolution in Iraq (SCIRI) during 2002. Although its leaders had not been as vehemently hostile to the idea of a federation as other Islamists during the 1990s, and indeed on certain occasions had signaled a degree of conditional acceptance of such a scheme,[90] still in 1997 one of its leading members in a historical analysis described "Shi'i demands for decentralization for the Shi'i areas" as a "fabricated accusation" which had to be refuted.[91] Furthermore, for most of the 1990s, SCIRI's participation within INC (widely seen as the main promoter of the federal scheme) remained low-level and reluctant, and at the end of the decade SCIRI was still refusing to participate in US-sponsored conferences where the INC had a prominent role.[92]

Much of this appeared to have changed by the summer of 2002, when 'Abd al-'Aziz al-Hakim, a prominent figure in SCIRI and the brother of its spiritual leader Muhammad Baqir, said that they would have no problems with federalism for all of Iraq if that proved to be the choice of the people. In support of this position, he referred to the fact that "administrative (*idari*) federalism" was working in Switzerland, the US, India and Pakistan and consequently there was nothing to prevent its application in Iraq.[93] A virtually identical answer was given to the Sawt al-Thawra al-Islamiyya Radio (broadcasting from Iran for an audience inside Iraq) a few days later, on this occasion specifically rejecting "ethnic" or "sectarian" federalism, and repeating the same examples of successful systems based on federal principles worldwide.[94] However, no expressly Islamic justification was presented for this particular choice of state model.

On other occasions, leading SCIRI members went further, presenting federalism as something distinctively positive for Iraq. Far from being seen as a product imported from abroad, it was rendered as a system of government not only compatible with Islamic principles, but in fact with firm roots in the Middle East. This interpretation of federalism, suggesting that the idea had long been present in the region, had already been discernible in some of the debates on Kurdish autonomy in the early 1990s. At that time, the term "the rule of the provinces" (*hukm al-wilayat*) had been employed to demonstrate that Kurdish aspirations could be preserved by

---

90 'Adil Ra'uf, *Al-'amal al-islami fi al-'iraq bayna al-marja'iyya wa-al-hizbiyya* (Damascus, 2000), pp. 327–329; interview with Muhammad Baqir al-Hakim, *al-Hayat*, April 1, 1996.

91 Hamid al-Bayati, *Shi'at al-'iraq bayna al-ta'ifiyya wa-al-shubhat* (London, 1997), pp. 6, 229–236.

92 *Al-Milaff al-'Iraqi* no. 85 (1999), p. 25; *al-Hayat*, October 29, 1999, p. 10.

93 *Al-Hayat*, August 13, 2002, p. 2.

94 Transcript of press conference held by Hakim on August 19, 2002, www.al-hakim.com.

resorting to traditional, Islamic solutions with which the Iraqis had been acquainted "during the period of Islamic rule".[95] A variant of this emerged again in 2002, when a leading SCIRI official maintained that the system in use in Ottoman times and "during the rule of the previous Islamic government" could be brought into place again in Iraq as a system of federalism for the whole country.[96]

Here it should be pointed out that these references to an Islamic system of provincial government represent reclassifications of historical experiences (of a rather revisionist character)[97] rather than a development or refinement of Islamic theories for decentralized government, and they do not address some of the doctrinally problematic issues of Shi'ism and state power. It is also interesting that this official referred to the rule of the caliphs. By reportedly stating that "Iraq in the past was made up of wulias of Baghdad, Basra and Kufa" he was apparently going back to Abbasid times rather than to the period before Baghdad's foundation and the rule of 'Ali, whose regime has more unquestionable Shi'i connotations. On the other hand, the later caliphate – historically a central symbol of the usurpation of the rule of the imams – is overshadowed (and in practice replaced) in Shi'i political theory by the debates over the deputyship of the Hidden Imam and its legitimate forms. With regard to this rendition of federalism, the potential for skepticism or accusations of fudge (whether from doubters of the historical reinterpretation presented or from Shi'i theoreticians) therefore remains considerable, although antisectarian, ecumenist readings could also be perfectly plausible.

Given the heritage of the Islamic revolution in Iran and the closeness of SCIRI to circles where radical renewal of Shi'i political theory had taken place since the 1960s, it is somewhat remarkable that these Islamists refrained from a more vigorous public effort to link their political visions to less controversial sources of Islamic legitimacy. Instead, they reinvented the Ottomans as great defenders of the faith and referred to the successes of various non-Muslim countries in building

---

95 *Sawt al-Da'wa*, December 1, 1992, p. 6. Some of the ambiguity about federalism was preserved in an official statement released by the political committee of the INC after the Salah al-Din conference in 1992, where "federal system" (rendered first as *al-nizam al-fidirali*) was accompanied by a parenthesis which added "[system of] provinces" (*wilayat*), possibly to make it semantically more palatable to the many Islamists who had objected to "federalism", see INC, *Al-waraqa al-siyasiyya, salah al-din* (1992).

96 Transcript of a discussion held at the American University Center for Global Peace Forum, Federal News Service, June 8, 2002.

97 The most substantial – as well as voluntary – examples of devolution within the Ottoman Empire had been in the shape of corporate rather than territorial autonomy, accorded to the recognized non-Muslim communities. On the other hand, decentralization in territorial terms had tended to emerge after international intervention (as in Lebanon and Egypt) or as negotiated settlements or tacit concords which limited the state's intervention in peripheral zones where its resources were limited (seen in parts of Syria and Arabia). Some analyses of earlier Islamic history describe tendencies to devolution beyond the mere delegation and decentralization of power associated with a unitary state structure as something which was harmful to the interests of the Islamic state, and led to the decline of the caliphate and the emergence of independent states outside its authority, Mas'ud Ahmad Mustafa, *Aqalim al-dawla al-islamiyya* (Cairo, 1990).

federal systems. However, quite apart from the numerous press briefings and conferences held in 2002 and 2003, the leader of SCIRI had also published papers on his views on forms of Islamic government where concepts such as "provinces", "decentralization" and even "federalism" and "confederalism" (the latter as loan words) were used in a wider, more theoretical context. In these writings, decentralization appears as a perfectly integral feature of an Islamic government, although it is not a system in which Baghdad is necessarily the ultimate capital.

A fundamental premise in Hakim's contributions from the 1990s is a belief in the concept of *wilayat al-faqih* and its institutionalization in the form of a paramount *faqih* for all Muslims in the world. In matters of central importance to the Islamic community as a whole (examples include strategy towards Israel, how to confront international hegemonies and how to face up to challenges from the West in the cultural sphere), the decision of the *faqih* is not to be contested, whereas matters of detail (*tafasil*) can be delegated to local governments (*wilayat mahalliyya*) in a decentralized (*lamarkaziyya*) system.[98] It is thus essentially a hierarchical system, in which reference to the supreme leader (*wali amr al-muslimin*, a term which supporters of the Islamic revolution in Iran use synonymously with the office of the ruling *faqih*) is required in a number of contexts. Hakim's texts also highlight the similarities between this system and the historical experience of the Islamic state in the "system of provinces" (*nizam al-wilayat*), as well as the resemblance to "federalism or confederalism" in the Western world in modern times.

Iraq has a place within this system as a region (*iqlim*), and positive values are ascribed to regional and local political leadership within the bounds of the larger system. Even within the unified Islamic community, one should "not deny the particular nature of the various peoples of this [larger Islamic] community with regard to their political problems and cultural circumstances".[99] Moreover, Hakim's vision of a pan-Islamic order must be distinguished from a model of Iranian expansion. This is perhaps best illustrated in the distinction drawn between the office of 'Ali Khamenei, the current *faqih* and *wali amr al-muslimin* on the one hand, and the Iranian state on the other, which is merely a "particular state" (*dawla khassa*) or "a state with a system of government, institutions, decisions and officials" within the larger system.[100]

There is a conspicuous convergence between the terminology employed by Hakim in this treatise and the less elaborate attempts to define "the rule of the provinces" as an Islamic variant of federalism in the discussions of decentralization among the Iraqi opposition quoted above. Even though the main focus is on the

---

98 [Muhammad Baqir al-Hakim], *'Aqidatuna wa-ru'yatuna al-siyasiyya*, an undated booklet written probably around 1992 and published on www.al-hakim.com. For more recent indications that SCIRI as an organization inclined towards this sort of state model, see quotes from various publications considered close to Hakim in al-Shaykh 'Ali, *Ightiyal*, p. 79.

99 Al-Hakim, *'Aqidatuna*, part 3.

100 Ibid., parts 1 and 9.

distinction between the central and the regional (for instance the "Iraqi") level, Hakim's writings do offer a wider doctrinal framework in which federal units in Iraq could belong to a larger Islamic system. Most importantly, it is a Shi'i theory of the state where concepts such as federalism and decentralization can neatly find a slot without appearing to be ideological imports from the West.

The timing of the move from a preoccupation with the regional unit of Iraq as a whole to the new focus on smaller, federal subdivisions within the country can possibly be explained with reference to the organizational development of SCIRI during the 1990s. Several sources indicate that the movement was under pressure from a number of competing forces in Iraqi politics in the 1990s, at the same time as its paymasters in conservative circles in Iran close to Khamenei were experiencing complications in the domestic arena. Already in the 1980s, the unwillingness of the Da'wa party to subject themselves fully to SCIRI as an umbrella organization had been interpreted as discontent with SCIRI's support for *wilayat al-faqih*. Further blows to the prestige of the organization came in the 1990s, as the Iranian attempt to regain control of the Da'wa failed in 1998, and it became clear that local religious leaders in Iraq (Muhammad al-Sadr) as well as exiled ulama critical of SCIRI (Muhammad al-Shirazi) had acquired significant numbers of supporters even among Iraqi exiles in Iran, a domain which earlier had constituted the organization's home turf.[101] Towards the late 1990s, criticism of *wilayat al-faqih* emerged as a main issue also on the domestic front in Iran, and an increasingly vocal, reformist Islamic opposition became a threatening factor for the regime alongside the quietist camp which had rejected the idea of the rule of the jurisprudent throughout the 1990s and had looked to Khu'i and later Sistani in Najaf for spiritual guidance.

In this context of strong pressures from the outside, it appears that even closer links were forged between Iraqi elites exiled in Iran and hardliners in Teheran. One possible indication of this may be seen in the fact that Khamenei, after 1999, appointed several Iraqis with loyalties to him after years of work in the exiled opposition, to key positions in the Iranian government.[102] And when Washington stepped up its rhetoric about a change of regime in Baghdad, conservative Iranians must have followed with considerable interest the prospect of a new order also in Najaf – the Achilles heel of the Islamic Republic because of the presence of Sistani and other prominent quietist clerics. The remainder of the argument concerning this development is necessarily limited to conjecture, but at least some of the advantages that could be gained both by SCIRI and hardliners in Iran by changing their position on Iraq seem fairly obvious. One way for the Iranians to get around the challenges posed by both greater competition from within the Iraqi opposition as well as the heightened likelihood of a revival of Najaf outside the scope of

---

101 Al-Shaykh 'Ali, *Ightiyal*, pp. 309–364; *al-Milaff al-'Iraqi* no. 88 (1999), pp. 49–51; "Iranian Security Forces Seize Body of Ayatollah Shirazi", www.shianews.com, December 19, 2001.

102 Wilfried Buchta, *Who Rules Iran?* (Washington, 2000), pp. 192–194; "Why Does Khamenei Co-opt Iraqi Shiite Oppositionists", *Daily Star*, March 18, 2003.

Iranian influence would doubtless be to make a tactical decision to enter the US-backed opposition conferences and use these meetings as a means to regain control in the political sphere.[103] And one of the magic words that could be embraced in order to perform this exercise was "federalism", the door-opener to the Kurds, the INC and the US.

As seen above, Hakim's theories of government for an Islamic state already included provisions for decentralization, and would merely require a shift of emphasis from the regional to the local level of government, while the fundamental principles of the system could be left intact. Even the ideologically problematic move of co-operating with the US could be addressed through ventilating the issue in the conservative Iranian media, where, in April 2003, Hakim faced tough questioning from circles considered to be politically close to him.[104] Through its participation at the London conference in 2002, SCIRI managed to achieve a dominant position as the main Shi'i representative *vis-à-vis* the US,[105] to the extent that other members of the community considered it tantamount to a monopoly.

It is important to counterbalance the picture of SCIRI as an organization with certain pan-Islamic ideals with the pronounced realism and pragmatism which have characterized the movement over the past years. Repeated public statements have referred to Iraq as a setting where a replica of Iranian institutional arrangements would be impossible, maintained that the multi-ethnic and multi-confessional character of the country would have to be reflected in its system of government, and even included mildly nationalist comments such as the assertion that Iraq in its present form "has existed for many centuries".[106] Schemes for larger integration and pan-Islamism have tended to have the character of long-time projects, coexisting with more immediate ambitions – perhaps in the same way as many European parliamentarians cherish dreams of a future federation and super-state while continuing to work within their national arenas. In the final year before war erupted in Iraq, these more grandiose visions did not constitute a prominent factor in the public rhetoric of SCIRI, and the movement also explicitly distanced itself from another, more radical trend on the rise in Iraqi politics.

Federalism as an Irrelevant Debate and a Non-issue

Away from the conferences held in European hotels during the autumn of 2002, there was little to suggest that federalism had become a key concept for Iraqi Islamists more generally. Certainly this appeared to be the case with respect to the

---

103 Limited contacts between SCIRI and the US also took place in the 1990s (see Ra'uf, *Al-'amal*, pp. 350–356), but the more dramatic reversal of attitude towards public co-operation seems to have occurred some time early in 2001, *The Middle East*, July/August 2001, p. 9.

104 "Ayat allah sayyid muhammad baqir al-hakim dar musahabah-i ikhtisasi: mu'aridin-i 'iraqi hukumat-i mardumi mikhahand nah-amrika'i", *Jumhur-i Islami*, April 29, 2003.

105 "The Iraqi Opposition Conference in London", *'Ayn al-Yaqin*, December 20, 2002.

106 Interview with Hakim in *Argumenty i Fakty*, May 7, 2003, published by FBIS.

many sympathizers of various Islamist groups who were still inside Iraq. However, the absence of a local debate on federalism among the Shi'is of Iraq cannot be attributed to the repressive practices of the regime alone, for an underground Islamist movement with a distinctly new political orientation had in fact been on the rise since the late 1990s. Brought to the notice of the outside world by the assassination of its leader Muhammad al-Sadr in 1999, it continued as a significant challenge to the regime in the subsequent period also, particularly in the urban slums of the larger cities. It also enjoyed popularity among Iraqi refugees in Iran.[107] After the war in Iraq, this movement attained a prominent position on the emerging political scene in the country, and Sadr's son Muqtada played a prominent role as the charismatic focus of the current also known as the Sadrites (*al-sadriyyun*).[108] The flare-up of public propaganda from this movement immediately after the war in 2003 can also provide some clues about its ideological development during the final years of the Ba'th regime.

In the course of the initial weeks of the US-led administration, this new direction in Iraqi Islamism focused on other issues quite apart from the vexed question of federalism. The very concept of decentralization may well have held limited interest for a movement led by clerics who on one occasion denounced "freedom, democracy, culture and civil society" as vehicles through which corrupting influences could be imported into Iraq.[109] Instead, the main policies advocated by supporters of this trend focused on creating unity among the inhabitants of Iraq on conditions laid down by themselves, including measures such as gender segregation, the veiling of women, encouragements to men to grow beards, and a ban on alcohol, cinema, gambling and other activities considered as sources of Western corruption.[110] In territorial terms, the movement seemed eager to increase its influence beyond the traditional Shi'i bastions, instead of erecting fences which would only serve as barriers to expansion. One manifestation of this tendency came with the forceful takeovers of Sunni mosques by supporters of this current in the wake of the US occupation.[111]

Despite the absence of detailed statements by the Sadrites on the precise nature of their ideal future government for Iraq, occasional hints in the media as well as their connections to more well-established circles in the Shi'i world revealed views both on territoriality and questions affecting the degree of centralization in a future system of government. On the one hand, there was a fierce defense of a specifically

---

107 On this movement generally, see al-Shaykh 'Ali, *Ightiyal* and 'Adil Ra'uf, *Muhammad muhammad sadiq al-sadr* (Damascus, 1999).

108 Despite the obvious danger of being accused of parochialism, some supporters of the Sadr movement used this name themselves, see "Mudhakkirat mu'aridin 'iraqiyyin ila a'da' lajnat al-mutaba'a li-mu'tamar landan", undated document published on www.irqparliament.com early in 2003.

109 *Al-Hayat*, April 19, 2003, p. 4; "Shiite Clerics' Ambitions Collide in an Iraqi Slum", *New York Times*, May 25, 2003.

110 *Al-Hayat*, May 3, 2003, p. 1; "Reverberations from an Iraq Prayer Meeting", *Christian Science Monitor*, May 19, 2003.

111 "Lam nursil mumaththili al-marja'iyya ila masajid al-sunna", *al-Zaman*, April 27, 2003.

Iraqi identity in some of the writings of people close to Muqtada al-Sadr. In an article written to refute accusations that the movement was exerting pressure on the apolitical clergy in Najaf, Haji Abu 'Ali divided the Shi'i clergy into those who belonged to Iraq and were "its sons", and the outsiders who had come to "Iraqi territory" after the fall of the regime in order to exploit it.[112] He complained that 'Abd al-Majid al-Khu'i (whose family hails from the Azeri-speaking parts of Iran) had been able to come to Iraq before Muhammad Baqir al-Hakim, and that Muhammad Taqi al-Mudarrisi (also of a family with Iranian roots) had arrived before Muhammad Baqir al-Nasiri. Similarly, other Shi'i clerics critical of the Sadrites were denounced for their connections with Kuwait. This assertion of a separate Iraqi identity echoed views which Sadr's father had articulated in the late 1990s, when he had made the case for a separate jurisprudent (*faqih*) for Iraq.[113]

However, a contradictory element in the thinking of the Sadrites with regard to the state has arisen because of the peculiar circumstances in which the current incarnation of the movement developed under the leadership of Muqtada al-Sadr. Sadr was a very young man when his father and two of his brothers were assassinated early in 1999.[114] He was then, and continued in 2003 to be, a student in the religious schools of Najaf (under the quietist Muhammad Ishaq al-Fayyad)[115] who had not reached the stage that would allow him to practice legal interpretation (*ijtihad*), hitherto considered a fundamental criterion for anyone aspiring to a role as a paramount religious leader within Shi'ism. Nevertheless, Sadr assumed the leadership of the considerable social movement which had developed around his father's increasingly oppositional religious sermons, and for some time solved the question of the ultimate religious source of emulation by referring to the judicial opinions of his late father. This is a practice which is frowned upon by 'Usuli Shi'is because the rulings of a deceased *marja'* will not be able to address the temporal dimension considered vital in legal interpretation, but nevertheless has been used in the wake of the deaths of several grand *mujtahid*s, including Khomeini and Muhammad al-Shirazi.

In April 2003, around the time the Iraqi regime collapsed, Sadr found a new way to address the issue of spiritual authority. He made an arrangement with Kazim al-Ha'iri, an Iraqi cleric living in Iran who had formerly been a Da'wa member but had left the movement after a quarrel over *wilayat al-faqih* (whose application Ha'iri favored), by which Sadr would become Ha'iri's representative in Iraq, and Ha'iri would act as *marja' al-taqlid* for Sadr and his followers.[116] Although some have suggested that this was a marriage of convenience, there are in fact sources

---

112 "Al-radd 'ala al-sha'i'at allati tatahaddathu 'an hisar al-marja'iyya fi al-'iraq", www.alsader.com, May 2003.
113 Ra'uf, *Al-sadr*, pp. 56–57.
114 In 2003, Sadr was believed to be in his early 30s (rather than 22, as first rumored), "Man huwa al-sayyid muqtada al-sadr?", *al-Mustaqbal*, April 14, 2003.
115 "Man huwa samahat al-sayyid muqtada al-sadr?", www.alsader.com, May 2003.
116 "Al-ha'iri murashshah li-qiyadat tayyar al-sadr al-thani", *al-Mustaqbal*, April 24, 2003; "Iran Edict Directs Iraq Shiites to Take Power", *New York Times*, April 26, 2003.

dating back to 2002 which indicate that, on at least one occasion, Sadr's father had alluded to Ha'iri as an ideal successor if his own leadership should come to an end.[117] Whatever the precise background, the newly forged alliance had important implications for the political orientation of the Sadr movement.

When Ha'iri was chosen as the ultimate source of authority for the Sadrites, they became connected to a theoretician who had written several works on the Islamic state, and whose views to some extent might appear discordant with the strong defense of an Iraqi identity articulated by some rank and file members of the movement. Despite tendencies to a pluralistic interpretation of *wilayat al-faqih* (allowing for multiple representatives of the Hidden Imam in a common Islamic system, as well as collective religious leadership) in some early writings,[118] books from the 1990s as well as fatwas published by Ha'iri in later years suggest a clear preference for a unified, centralized and highly hierarchical system of Islamic government, in which criticism of the leadership is to be avoided.[119] Ha'iri emphasizes the "political" qualifications of the *faqih* as opposed to mere eminence in traditional legal studies, as well as his guiding role in important societal and political matters in which the textual sources of the Islamic law sometimes do not provide unequivocal answers. He views this as the domain of executive rulings (*ahkam wala'iyya*), where the traditional Shi'i process of consulting a *marja'* is simply aborted and overridden by the decision of the supreme *faqih* who in these contexts is rendered immune to criticism from the established hierarchy of learning.[120]

With respect to territoriality and the extension of the authority of the jurisprudent in *wilayat al-faqih*, Ha'iri is more specific in some of his fatwas. Thus, to a question whether there can be more than one supreme leader (*wali*) exercising power under this system, his answer is that "from a judicial point of view this would be permissible, but the interests of Islam require a unification of the supreme leadership".[121] A follow-up question about the possibility of having several *walis* "each in his country" emphasizes the problem of the geographical extension of leadership across international borders. To this Ha'iri replies that such an arrangement would "lead to chaos and is not permissible". A similar attitude with regard to the universality of the *wilayat al-faqih* system is seen in more practical examples. For instance, when Ha'iri is asked about the legitimacy of certain Shi'i initiatives to extend active support to secular state structures in Bahrain, the answer is stern: "Any law made by [human] society will lack legitimacy unless it carries the signature of the *faqih* and is implemented by him."[122] The necessity of rising above indi-

---

117 Ra'uf, '*Iraq*, pp. 572–574.
118 Kazim al-Ha'iri, *Asas al-hukuma al-islamiyya* ([Beirut], 1979); al-Husayni, "Al-takyif".
119 Kazim al-Ha'iri, *Al-marja'iyya wa-al-qiyada* (Qum, 1998), part 3.
120 Ibid., appendix "buhuth fi al-qiyada wa-al-hukuma". See also Ha'iri's answers on the subject of head-cutting (*tatbir*, which sometimes occurs during the Muharram commemorations of Imam Husayn's martyrdom), www.alhaeri.org.
121 Undated fatwas on questions concerning *wilayat al-faqih*, www.alhaeri.org.
122 Undated fatwa, www.alhaeri.org.

vidual concerns in order to avoid anarchy and collective irrationality is a theme which runs like a red thread through many of Ha'iri's publications, and it is easy to see that some of the problems of individual versus collective interests outlined by him in his defense of *wilayat al-faqih* would become repeated at the international level if the population of another state were suddenly to adopt the system of government established in Iran by Khomeini and thereby become part of the same Islamic community.[123]

In this manner, the movement of Muqtada al-Sadr was linked in 2003 to a spiritual source of reference whose views on political leadership could potentially collide with existing state structures if they were to be implemented. Indeed, they could also collide with the views of Sadr's followers themselves, who exhibited little enthusiasm for an Iranian regime which had treated their previous leader Muhammad al-Sadr with both suspicion and outright obstruction.[124] The significant point here is that for all their youthful energy and sometimes radical public statements, Muqtada al-Sadr and his companions did not create a revolution in the world of Shi'ism in the first half of 2003. By opting for an alliance with Ha'iri, they ultimately confirmed the stratification between *muqallid*s and *mujtahid*s which lies at the heart of 'Usuli Shi'ism, and thereby imposed on themselves certain restrictions with regard to the development of strategies for the future. The Sadrites, at this stage at least, stopped short of adopting the common Sunni Islamist contention that the traditional ulama and their heritage can be bypassed altogether, and also refrained from proceeding along the millenarianist path used by many earlier nonconformist currents within Shi'ism, as seen in various Mahdist movements. This is of considerable significance for interpreting the political potential of the many thousands of Sadr's followers who may well have disagreed with (or even been quite unaware of) Ha'iri's contemplations of the Islamic state, but who nevertheless became connected to these visions in April 2003 through hierarchical structures of 'Usuli Shi'ism. Despite significant uncertainties about the real degree of his popular support, the result of Sadr's maneuvers regarding the selection of a *marja'* was that Ha'iri's thinking on a state ruled according to the principles of *wilayat al-faqih* became an additional element in the debate over Iraq's future.

Shi'i Politics in Iraq during the First Weeks after the Fall of the Ba'th Regime

Prior to the war in Iraq in 2003, some Shi'i protagonists for a federal Iraq claimed that almost all the Shi'is supported this model as the best future system for the country.[125] As seen above, significant objections to this point of view could be found in circles which did not frequent the US-sponsored conferences, and little

---

123 Kazim al-Ha'iri, *Al-imama wa-qiyadat al-mujtama'* (Qum, 1995), part 3.
124 Al-Shaykh 'Ali, *Ightiyal*, pp. 339–344.
125 "Iraqi Opposition Goups Want a Federal State But Have Yet to Agree on Form", Radio Free Europe/Radio Liberty, November 5, 2002.

could be known about the opinion of the Iraqis still living under the authoritarian Ba'th system. As the war progressed and spaces for political debate opened up in Iraq, the various Islamic parties of the exiled opposition gradually returned and started to interact with both members of their own organizations who had remained in Iraq as well as the new political movements which had developed during the final years of the former regime.

Attacks on Pro-US and Apolitical Religious Circles

It was the most enthusiastic supporters of federalism who, at least in an indirect sense, suffered the first casualty in the political chaos of post-war Iraq. On April 10, 2003, the newly returned 'Abd al-Majid al-Khu'i was stabbed to death by an armed mob in Najaf only days after his arrival in the area in an operation made possible through co-ordination with the US.[126] Khu'i had oscillated between an apolitical attitude and active partnership with the US, but at least in the final months of his life, there had been a marked shift towards political participation, and Khu'i had even made specific proposals for how power could be divided between the largest communities in a future government.[127] Although he had often dodged the federalism issue, his keen participation in the work of the exiled opposition in late 2002 suggested that he was not hostile to the idea, and for the pro-federalist camp he doubtless represented a potential intermediary *vis-à-vis* the more apolitical but highly important Sistani.

Shortly after his arrival, Khu'i became engaged in work to restore normalcy in Najaf and was in the process of effecting a reconciliation between the local population and a Shi'i who had been in the employ of the former regime when he was murdered. While some explained his death as a tragic accident that happened when the people of Najaf took their revenge on a collaborator with the Ba'th party, it was equally evident that others attributed his death to larger ideological issues. His increased co-operation with the US had been criticized by Iraqi exiles in Iran shortly before the war,[128] people in Qum close to Sistani had publicly indicated growing discord between the leading *marja'* and Khu'i shortly before he was murdered,[129] and it was openly suggested that his death was the result of his having entered the

---

126 "Shahid 'ala rihlat al-khu'i ila al-'iraq", serial in *al-Sharq al-Awsat*, April 23–29, 2003.

127 Shortly before his death in 2003, a sharp contrast had developed between the position of Khu'i the father, who during the rebellion against the regime in 1991 had limited his involvement to an appeal for public committees to be established to take care of law and order, and Khu'i the son, who by now had entered the discussion about sectarian spoils in a future regime by calling for a Shi'i president for Iraq with three vice-presidents (for the Shi'is, the Sunnis and the Kurds respectively), see interview in *al-Qabas*, January 11, 2003, published at www.iraqishiacouncil.com.

128 "Opponents Disrupt Meeting of Iraqi Shiite Moderate", *AFP*, January 9, 2003.

129 "Namayandah-i ayat allah sistani: ishan hich kas az jumlah-i sayyid majid khu'i-ra bih hudur napadhiruftah and", www.baztab.com, April 10, 2003. Similarly, in the wake of the assassination, Iranian media portrayed Khu'i as someone who had departed from the traditional path of the Najaf clergy, *al-Wifaq*, April 12, 2003, pp. 1–2.

area "riding on foreign tanks".[130] After the murder in Najaf, some newly returned exiled clerics, such as Iyad Jamal al-Din, took up the role Khu'i had been expected to play by promoting a secular state at the carefully orchestrated meetings of politicians which were held under US auspices in Nasiriyya[131] and later in Baghdad.[132] In May, Muhammad Bahr al-'Ulum returned to Iraq and quickly became engaged in dialogue with other segments of the opposition in Baghdad.[133] But this activity by the religious forces thought to be most receptive to the idea of federalism appeared restricted to the level of elite politics, with few signs of persuasive symbolic power or widespread public support.

Also the apolitical clergy, which probably constituted an abstainer rather than an oppositionist in the debates over federalism, came under pressure as Iraq started to change. In the wake of the murder of Khu'i, rumors emerged that Sistani's house in Najaf had been besieged and that he had been ordered by political activists critical of his quietist stand to leave the city.[134] The stand-off did come to a peaceful end, but reports of a precarious state of security in Najaf persisted. Sistani subsequently moved to consolidate the traditionalist faction of leading ulama in the holy cities by deepening his links with the three *mujtahids* generally considered to follow next to him in rank.[135] Nevertheless, in May he remained isolated from the public, and there were suggestions that he planned a pilgrimage to Iran or Syria to escape the mounting conflict over control of the holy cities.[136]

Power Struggles among Political Activists

Some of the more outspoken skeptics with regard to federalism had belonged in one way or another to the Da'wa party or the various factions which all claimed to be the real heirs to the original movement. In the times of the Ba'th regime, these circles had often been credited with a significant underground presence in Iraq, and were among the most vocal critics of conferences attended by exiles who were "not representative of the real opposition on the ground". Despite the opening up of headquarters in Iraq for some of these organizations in the weeks immediately following the war as well as reports about the presence of armed groups loyal to the Da'wa in several locations in Iraq, the public appearance of the movement in this period (when demonstrations were arranged and posters of potential future leaders were popping up all over Iraq) did not quite live up to the expectations of a unified movement with a strong public appeal which its exiled members had generated. In

---

130 Interview with Muhammad Mahdi al-Khalisi, *al-Mustaqbal*, April 19, 2003.
131 The idea of a federal Iraq was reiterated at this meeting, which was boycotted by most of the Islamists, Al-Jazeera Television, special news bulletin *Ma ba'da saddam* presented by 'Abd al-Samad Nasir, April 15, 2003.
132 "Jamal al-din yuhadhdhiru min tasalluh al-azhab", *al-Zaman*, April 29, 2003.
133 "Bahr al-'ulum yaqtarihu sab'a mustaqillin muhayidin", *al-Zaman*, May 26, 2003.
134 "Jama'at muqtada al-sadr tuhasiru manzil al-sistani" *al-Sharq al-Awsat*, April 14, 2003.
135 "Harakat al-sadr tunassibu al-ha'iri marja'an", *al-Zaman*, April 29, 2003.
136 "Al-sistani yanwi ziyarat iran", *al-Sharq al-Awsat*, May 26, 2003.

particular, there seemed to be no public figure around whom the supporters of the movement could rally.

During the 1990s, the leading branch of the Da'wa had repeatedly refused to establish links with any particular *marja'*, leaving this issue to the individual member.[137] But for a movement claiming to be the successor to the spiritual heritage of Baqir al-Sadr, the lack of a strong link to a leading, activist cleric in Iraq appeared to create a deficiency in the symbolic repertoire. Fadl Allah, seen by some as a potential future leader, remained in Lebanon despite speculations about a possible return,[138] whereas others who had supported Muhammad al-Sadr in the past were now faced with competition from the movement led by his son, apparently without being able to offer any weighty political alternative. At the same time, no personalities from the lay leadership of the party managed to acquire a very prominent position in Iraqi politics during the initial period after the war. In April, the Da'wa participated with some delegates at the Madrid conference of the opposition (where federalism was mentioned as a key principle in the concluding declaration), and in May, its largest faction joined the US-backed process of preliminary consultations for the establishment of an interim government.[139]

SCIRI, on the other hand, had often been accused before the war of being merely the brainchild of the Iranian regime, completely dependent upon hardliners in Teheran for support. There is little doubt that the organization profited immensely from the link to Iran in terms of material support which facilitated the logistics of its swift return to Iraq in April 2003 and enabled it to play a prominent role during the first, large-scale religious celebration in Karbala on the occasion of the *arba'in* (end of a forty-day mourning period) of Imam Husayn.[140] But the grand receptions accorded to Muhammad Baqir al-Hakim during his triumphant homecoming to Iraq in May indicated something more than an Iranian marionette, and despite counter-demonstrations in certain areas,[141] these events surpassed the displays of public support accorded to most other political figures in Iraq at the time. SCIRI proceeded quickly to establish a presence in Baghdad and the holy cities where it began work to open an Islamic university,[142] and seemed able to continue its pragmatic course *vis-à-vis* the US while retaining legitimacy among its followers. The organization had adopted a businesslike position towards federalism in 2002, and while the concept failed to appear as a central theme in the

---

137 Ra'uf, *Hizb al-da'wa*, p. 20; Sakai, "Modernity", p. 46.

138 Interview with Fadl Allah, *al-Sharq al-Awsat*, May 2, 2003.

139 It has been suggested that the decision of the Da'wa to join these discussions resulted from advice from Fadl Allah (whose anti-federalist position is described above), see "Washington May Find Unusual Ally in Fadlallah", *Daily Star*, May 31, 2003.

140 "Al-hakim yad'u li-tajammu' fi karbala' ", www.aljazeera.net, April 17, 2003. The skillfulness of the Iranians in promoting their points of view among an Iraqi public was also evident in the success of the 'Alam television channel, established shortly before the war and reaching huge masses of Iraqis by using terrestrial rather than satellite technology.

141 *Middle East International*, April 18, 2003, p. 27.

142 *Al-Wifaq*, May 8, 2003, p. 1.

propaganda of the party, there was nothing to suggest that its stand on the issue had changed dramatically in the first weeks after the war.

The third main grouping among the Islamic activists in Iraq in early 2003 was the movement led by Muqtada al-Sadr. This political faction quickly acquired notoriety because of allegations of its involvement in the killing of Khu'i and the siege of Sistani in Najaf in April, and it is not improbable that the subsequent media interest blew the image of its public influence somewhat out of proportion. In particular, it is unlikely that all the posters of the late Muhammad al-Sadr carried in the anti-American demonstrations in Iraq necessarily represented signs of loyalty to his son. Nevertheless, it soon emerged that the young Sadr did have an extensive network of contacts in Iraq, and his influence grew quickly as people loyal to him stepped in to fill the power vacuum after the collapse of the Ba'th regime and the subsequent spectacular failure of the coalition forces to address basic issues of human security in areas under their control.[143] The position of the Sadrites was consolidated through anti-American demonstrations and well-attended Friday prayers (particularly in the poorer areas of Baghdad, where one vast suburb was renamed Madinat al-Sadr after the fall of the regime) and profited from the powerful symbolism associated with Muqtada's father, considered by many Iraqis as a martyr who died in a struggle against the former regime. In Basra, clerics began to promote radical policies similar to those backed by the followers of Sadr,[144] and in other cities of the south, there were forced takeovers of Sunni mosques resembling acts carried out by his lieutenants in Baghdad.[145] In May, after Sadr had forged his new alliance with Ha'iri, posters of this leading cleric (who remained in Iran) became another element in the public demonstrations headed by this movement,[146] and a subsequent visit by Muqtada al-Sadr to Qum in conjunction with the commemoration of Khomeini's death resulted in contacts with leading conservative Iranian politicians.[147]

Perhaps most importantly, people in Sadr's circles appear to have spearheaded the development of political slogans which gave hints about possible future directions in Iraqi politics, rallying cries which actually proved to have resonance among the Iraqi public instead of being confined to the theoretical discussions of political elites. With regard to the future system of government, these slogans were noteworthy for the recurrence of the concept of the religious schools in Najaf (*al-hawza*) as the sole representative (*al-mumaththil al-wahid*) for the Shi'is (or the

---

143 "Shiite Clerics Move to Assume Control", *Washington Post*, April 14, 2003; "Rijal al-din al-shi'a yandafi'una li-mal' al-faragh al-siyasi", *al-Quds al-'Arabi*, April 18, 2003; "Le chérif des chiites fait la loi à Saddam City", *Le Figaro*, April 16, 2003.

144 *Al-Hayat*, May 19, 2003, p. 4.

145 " 'Anasir min hizb al-da'wa la tusghi li-fatwa al-maraji' al-shi'iyya al-'ulya", *al-Zaman*, May 20, 2003.

146 Al-Jazeera Television, evening news bulletin, May 19, 2003, 2000 GMT.

147 "Safar-i sayyid muqtada sadr bih iran", www.baztab.com, June 6, 2003.

Iraqi Muslims in their entirety, as some claimed). [148] Further down the political hierarchy, in interviews with ordinary citizens, the notion of "a clergyman to be the future president of Iraq" was frequently heard.[149] Such preparedness to delegate authority more or less blindly to those within the *hawza* who were prepared to take up a political role seemed at variance with earlier claims by the exiled opposition about the strong aversions to clerical rule said to distinguish Iraq from Iran, and formed a contrast to the perception of Najaf as a city where quietism had a strong appeal.[150] It was posters of the activist martyr Muhammad al-Sadr, who had spoken of an "articulate *hawza*" (*al-hawza al-natiqa*), rather than images of Sistani (seen by the Sadrites as the representative of the "dormant *hawza*") which dominated in the public demonstrations in Iraq in April and May 2003. After having declared his new association with Ha'iri, a firm adherent of *wilayat al-faqih* who had earlier severed links with the Da'wa over the issue, Muqtada al-Sadr too publicly voiced his support for this model of government. [151] With these developments, the issue of federalism showed signs of having faded into the background in May 2003, at least temporarily.

Traditionalists, Islamists and New Radicals

With the appearance shortly after the fall of the Ba'th regime of death threats against prostitutes and vendors of alcohol,[152] warnings from prayer leaders to un-veiled women and cinema proprietors,[153] and suggestions from religious clerics that Christians too should be subjected to Islamic laws or "Islamic manners",[154] the impression that Iraq was headed into uncharted waters was strong indeed. This new radicalism was accompanied by material efforts to establish control on the ground by loyalists of Muqtada al-Sadr, whose well-armed followers had a lead on most of the competing Islamist movements because of their established presence in Iraq

---

148 Other variants of this theme were found in slogans and statements such as "Our voice is the voice of the *hawza*" (*sawtuna huwa sawt al-hawza al-'ilmiyya*) and "The selection of the representatives of the people is a matter for the *hawza*" (*ikhtiyar mumaththili al-sha'b amr ya'udu ila al-hawza al-'ilmiyya*), see *al-Hayat*, April 16, 2003, p. 1; extracts from press conference held by 'Abd al-Hadi al-Muhammadawi, www.alsader.com, May 2003; "Alaf al-'iraqiyyin yatazaharuna didda ijtima' al-mu'arada fi al-nasiriyya", www.aljazeera.net, April 15, 2003.
149 BBC World, news bulletin, June 10, 2003, 1800 GMT.
150 Political quietism is inevitably less spectacular than hard-line Islamism, but in early 2003 it looked as if the old fallacy of reducing Shi'ism to an Iranian phenomenon had been overtaken by an equally problematic counter-stereotype of an Iraqi Shi'ism supposed to be tribal, rural, focused on religious rituals and almost militantly averse to the idea of clerics assuming the reins of political power.
151 Interview with Muqtada al-Sadr, www.alsader.com, May 2003.
152 "Mutahammisun li-tatbiq al-namudaj al-irani...", *al-Zaman*, May 28, 2003.
153 "Imam shi'i 'iraqi yatawa'adu nisa' wa-ashab dur sinima wa-ba'at al-khamr", *al-Sharq al-Awsat*, May 17, 2003.
154 "Al-sadr yad'u min al-najaf ila dawla islamiyya tulzimu al-masihiyyin bi-al-islam", *al-Zaman*, May 5, 2003.

prior to the war. In particular, Sadr made an effort to acquire control of the *hawza*, by claiming to speak in its name, denouncing its apolitical members as unworthy representatives of the Shi'is, and even making suggestions that new political parties should be subject to screening for political correctness at the hands of the *hawza*.[155]

At first sight, the concept of a centralized *hawza*, speaking with a single voice and opening up offices as if it were a perfectly bureaucratic organ,[156] appears antithetical to the ethos of scholarship that had characterized Najaf in the past.[157] The traditional system of education was essentially decentralized, to the extent that a Shi'i student attempting in the early 1990s to analyze the "position of the *hawza*" on educational matters historically complained about the absence of a unified strategy and ended up studying the points of view of individual clerics.[158] To a certain degree, the subsequent centralization may have been the result of an increasingly bureaucratic and authoritarian state that demanded a representative to deal with in issues such as military conscription and international visiting students (Khu'i had fulfilled this role in his time as the unrivalled grand *mujtahid* in Najaf),[159] but there are also indications that the authoritarian state fostered an opposition movement which adopted a centralizing counter-strategy: Muhammad Baqir al-Sadr had propagated the idea of institutionalizing the *hawza* in the past, for instance through the certification of prayer leaders as well as the establishment of a collegiate council to safeguard the process of succession within the political leadership in times of crisis,[160] and many Islamists favored such arrangements as a means to consolidate the position of the religious schools, bemoaning their current "chaotic" conditions.[161]

In a development which started with an initiative from the Ba'th regime, Muhammad al-Sadr assumed in the 1990s a number of official tasks in Najaf to the extent that a concept of a more centralized leadership for the *hawza* emerged, and a journal issued in its name also came into existence, where Sadr's son Muqtada had an editorial role.[162] Although the Iraqi state at first attempted to use Sadr to gain control among the Shi'is, even his political opponents later acknowledged that he

---

155 "Al-sistani yuharrimu intiza' al-jawami' min ahl al-sunna wa-akharun yunshi'una hay'a shar'iyya li-al-ishraf 'ala al-azhab", *al-Sharq al-Awsat*, May 3, 2003 and interview with Jalal al-Hasanawi, www.alsader.com, May 2003.
156 "Power Play at Shiite Holy Institution", *Christian Science Monitor*, May 14, 2003.
157 Even SCIRI officials who had been in exile expressed a degree of bemusement at the notion of *hawza* with a defined leadership role, see "Return of the Ayatollah", *Al-Ahram Weekly*, May 15–21, 2003.
158 Al-Bahadli, *Al-hawza*, pp. 385–391. See also Fadil Jamali, "The Theological Colleges of Najaf", *The Muslim World*, vol. 50, no. 1 (1960), pp. 15–22.
159 Ra'uf, *Al-sadr*, p. 107.
160 Chibli Mallat, "Religious Militancy in Contemporary Iraq: Muhammad Baqer as-Sadr and the Sunni-Shia Paradigm", *Third World Quarterly*, vol. 10, no. 2 (1988), p. 727; Faleh Abdul-Jabar "The Genesis and Development of Marja'ism Versus the State" in idem (ed.), *Ayatollahs, Sufis and Ideologues* (London, 2002), pp. 84–85.
161 Al-Bahadli, *Al-hawza*, pp. 251–253.
162 Ra'uf, *Al-sadr*, p. 442, "Man huwa samahat al-sayyid muqtada al-sadr?", www.alsader.com, May 2003.

eventually managed to use his position to further Shi'i interests in a manner which threatened the regime and ultimately led to his murder in 1999.[163] However, one legacy of his period as formal leader of the *hawza* was a pronounced tension between Sistani, the quietist cleric now considered the only possible leading figure for Najaf's religious establishment in traditionalist circles, and the memory of a far more activist *hawza* under Sadr's leadership. It was the spirit of this new force in Iraqi politics which the Sadrites attempted to build upon when they began to issue statements in the name of the *hawza*, sent enforcers on its behalf,[164] and addressed their own master as the leader (*za'im*) of the religious schools in April 2003.[165]

However, Muqtada al-Sadr's attempt to monopolize the *hawza* and to turn it into a tool for furthering some of his more radical ideas faced resistance from several quarters. In the first place, as noted above, Sadr had already submitted to one of the basic axioms in 'Usuli Shi'ism which demands that someone who is not schooled in *ijtihad* must defer to a person who possesses this ability. This raised the prospects for conflicts even with close political allies: the religious prestige of his source of emulation, Ha'iri, could potentially be drawn into controversy over unconventional practices carried out by Sadr in the name of Islam, thus constituting at least a temporary barrier that would have to be negotiated. Ha'iri, in Qum, had himself seen the Afghan Taliban exposed to severe criticism in Iran, partly for policies not altogether different from those pursued by Iraq's new radicals.[166] Many of the same barriers were relevant for the prospect of rapprochement between Sadr and SCIRI (whose leader included explicit warnings against "Taliban" and the curtailment of women in his first public speeches in Iraq),[167] in addition to a long history of personal animosity between Sadr's father and prominent SCIRI leaders.[168]

Secondly, by acknowledging the basic stratification of Shi'i society according to knowledge of Islamic law, the young and radical preachers close to Sadr also made themselves vulnerable to criticism on the terms of the more traditional ulama, as well as Islamists of the old school who were less loyal to Iranian hardliners than Ha'iri and SCIRI. Thus, in May, Muhammad Baqir al-Nasiri, a cleric, a former Da'wa activist and a student of Muhammad Baqir al-Sadr, attacked preachers who in the name of Islam demanded that people wear a certain style of clothes, denouncing such persons as ignoramuses (*jahala*), a strong accusation which questioned the very integrity of these activists.[169] Others who opposed the Sadrites could benefit

---

163 See for instance the posting "Al Sadr Phenomena", www.aliraqi.org, May 2, 2003.

164 "Baghdad Cinemas and Shops Attacked", *Daily Telegraph*, June 1, 2003.

165 "Al-qissa al-kamila li-sa'atayn wa 35 daqiqatan min al-hisar al-musallah intahat bi-ightiyal al-khu'i", *al-Sharq al-Awsat*, April 22, 2003.

166 Some Iraqi Shi'is used the term "the Shi'i 'Taliban' " to refer to Sadr and his followers, "Hizb al-da'wa al-islamiyya yu'idu tanzim sufufihi", *al-Mustaqbal*, April 16, 2003.

167 Transcript from Voice of the Islamic Republic of Iran Radio, May 11, 2003, published by FBIS; "Excerpts of Remarks by Iraqi Ayatollah", *AP*, May 10, 2003.

168 Al-Shaykh 'Ali, *Ightiyal*, pp. 73–81.

169 Interview with Nasiri, *al-Zaman*, May 28, 2003. On his background, see Muhammad al-Gharawi, *Talamidhat al-imam al-shahid al-sadr* (Beirut, 2002), pp. 295–297.

from fatwas from both the politically inclined Fadl Allah as well as the more
quietist Sistani, who pointed out that the forceful takeover of Sunni mosques by
Shi'is (such as those carried out by people loyal to Sadr) were unlawful according
to Islam,[170] and a declaration was issued saying that neither Sistani nor any of the
other leading ulama in Najaf had made any fatwa imposing the veil on women.[171] In
addition to this, Sistani signed a declaration underlining the traditional role of the
hawza as a purely educational establishment,[172] as well as a fatwa regarding the
many attempts to speak in the name of the *hawza* where he firmly redirected the
believers to traditional practices and the necessity of listening to the advice of
individual clerics and the declarations and fatwas issued by them in person.[173]
While Sadr's preachers apparently tried to push the limits in some of their Friday
prayers, their acknowledgment of certain basic structures in Shi'ism to some extent
could work as a deterrent against this capriciousness, with the traditional hierarchy
forming a source of restraint which could not be circumvented as easily as has been
the case in certain Sunni contexts. Even the more quietist ulama showed signs of
increased assertiveness after the initial weeks of hardliner dominance, an interesting
new development possibly induced by the upsurge of radicalism but performed
according to their own, traditionalist terms.

Thirdly, even in certain Islamist circles potentially receptive to some of the
criticism of the traditional system found in Sadr's rhetoric,[174] fundamental
differences of agendas *vis-à-vis* the new radicals remained, particularly at the elite
level. The Da'wa's focus on Iraqi unity had earlier led them to adopt a basically
pragmatic view on politics in a multi-ethnic society with a number of political
currents, where secular political parties have also historically had a strong position
among the Shi'is. There had already been angry reactions when, in the autumn of
2002, Ha'iri banned co-operation with the Iraqi communists because of their
atheistic orientation,[175] and attempts to take over Sunni mosques by force, seen in
Iraq after the war in 2003, were clearly at variance with the more tolerant strategies
for achieving Islamic unity cultivated by the Da'wa in their writings. Friction
between the two camps was further accentuated by the ongoing personal rivalry
between their main spiritual patrons, Ha'iri and Fadl Allah,[176] and there was an

---

170 "Lajnat al-difa' 'an ahl al-sunna fi janub al-'iraq tahsulu 'ala fatwa bi-'adam jawaz
   ihtilal masajid al-sunna min qibl al-shi'a", *al-Sharq al-Awsat*, May 30, 2003. The fatwa
   from Fadl Allah was significant because some activists were disinclined to follow the
   advice of the traditionalist Sistani.
171 "Lam nusaddir fatawa tulzimu al-nisa' bi-al-hijab", *al-Zaman*, June 11, 2003.
172 "Tawdih hawla mustalah al-hawza al-'ilmiyya", www.najaf.org, May 26, 2003.
173 Fatwa, www.najaf.org, April 20, 2003.
174 See for instance the elements of a critique of the traditional system of learning, its
   system of examinations, familist tendencies and even the problem of forged permissions
   to practice *ijtihad* in Ra'uf: *'Iraq*, pp. 129–130, 407–408. In the same work, the writer
   lauds the contribution of the two Sadrs (Muhammad Baqir and Muhammad
   Muhammad Sadiq) to Iraqi Islamism.
175 "Bayan hawla fatawa tahrim al-i'tilaf", www.rezgar.com, September 26, 2002.
176 Ra'uf, *'Iraq*, pp. 85–98.

evident potential for more general disagreements similar to those seen in Iran between reformists and hardliners.

Despite the existence of such forces of resistance to Muqtada al-Sadr, it appeared as if the emergence of his movement during the tumultuous period of transition after the fall of the Ba'thist regime did introduce a wild card in the debate over the shape of the state model for the future Iraq. While the established traditionalist and Islamist elites with their well-defined doctrines had little sympathy for Sadr's volatile manners, there were indications of defections to the Sadrites by rank and file members from both camps.[177] And the constraints imposed through the Shi'i hierarchy of learning take on a somewhat academic character if extra-judicial proceedings and vigilantism are allowed to take place with the tacit support of ulama who themselves may continue to play by the rules of traditional jurisprudence, a phenomenon increasingly seen in Iran in recent years.

Through their new relationship to Kazim al-Ha'iri, the Sadrites linked up with a cleric with a clear vision of an Islamic state, where unification and centralization of Islamic leadership are emphasized, and safeguards against over-centralization and the protection of provincial autonomy receive less attention. As long as the nucleus of that regime is located in Teheran, a degree of friction is likely to remain between Ha'iri and his Sadrite followers, with rather unpredictable implications for their contribution to the debate on a new political system in Iraq. On the other hand, for all the media attention accorded to Sadr, it is important to keep in mind the many other forces that make up the Shi'i Islamist scene in Iraq. In these circles, those who favored the US-sponsored vision of a federal democracy were on the defensive in the first weeks after the war ended, but the pragmatism of SCIRI contributed to keeping the concept alive at least as a possible solution for the future. Ironically, in this setting where many of the involved parties entertained some sort of pan-Islamic vision, the federalism issue remained one of several factors that seemed to complicate relations between INC and the Islamist party most consistently devoted to a separate Islamic regime for Iraq, the Da'wa, although the party's participation in the Madrid conference in April could possibly signal a significant shift in attitude in this regard.

Federalism in the Democratization of Iraq

In many ways, it is paradoxical that proposals about federalism should arouse so much controversy among the Shi'is. If implemented on a purely "administrative"

---

177 Certain press stories linked the Da'wa with the new Sadr movement, and some of Sistani's representatives also made surprisingly activist statements during the first critical weeks in April 2003, *al-Hayat*, April 11, 2003, p. 6; "Fi baghdad qa'at al-sinima taghussu bi-al-ruwwad mutajahilatan tahdhirat al-fartusi", *al-Sharq al-Awsat*, May 19, 2003. Sadr's decision to formalize his links with Ha'iri (rather than Hakim or Fadl Allah) clearly had the appearance of a desire to stay politically independent from the established parties.

basis with five or six medium-sized provinces, it could offer an attractive option for removing some of the intense pressure in Iraqi politics from a single center of power, while guaranteeing a minimum level of Shi'i representation without resort to arrangements of an explicitly sectarian character.[178] It could even help the Shi'is sort out some of their internal differences over the principles to be adopted in a new system of government, as several visions for the future could be kept afloat at the same time within one polity but in different geographical areas.

So far, this sort of arrangement has been enthusiastically embraced only by some of the religious Shi'i factions. Indeed, also after the outbreak of the war in 2003, Islamist circles continued to suggest political arrangements for the future where federalism had no place.[179] On the other hand, it is not unthinkable that several of those who have thus far voiced skepticism or remained on the sidelines may ultimately find federalism in one form or another to be compatible with their own schemes. For the quietists around Sistani it is a basic hostility to intimate involvement with *any* sort of state structure, federal or not, which has been the dominant theme. Although some interesting signs of increased attention to politics emerged in this camp as the situation in Najaf stabilized, there was still little in the way of specific advice on state structures for the future beyond a more general call for the formation of an elected Iraqi government.[180] And for many other important players in Shi'i politics, it is difficult to pinpoint theoretical issues that would definitely rule out the possibility for at least rethinking federalism, although several aspects of their current discourse on decentralization would have to be reconsidered if the concerns of proponents of a secular state model were to be taken into account. Some of these secular federalists in reality call for a confederation and are unlikely to be impressed by attempts at verbal masquerade.

The objections of the Da'wa have focused on an ethnic or sectarian interpretation of federalism, and could become less vociferous if a system demarcated according to less controversial and politicized criteria were arrived at. Moreover, even though some of their spiritual sources of inspiration have defended the concept of a unitary state both in Lebanon and in Iraq, it is less clear to what extent this stand is the direct product of their theories of the Islamic state. In these theories, pluralism is a fundamental value, and the attachment to the particular state system of the Middle East as it emerged after the First World War seems more spurious. There would probably be limits as to the extent to which a legitimate representative of the Hidden Imam could be directly involved in a state structure where some ar-

---

178 A federal system of this category would certainly be less sectarian than the key for distributing representatives operative at the INC level in the 1990s, where even ideological parties were transformed into sects – the category "liberals" figured alongside Kurds and Islamists of various denominations, all with a specified number of representatives.

179 See for instance *bayan* from Sadiq al-Shirazi, April 11, 2003, www.alshirazi.com.

180 A meeting in June 2003 between Sistani and a prominent Kurdish advocate for a federal Iraq, Mas'ud Barzani, suggested that the Shi'i cleric at least was open to dialog with representatives of this current of thought, *al-Hayat*, June 7, 2003, p. 3.

eas of government, notably defense and foreign policy, were excepted from his authority. On the other hand, Shi'i thinkers have in many contexts accepted the "existing political circumstances" as a given, underlining that political leaders should focus on improving society as far as circumstances permit.

SCIRI, originally an organization with tendencies to long-term pan-Islamist ambitions, has settled for a pragmatic approach to a concept of federalism which its leaders have managed to fit into their own political nomenclature. However, in this case certain theoretical issues could potentially prove problematic, for while Hakim's writings on government do pay ample attention to the local level in the *wilayat al-faqih* system, the assumption is that local administrative structures should be subordinated to the apex of this system, currently the office of 'Ali Khamenei in Teheran.[181] If, for instance, this sort of state model were to be implemented in some parts of Iraq through a federal system, without any connections to the supreme *faqih*, problems of legitimacy could arise because the local ruler, in some areas of government (such as relations with Israel, or oil-pricing policy), would have to abide by decisions taken by a federal government which might contradict the interests of the greater Islamic community as formulated by the paramount *faqih*.[182] On the other hand, the example of Lebanon shows that supporters of *wilayat al-faqih* may also find a perfectly constructive role within a non-Islamic system, with their sources of spiritual influence remaining on the sidelines of those particular state structures, and the pyramidal web of Islamic loyalties to external patrons perhaps also assuming a more theoretical character over time.[183]

Quite apart from the discussions of Islamic state models developed over the last decades, federalism might hold a special appeal to all the different movements discussed here, because of the general trend in Islamist circles towards an emphasis on gradual reform starting with the local society, and the increased attention to concepts such as "Islamic spaces" in a territorial sense. In fact, in the context of Shi'ism, the strongest propensities for such a conception of territoriality have been manifested among some of the most loyal supporters of a dirigiste interpretation of *wilayat al-faqih*, with uncompromising supporters of Khamenei in Iran declaring a

---

181 The intention of SCIRI to attempt to reconcile a federal scheme with Islamic law seemed evident in comments made by Hakim after his return to Iraq, "Ayat allah hakim: shura-yi muntakhab-i amrika bara-yi idarah-i 'iraq namashru' ast", *Kayhan*, June 8, 2003.

182 Interestingly, one of Hakim's writings addresses the problem of exercising legitimate authority in a territory to which the supreme ruler's effective authority does not or cannot extend. Among the various possible settings listed by Hakim is the situation in which a local *faqih* assumes power and the supreme ruler chooses to acquiesce through his silence (*sukut*). Muhammad Baqir al-Hakim, *Al-qiyada al-siyasiyya al-na'iba*, from www.al-hakim.com.

183 Hints by SCIRI officials to the press that Hakim might in the future concentrate on affairs connected with his role as a *marja'* may have been an important signal about an increased focus on Iraqi, rather than pan-Islamic, affairs on his part, as his followers were mostly limited to Iraqi Shi'is, *al-Hayat*, May 5, 2003, p. 4.

ban on the entry of reformist politicians to the territory of the city of Mashhad,[184] and with Sadrites in Basra fronting the demand that coalition forces regroup and remove their physical presence to the outskirts of the city.[185]

Intimately linked to the controversy over federalism as a future system of government in Iraq is the perception of it as a model imported or even imposed from abroad. Understandably, some Islamists are put off when Iraqi exiles declare that this is a new system of government with practically no precedence in the region,[186] just as others may react to the Islamist argument that the Ottoman Empire in fact exhibited federalism in its most virtuous shape. Between these extremes, however, several Islamic movements in Iraq cherish political aspirations where some form of decentralization can play a positive role. Here it seems to be of paramount importance that it should be left to a representative assembly of Iraqis to hammer out for themselves the particular shape of any new, federal structures, as this could serve to remove accusations about imperialist plots to divide Iraq which have impeded discussions in the past and made them less constructive.

Signals from the US administration in this regard during the first months of their rule in Iraq in 2003 did raise serious questions about what sort of restrictions they would impose on democratic development in the country. The political meetings held to inaugurate the new democratic Iraq were characterized by secrecy, heavy representation of exiles hastily flown in from abroad and exclusion of some of the movements which had emerged underground in Ba'thist Iraq. There were hints in the press that US officials were trawling the countryside for amenable village imams,[187] as well as rumors that they were interested in an alleged Akhbari revival within Shi'ism which supposedly would translate into political quietism.[188] In Basra, the British chose to sideline religious forces and for a while worked through a tribal leader accused of links to the former regime, giving him wide powers to decide on the composition of a local council.[189] Signs of political dissent in Iraq in April and May were in several cases attributed to "influences from Iran",

---

184 *Al-Hayat*, June 10, 2003, p. 1.
185 "Shiite Muslim Protest Demands British Withdrawal from Basra", *AFP*, June 7, 2003; "Maqtal jundi amiriki...", www.aljazeera.net, June 8, 2003.
186 Paper by Kanan Makiya presented at the American Enterprise Institute, October 3, 2002.
187 "U.S. Tells Iran Not to Interfere in Iraq Efforts", *New York Times*, April 24, 2003.
188 "Defense, State Differ on How to Handle Shi'ites", *Reuters*, April 25, 2003. The notion of Najaf as a "city [that] has long been aligned with Akhbari Shiism" also appeared in "Shiite Struggle is Crucial for Iraq", *International Herald Tribune*, April 18, 2003, a proposition both astonishing and esoteric which could possibly be related to the same development. The idea that Akhbarism (today a minority branch within Shi'ism, in Iraq concentrated in certain areas around Basra) would automatically induce political docility is itself problematic, for Akhbari ulama have historically covered the whole political spectrum. One leading cleric agitated against the British after the First World War, see 'Abd al-Jalil al-Tahir, *Al-'asha'ir al-'iraqiyya* (Beirut, 1972), p. 143.
189 "British Forces Turn to Tribal Leaders for Help", *Guardian*, April 9, 2003; "Marja' dini fi al-basra: narfidu tawalli shuyukh 'asha'ir al-amn", *al-Sharq al-Awsat*, April 11, 2003.

and conservative US politicians declared that a popular wish for an Islamic state along Iranian lines would not be respected.

Many of these tendencies come across as somewhat alarming if past developments in Iraqi politics are taken into account. The strategy of packing political councils with docile representatives of the countryside in order to sidestep the complicated political demands of urban, intellectual centers was pursued during the Iraqi monarchy with catastrophic consequences. The long-standing and dishonorable tradition in Iraqi history of blaming Iranian "agents" for any hitch in Shi'i politics in the country has proved equally counterproductive. And the US policy of promoting selected religious currents among the Shi'is runs the risk of backfiring if it is carried to the extreme at the expense of mainstream Shi'i groups, in an attempt to define the sort of Shi'ism Washington could tolerate. This could easily degenerate into gerrymandering and attempts to reclassify or obstruct hostile political tendencies, instead of engaging these forces in a democratic process that in itself could contribute to rapprochement between different points of view. If the US attempt at building a federal "mosaic" in Iraq implies deliberately weakening all coherent social movements found in the country in order to make space for as many different pieces as possible, then the resultant product may well end up with frailty and instability rather than balance and harmony as its basic characteristics.[190] On the other hand, if a genuinely democratic process can be embarked upon, it seems likely that many groups in Iraqi society, including the religious parties among the Shi'is, would see certain favorable dimensions in a project of political decentralization.

Conclusion

The concept of federalism received increased attention among Shi'i religious parties of the Iraqi opposition during the build-up to war in 2002 and early 2003. Before the war, several political leaders who had earlier signaled various degrees of skepticism towards federalism decided to embrace the concept – in an "administrative" variant, emphasizing non-sectarian and non-ethnic criteria for the demarcation of federal provinces – as a sustainable scheme for the future of Iraq. As they had done throughout the twentieth century, the Shi'is refrained from a purely sectarian approach to the geopolitical (and hydrocarbonaceous) realities of Iraq, and instead painstakingly emphasized the unity of the country as a cardinal principle for future political negotiations over federalism.

However, during the initial period after the war, the emerging Shi'i political scene in Iraq came to be dominated by quite different issues, with the basic dichotomy between pro-American and anti-American positions attracting more of the attention, and the latter apparently enjoying far greater symbolic power through new

---

190 In June 2003, British military authorities reportedly used the religious complexity of the Basra area as a pretext for not holding local elections, see "Al-Jazirah TV: Basra Citizens Reject Appointment of British Governor", June 1, 2003, published by FBIS.

and radical forms of Islamism. According to supporters of these trends, questions of administrative decentralization were at best secondary to more pressing matters of cultural and religious reform at the local level. As far as the formulation of a political system was concerned, the new current in Iraqi Islamism was surprisingly prepared to delegate authority to the religious *hawza* and individuals who claimed to speak on behalf of this awe-inspiring yet somewhat intangible institution, instead of maintaining the sharp distinction between the clergy and politics highlighted by many Iraqi exiles as a distinguishing characteristic of Iraqi Shi'ism. Through their new alignment with an Iraqi cleric based in Iran, at least one segment of this tendency also became linked to a state model which emphasizes unity in an Islamic system led by a paramount *faqih*, rather than checks and balances against the concentration of power of the kind that a federal system would imply. Nevertheless, both the long-established Islamist parties as well as supporters of the quietist ulama (in addition to considerable blocs of secularists) continued to contribute to a high level of political diversity within the Shi'i community as a whole.

The other important feature of this period was the relatively static character of the different ideological approaches to federalism. Despite some significant movements of persons from one camp to another, there was less in the way of radical developments and changes as far as political theory was concerned. The pro-federalist argument remained based upon three paths to devolution, sometimes appearing in isolation and sometimes in hybrids: an "administrative" federalism marketed with secular and utilitarian rather than specifically Islamic arguments; an Islamic variant of federalism essentially limited to a reinterpretation of the experiences of former Islamic empires and by no means a detailed program for putting federal principles into operation; and finally an Islamic form of federalism developed in the context of a total, Shi'i, Islamic form of government, ruled by a supreme cleric, a council of clerics, or, as a minimum, subjected to clerical vetting of legislation at all levels of government – with recognized non-Muslim minorities forming the only candidates for partial exemption from this regime on a corporate basis. Reconciling these visions with both pressures from core Shi'i constituencies for Islamic legitimacy, as well as with non-Islamist demands for an overarching, secular framework for a federal system, remained an important challenge for Shi'i advocates for decentralization in May 2003.

Chapter 7

Understanding the Complexities of the Gulf: Concluding Remarks

Helge Hveem

The world of oil and gas has undergone major changes in the last decade. Needless to say, the wars in Iraq 1990–91 and 2003 are closely related to these changes. Wars aside, however, practically all the changes are related to both economic and political factors, often integrating both aspects. To understand them, we need a political economy perspective. The petroleum market is only partially run by the mechanism of supply and demand. Cultural factors related to religion frequently interfere, as do issues of national identity and prestige, making the political economy of petroleum even more complex.

The changes that have taken place and that create such complexity include mega-mergers in the industry, large and rapid price fluctuations, agreements for dealing with climate change, the mobilization of Islamic fundamentalism as a political force, nation-building and the collapse of nation-states, and tensions or armed conflicts in regions vital to the industry. The key geopolitical doctrine – that the space where a vital strategic element (oil resources) is found must be controlled – has remained a constant amidst this complexity. But a new dimension has entered, with the acute challenge of terrorism that faces the post-9/11 world. Today's terrorism is perceived as a new phenomenon that draws its leadership and resources from the region where most of the world's petroleum resources are located: *the Middle East and the Gulf.*

The main purpose of the present work has been to offer an original, thoroughly researched and up-to-date analysis of the complex relationship between geopolitics, religion, cultural identities and domestic political pressures in this core region of the world's oil industry. This relationship – or, more precisely, the interaction between domestic political processes in major petroleum countries and the political economy of international relations in the region – is an important focus for research. In the past, the great powers could perhaps hope to contain and control domestic politics in these countries: but this is no longer the case. Today the internal politics of the countries of the Middle East and the Gulf would appear to be shaping international affairs as often as the latter are shaping the former. The Iranian revolution of 1979, the Palestinian *intifadahs* and the recent revelations that al-Qaida is a transnational movement with a base in Saudi Arabia are but a few illustrations among many. Moreover, post-war Iraq is likely to prove nigh-impossible to organize and rule from the outside.

In sum, shifting combinations of socio-economic and political factors in the Middle East and in particular the Gulf region have become critical in shaping the world's petroleum market. The interaction between these factors also affects the prospects for economic development and for democracy in the region.

How and why has this come about? Here also, the answer is complex. One important reason why we can find no common pattern throughout the region is that political conditions in these countries vary considerably, across borders and over time. Another reason is that international relations in the region are unstable.

This book has presented in-depth analyses of several states. At the same time it has examined some phenomena that relate to most or all of the states, phenomena that shape the dynamics of the region. In so doing the authors have employed various analytical perspectives and methodologies, from political science and history, to economics. The chapters have thus not been designed to serve a systematic comparative purpose, but reflect different ways of understanding the issues and cases under study. This in turn reflects the multidisciplinary character of the research program underlying most of the reports.

We have looked at the differences that the various Gulf states demonstrate with respect to the factors referred to above, and noted the evolutionary character of these factors. We have also shown how geopolitics interacts with domestic politics, oscillating between extremism and reformism to create instability, but also creating opportunities for building stable relationships through economic co-operation and political alliances. The focus has been on whether – and if so, how – prospects for economic development and democracy are affected by these factors and processes, and how the two influence each other.

After 9/11 and the War on Iraq

The terrorist acts of September 11, 2001, and the subsequent war on terrorism have been widely identified as a turning point in international politics. One entire chapter in this book is devoted to an assessment of the terrorist threat to the oil industry in light of what happened in New York and Washington DC, on that date.

Many people would say that, in the wake of these events, our threat perceptions and security responses have been transformed, and that the psychology of a new perception of threat and insecurity will now prevail. However, it is mainly in the West – and primarily in the United States – that this transformation has taken place. It has led to radically changed perceptions of the Middle East and the Gulf in many quarters where decisions are made. To most people in the West, the economic outlook is also different now: they perceive greater uncertainty and more risk for themselves as investors, traders and travelers. *The most immediate effect of 9/11 is therefore that political and economic decision-makers in the West, and the USA in particular, look differently at the Gulf region.*

But terrorism has a long history, its sources are not found solely in the Gulf – and these facts have been known for some time. It would be a gross error to equate all political opposition in the Gulf and elsewhere with terrorism. Much of the research on which this book is based has, from the outset, focused on political dissent and contradictions, including struggles between state elites and their populations. Anyone aware of the practices of state institutions and the dynamics of socio-political processes in the Gulf will realize how complex and fluid is the situation, within as well as between the states of that region.

It is too early to say in which direction Iraq will move after the 2003 war and under US occupation, a matter to which we return below. However, for Iraq as well as for the rest of the region, the actors, factors and processes that were at work long before 9/11 will remain decisive. Iran, on the other hand – despite the continued rule of conservative religious leaders and periodic setbacks for the reform movement – appears headed on a reform course. In Saudi Arabia, demographic and socio-economic pressures seem to be leading not only to recruitment to transnational terrorism, but also to increasing pressures on the kingdom to open up to the outside world.

Many would claim that, after 9/11, international factors have become relatively more important than domestic politics in shaping developments. Put differently, one might say that international-level factors were dominant throughout the decades of imperialism and up until the 1960s. The CIA-staged *coup d'état* in Iran in 1953 is but one example. Then, with the transformation of the petroleum industry to become more of a national project and a matter of collective action by OPEC, power shifted towards factors at the domestic and regional levels. And now power has been shifted back to the international level again.

This, however, is an over-simplified view of reality. *What we are witnessing today is that interactions between domestic politics and international have become intensified.* This is happening not only because of events in the Gulf, but also as a result of the heightened geopolitical game being played out in Central Asia and Caucasus between the superpower, an ambitious (and petroleum-hungry) China and a reassertive Russia. One illustration of this is the question of whether major pipelines connecting the new petroleum provinces of Central Asia with global markets should be constructed through Turkey (the least economically efficient solution), or through upgrading old lines through Russia, or by building new ones through Iran and the Gulf – the most cost-effective alternative.

There have indeed been dramatic changes in the region: among them the 1953 *coup d'état* and the 1979 Islamic revolution in Iran, the domestic and foreign political strategy of Iraq under Saddam Hussein and the war that toppled his regime, and finally the unresolved conflict between Israel and the Palestine National Authority. In their various ways, all illustrate the complex interaction between international and domestic politics.

Geopolitics and the Gulf

Within a few weeks of the attack on the World Trade Center, US diplomacy had managed to put together an impressive coalition to back its anti-terrorism campaign. Even such not-so-obvious allies as China joined in. Why did China as well as Russia and India join, apparently without many second thoughts? The explanation is perhaps fairly straightforward: all shared with the world's hegemonic power a common interest in combating terrorism – which, their governments argued, threatened their own countries as well. Never since the nineteenth-century Concert of Europe had the world seen such an overwhelming expression of great-power co-operation.

But the resilience of this unusually strong coalition was soon to be put to the test. The main cause was the policy of the United States under the present administration of George W. Bush. Fighting the "new" transnational terrorism network(s) is certainly a general policy principle that is easy to applaud. The problem lies in the practice. When the US government issued a statement naming two of the regimes in the region, Iran as well as Saddam's Iraq, as parts of "an axis of evil", US leaders were helping the conservatives against the reformists in Iran. When they took up the issue of attacking Iraq militarily to topple Saddam, they boosted rather than weakened Saddam's position in the region. And in Afghanistan, the speedy pull-out left room for local clan leaders to resume their destabilizing power struggles, even making it possible for the Taliban to re-emerge. These steps put strains on the new anti-terrorism alliance as well.

But then the USA managed to topple Saddam by military action, in the face of opposition from all but one of the veto powers in the UN, and with little opposition on the ground in Iraq. That success has silenced much of the previous war protests and further augmented the status of the USA as the world's pre-eminent superpower. Will that apparent success lead to a restoration of the strained anti-terrorist alliance? And if so, will the US administration feel confident that it can attack Iran's nuclear installations?

US diplomacy in the region appears to have reverted to a fairly elementary version of geopolitics. True, things were somewhat easier during the Cold War, when containment of, and if necessary confrontation with, Communism was the chief doctrine. It was in line with this doctrine that the USA supported the *mujaheddin* in Afghanistan against the Soviet occupation. Its support of Saddam against Iran in the Iraq–Iran war may, however, be explained by another principle, that of classical balance-of-power politics: to maintain control of a region by balancing local powers that confronted one another, by "divide and rule". But the US support of Saddam was also motivated by fury at being humiliated by the radical Islamic regime of Khomeini when its militants were allowed to take control of the US embassy in Teheran.

While many of the US policy choices may be well understood in the West and indeed have been popular in the United States itself, they have alienated great parts of the populations and some of the leaders in the Middle East/Gulf region. The strategy adopted by the Bush Jr. administration is not only putting great strains on the global anti-terrorism coalition, it also appears to be splitting NATO and resulting in a loss of confidence in US policy among much of Western public opinion. On the other hand, such a split – apparent during the summer and fall of 2002 when Germany and France agreed to oppose attacking Iraq without full UN support – may recede if new acts of terror occur that can be related to transnational terrorist movements. Even at home in the USA, the neo-conservative foreign policy doctrine of employing proactive strikes and unilateralism, as practiced in launching the war on Iraq, has been criticized not only by liberals but also by "realists" like Henry Kissinger.

On the other hand, analysis of the political economy of oil in the Gulf should not over-dramatize instability and fluidity, nor should it focus excessively on violence. The fact that OPEC has succeeded in maintaining oil prices at relatively stable levels over long periods demonstrates that actors in the region are capable of reaching compromises among themselves and of managing the political economy of one of the world's most important industries. Despite their historical conflicts, Iran and Saudi Arabia have managed to co-operate on oil price policy, and in recent years even Iraq has been allowed to take part in OPEC activities.

Less impressive, however, are the results that these states have achieved in terms of economic and above all social development. This widespread "development failure" has contributed considerably to the current lack of stability in the region. Repressive regimes, economic disparities, corruption and lack of democracy are found in other parts of the world as well. But in the Middle East these aspects have combined with Arab defeat in wars with Israel and continued Israeli occupation to create growing disillusionment with the failure to make ruling elites and the military accountable. This disillusionment has been an important factor behind the resurgence of political Islam from the late 1970s.[1]

Looming on the horizon is "the clash of civilizations" that Samuel Huntington predicted would follow if the West did not learn to live with political Islam. This prospect of clash is in total contradiction to the project of reformists in Iran, where a main ideological pillar is dialog among civilizations.

With respect to post-war Iraq, the rush by foreign corporations to secure for themselves a share in its rich oil resources is expected to impact strongly on the market, although probably not in the very short run. If or when Iraq's production capacity becomes fully operational, and if that occurs under foreign political control of the country, this should also have consequences for the position of Iraq in OPEC, and for OPEC's position in the petroleum world.

If this view of current developments and future prospects is correct, oil will certainly be caught in the middle of the general sense of a new insecurity. And it will be the focal point of clashes to come. Not only will oil prices be affected: reliability of supply and conditions of operation for oil corporations may be as well.

---

1   See Mahmood Monshipouri (2002), "The Paradoxes of US Policy in the Middle East", *Middle East Policy Journal,* Vol. IX, September, No. 3.

Foreign states, in particular the great powers, would appear to have contributed to aggravating tensions in the region, rather than easing them. Development assistance programs have not penetrated to the masses, and they have been dwarfed by military assistance from the same donors. Efforts to reach a peace agreement between the Palestinian Authority and Israel have been seen as too lukewarm; the perception in the region is that the West has not pressured Israel hard enough to make it move. Added to this is what is widely seen as an inconsistent political strategy in the region, in particular by the US administrations. In Afghanistan, the USA supported the *mujaheddin* and a broad alliance against the Soviets, only to withdraw without any plan for reconstruction. Having thereby left the arena to the Taliban, Washington subsequently went on to make them yet another main target. If such moves can be explained by the balance-of-power principle, then surely that principle is not well understood outside the command rooms of central decision-makers. Another instance: the USA helped Saddam re-arm Iraq – and then targeted him as the main opponent.

Democracy and Development: the Obstacles are Mainly Domestic

These intensified interactions accentuate the complexity and at times deepen the fluidity observed in the region. But they cannot alter a fundamental fact that remains as valid as ever: *economic development and democratization continue to be contingent upon domestic politics.*

The belief that successful democratization in one country will spread to others in the region through a "positive domino effect" is a gross simplification of matters. Or – could it nevertheless happen? And perhaps through foreign intervention?

One informal law of political science is that domestic institutions forced on a nation from the outside never last unless they are adopted by the local population, fairly immediately and in a truly voluntary spirit. Until disproved, this would imply that that the US democratization project in Iraq probably has less chances of success than does the reform movement in Iran. It also implies that the other countries in the region would feel greater pressure to democratize if Iran succeeded, than if the US project in Iraq were to be brought off with only moderate and not overly legitimate local support. If reformism should prevail and lead to major change towards a more economically open and politically liberal Iran, then this would also contribute to greater stability in the region. If, however, the conservative hold on power were to prevail and perhaps even become stronger, this would help to make the region even less stable.

Such an outcome would also have a marked effect on the oil market. Oil supplies would probably be less predictable, and prices would rise. If relations between Iran and Iraq were strained under the previous Iraqi regime, they seem unlikely to improve under continued foreign occupation and control over Iraq. A key factor here will be what happens in US–Iran relations, and that appears to be largely dependent upon whether the US administration follows up its provocative policy towards Teheran, branding it as a member of an "axis of evil".

If domestic politics are still vital, then the prospects for economic development and democracy in the short and medium term appear bleak in most other parts of the Gulf. There are, however, some promising openings.

The political systems throughout the region are generally classified under nondemocratic categories such as "totalitarianism", "autocracy", "patrimonialism", "elitism", "oligarchy" and "*rentier* state". These are states still far from respecting human rights, the rule of law and democracy – which in turn can explain why the oil assets have so often been squandered without benefit to the people as a whole.

In several of the chapters in this book, the *rentier* state phenomenon and the widespread practice of corruption are presented as major obstacles not only to economic development, but to democracy as well. In the paramount *rentier* state of the region, Saudi Arabia, the linkage between the economy and the polity of the country is particularly intimate. Here pressure for change has also been strong and visible for a long time. This has been dramatically illustrated by the rise of al-Qaida, but indirectly and directly it has been a factor of importance long before September 11. There is much to indicate that influential policy-making circles in the West, especially in the United States, have overlooked this factor over the years.

A simple but only partly valid explanation of the success of the al-Qaida network among Islamists in the region is that it builds on a combination of domestic opposition to the incumbent political regime and resentment at the geopolitical maneuvering and attempted hegemony of the West (read: the USA), past and present. The switch to reformism that now appears inevitable in the case of Saudi Arabia has already prevailed through electoral processes in Iran. In Iran, however, a religious oligarchy is in control of much of the economy and has the power to impose checks and curbs on policies introduced by the elected administration.

In Saudi Arabia, with its highly uneven distribution of political power, social privileges and economic wealth in favor of the royal family, the regime has attempted to buy off the people by offering them a share of the petroleum rent, as well as by supporting the introduction of a fairly radical interpretation of Islam financially and politically. This practice has meant blatant offences against human rights and is a development that would hardly have been tolerated in a great many other countries – and yet, most other governments have turned a blind eye to Saudi Arabia. The main reasons have been the country's position as the world's biggest exporter of oil, combined with the regime's firm support of US geopolitical goals. And the result? Today the kingdom finds itself hard-pressed politically and can no longer resort to the "gift" system in order to survive. Major economic adjustments are necessary in order to avert radical political change – if indeed that can be avoided at all.

Corruption and how best to fight it appear to be contingent on both cultural and contextual factors. Bonham and Heradstveit in their comparative study of Iran and Azerbaijan show that populations in the two countries attribute different causes to the phenomenon. In both countries, samples of the elite were asked about their view of the role of foreign oil corporations. Respondents were for the most part skeptical about the contribution such corporations can make to fighting corruption (and thereby to promoting democracy indirectly). In Iran the legacy of their role in the overthrow of a democratically elected government in 1953 still weighs heavily on the minds of many people. On the other hand, Iranians appear to blame corruption not on "the system" or "the culture", but on individuals. The position of most of the interviewed opposition leaders in Azerbaijan is the converse: when foreign oilmen are seen as unable to contribute to eradicating corruption, this is largely because they operate within a corrupt system ruled by the Aliev clan.

In Saudi Arabia, anti-US sentiment may have been building up throughout the 1990s, as a large US military force remained stationed in the country. In the wake of September 11, such feelings appear to have been radically strengthened. There are indications that the royal family is split over how to handle a most delicate balancing act: between its continued alliance with a US administration whose foreign policy in the region is hardening; and those in the region (and indeed in the Kingdom) who sympathize with the cause of the political opposition, including that of al-Qaida. The outcome is by no means a foregone conclusion. It will depend heavily on the conduct of US policy in vital areas such as the Palestinian issue, its continued role in Afghanistan and not least how it conducts its occupation and intended transformation of Iraq.

Whither Iraq?

The policy implications of the studies presented in the book are several. One follows directly from the theoretical implications, and could be stated as follows:

> In order to understand terrorism, do not link it solely to Islam: link it instead to the interaction between domestic social and political gaps and grievances on the one hand, and on the other hand to the geopolitical maneuvering of those powers, outside and inside the region, that desire to control the region in their own interest.

Culturally and politically, the Gulf is a pluralistic phenomenon whose various entities have a long history that informs much of their present practice. The region has to be understood as such, and not simplistically seen as a monolithic entity based on Islam.

Iraq will most probably present yet another proof of this. The issue of the future constitutional arrangement of the country after the overthrow of Saddam and Ba'th power has been widely debated since long before the war. Visser's thoroughly researched chapter on Iraq shows clearly how complex the political situation has become after the war, and how this impacts on the constitutional debates. One key element in what is widely expected to be the future political system – a federal structure of governance – has become more of an issue after the war than it was before it. Federalism is definitely preferred by Kurdish leaders who aspire to establishing considerable autonomy in the territories traditionally populated by the Kurds. The idea of a federal arrangement has also received manifest support from various other segments, including the majority Muslim population, the Shi'i. After the war, however, as various factions have worked to position themselves, support for federalism also has become more conditional. The issue appeared to be fading into the background, at least temporarily, during the spring of 2003.

Instead several leading Shi'i representatives, backed by street demonstrations, increasingly reflected radical Islamist views denouncing secular tendencies within the Shi'i population. These forces, apparently on the rise after the end of the war, have been demanding that a political order be established under a strict hierarchy that would put religious leadership at the top and adherence to its religious teachings as the basic principle for the political rank-and-file. They have been behind attempts to take over Sunni mosques, indicating their clear preference not only for a unitary state and the rejection of religious pluralism, but also a dislike of those policy principles that have been based on pragmatism concerning the future political order and that have accepted some form of federal system. The spring and summer of 2003 were marked by growing tendencies among the various aspiring new leaders in post-war and post-occupation Iraq to display disagreement over the future political order. Such disagreement was also increasingly seen within the Shi'i population.

Another controversial issue has also come to the fore: what sort of position will the future Iraq adopt with regard to pan-Islamist visions? During much of Saddam's rule, an important faction of the Shi'i leadership was exiled to Iran. Some within this faction, but also outside it, have been advocating a "pan-Shi'i" order to be established in Iraq – in other words, one that holds the office of the supreme leader of Shi'i Islam, currently held by Ayatollah Khamenei in Iran, as the apex of the local administrative structures to be established in Iraq. How powerful will this view prove to be? It is certain to be contested by Sunni Muslims and other religious groups in Iraq. But will it be acceptable to most Shi'i Iraqis – will religion definitely trump national identity?

No long-term solution may be found without the participation of the Shi'i population of Iraq. If numbers were all that mattered, it would stand to form a majority government in a future representative and parliamentary democracy – something it was denied during the rule of the Ba'th party, which represented the minority Sunni population. On the other hand: is the issue not that of introducing parliamentary democracy, be it federalist or otherwise, but rather that of introducing an Islamic republic instead of a secular one? Shi'i leaders may mobilize either way; Visser's study shows that this is what they have done so far. But he also points out that the split that emerged during 2003 might be overcome, if or when those who have voiced skepticism or who have remained on the sidelines could find federalism in some form or other compatible with their own schemes.

Most of these issues will probably remain unresolved for a long time to come. Exactly how long may be a matter of how long the US occupation forces remain in Iraq, and that is not at all known as this conclusion is written. To the extent that the

US administration before the war had prepared themselves and their allies among Iraqi exiles for a political solution, a federal constitution of some sort was one of the preferred options. As is to be expected, the US administration, in particular its conservative part, is not going to tolerate popular demands for an Islamic state along the lines of that in Iran. On the other hand, even some leaders and movements with which the US had not co-operated before the war also generally favored a federal solution: thus it may appear as a likely compromise solution. Also those Iraqi factions that would prefer to drop federalism might accept it as a temporary solution. Many of these factions perceive federalism as an American invention meant to divide and weaken the country, while also offering a preferred position for the Kurds.

If skeptical or hostile Iraqi leaders are willing to strike compromises with the US administration over future constitutional arrangements, Washington would in return have to accept these leaders as legitimate representatives of the population and of future Iraqi leadership – no matter whether their base is religious or secular. In so doing the Americans could rely on what has become a fairly general historical lesson: the political leadership of a country cannot in the main, and definitely not in the long term, be based in another country (Iran) – except when power is exercised by military occupation. And even that way of running a country cannot last forever.

Index

Petroleum Industry Regulation within Stable States

Edited by Solveig Glomsrød
and Petter Osmundsen

ISBN 0 7546 4252 6

Ashgate Studies in Environmental and Natural
Resource Economics

This book addresses the challenges facing stable democratic states in dealing with oil companies in order to secure general welfare gains. Political stability means that such states should be able to take a longer term perspective. The text focuses on petroleum industry regulation but also considers non-renewable natural resources and addresses the question of tax competition between producing countries.

Within the context of company and government relations the book examines current topics such as the challenges of dealing with merged companies and the strategic choices facing tax authorities.

ASHGATE

The Changing World of Oil
An Analysis of Corporate Change and Adaptation

Edited by Jerome Davis

ISBN 0 7546 4178 3

This timely book considers the nature of industrial change in order to explain what is happening in the oil industry. Uniquely, this book identifies firms within the industry as dependent variables and not the future production and demand for oil and gas. Particular attention is paid to the so-called 'mega-mergers' and to the on-going industrial downsizing and outsourcing.

The book explains why the oil industry behaves the way it does and considers society issues such as environmental policies and depleting resources.

The unique approach of this book will help extend readers' understanding of the oil industry beyond more conventional studies.

ASHGATE

DATE DUE

NOV 3 0 2012			

Library
Southern Maine Community College
2 Fort Road
South Portland, Maine 04106